THE REVENGE OF TEAM 33

By William R Barber

Prologue

A division-level military unit requires an on-the-ground intelligence-gathering source operating within enemy-occupied territory. The Marine Corps formed a Force Reconnaissance Company, which, when established in the 1950s, was envisioned to operate behind enemy lines. Specifically designed for a conventional war against the Soviet Union. The company was trained to operate in four-man teams, fifty to one hundred fifty miles behind enemy lines. The Vietnam War necessitated a diametrically opposite mission adjustment. Force Recon teams were dispatched by helicopter into the area where the North Vietnamese Army roamed. Conceptually, recon teams would verify and report the existence of NVA, map coordinates, and strength. On patrol, the recon team will call in air and artillery support and, on occasion, ambush NVA supporting units to gather documents such as mail and, in rare instances, capture an ambush survivor.

The Ambush: 1966

After vigilantly zigzagging their way through the terrain between Con Thien and Dong Ha, Force Recon Team 33 is on its final traverse to the alternate extraction site.

Homeward bound, the apprehensive and psychically edgy Team moves out of the jungle in tactical formation. The final trek to extraction involves stepping from the concealment of the jungle's tree line into an open, uphill field of elephant grass stalks that are shoulder-high, bending and oscillating in the wind.

Suddenly, after an ingress of two hundred meters, the whistling of incoming and the thunder of impacting mortar rounds shattered the silence. The shocking discovery automated a quickening pace and a surge of heart-pounding anxiety. Inbound rockets exploded, randomly flinging hot steel fragments aimed to sever flesh from bone. The screaming sound of the unseen fell from the sky. Though inaccurate, the unremitting barrage of mortar rounds confirmed McLeod's dissent over using this extraction site.

McLeod and Team, hearts jackhammering, ran through, around, and near the enormous patterns of earthly debris that blew heedlessly into the air. Running amidst a mix of earth, tree branches, and grass, suspended in midair, all falling and rising as if in slow motion. The stalking elephant grass and the wind-induced, wildly oscillating top camouflaged the Team's whereabouts from enemy gunners. Mortar rounds burst aimlessly around and overhead without causing any damage. Tracers from machine guns tore blindly through the elephant grass, marred the bright blue morning sky, and lit up racing lines of bouncing red into the horizon.

Nevertheless, the Team steadily traversed upwards to the flat top of the hill. The sound of the AK-47 rifles joined the piercing sirens of the incoming. With invigorated forcefulness, Team 33 raced toward the designated extraction site. Nearing the vantage point of a higher elevation, each Marine looked down upon scores of North Vietnamese troops. They were approximately five hundred meters away and closing in. Dillon was on point.

"Hold up," McLeod shouted, stationed behind Dillan as they neared the top of the hill.

The Team heard the order, and Dillon executed the proper hand and arm signal. Thomas and Archer immediately obeyed and formed a tactical defensive position. McLeod caught up to his Team as mortars continued to rain down ineffectively in an uneven hopscotch configuration.

"They have lost us in the elephant grass; they must have spotted us when we left the jungle's edge," a heavy-breathing McLeod deduced. "Dillon, stay on a beeline for that elevated mound. We're about 200 meters (about 656.17 ft) from where we need to be."

The mortar fire stopped as abruptly as it began. The Team could hear the North Vietnamese-trained bloodhounds barking over their commanders' orders.

"Their advance unit is too close to us for the assholes to continue with mortars," McLeod shouted as he slung a green canvas bag of claymores over his shoulder. "Listen up: Fire all three bandoliers of M79 ammo on the run. Save the two rocket launchers until we get to the extraction point. We'll fire them off before we board. Dillon, break out the tape recorder; turn the volume up high. Hopefully, it will confuse them and cause some hesitation."

McLeod confidently assured the Team, "The extraction folks are close; they'll vector in air support. We're going to be all right." McLeod held up two claymores, one in each hand, saying, "They'll walk right into these babies." McLeod placed the claymores along the path. The team, positioned in a tactical defense setup, set the detonation tripwires.

"Ready!" McLeod commanded, "Dillon, lead the way; I'll bring up the rear. Remember, loft those M79 rounds high. Now, let's boogie!"

As ordered, the Team expended M79 ammo toward the NVA while they made their way through the elephant grass toward the extraction point. Finally, the elevated clearing was within sight; their aim, now within reach, activated their inherent esprit de corps. The pace accelerated into a jog.

The claymores blasted loudly behind them. The explosions momentarily confused the enemy; nonetheless, the N.V.A. resumed the chase within minutes, closing in on the Team.

"It's as if these assholes know the extraction location and are herding us," McLeod murmured. He shouted, "Thomas, let's see if we can slow them down; launch your rocket!"

Thomas fired off one of the rocket launchers and returned to his former position.

The midmorning sun continued to beat down unmercifully. The sun's sparkling brilliance made eyes squint. The sticky mixture of sweat and fear clung steadfastly to their being. However, knowing that extraction was within reach and satisfied that each meter was homeward-bound, the team fought through the remaining meters of thick, heavy elephant grass. Their martial ethos squeezed out every ounce of residual strength.

McLeod had expected a full-on assault, but, to his surprise, the enemy stopped their advance. Then, McLeod saw a football-field-sized distance ahead on the extraction site atop the hill. There was no cover or concealment on flat ground where the Team would be most vulnerable; inexplicably, the incoming fire stopped. The Marines raced toward the landing site unimpeded by the hill's steepness. Focused on the extraction opportunity, McLeod signaled double time, and the Team enthusiastically responded.

"There!" Archer shouted, pointing with the barrel of his rifle; he could see the helicopter coming from the direction of Hill 283. The team members sighed with relief.

McLeod grinned, impressed that the helicopter was on-site with no radio link-up. The pilot McLeod, who contemplated this, must be a real veteran adjusting to a hot extraction. Air support must be right behind him. That must be the reason the N.V.A. held its ground.

The helicopter's whipping blades kicked up a thick cloud of brown dirt with straws of elephant grass. The engine noise was deafeningly loud.

The Team began their approach; the entry doors slid open within fifty yards. The mission was over; they were going home.

On the run from the rear, McLeod surveyed the helicopter. The first thing that caught his eye was that the bird had no markings. The second was that this was a hot landing zone, but no supporting gunships or fixed-wing aircraft were in sight. This extraction was a solo recovery. "Maybe this is a gunship pulled out of special operations," he thought, "hence, no markings." The first three members of the team were twenty-five yards from boarding the CH-47 Chinook.

Suddenly, he noticed two helmeted crew members peering out at him. One leaned over a mounted machine gun, fanning his left hand inward, pressing a thumbs-up come-on aboard to the approaching recon team while alternating a military double-time signal with his right arm. The other had a shotgun while waving at the Marines to double time.

Archer turned to relay the thumbs-up sign to his Team. Dillon and Thomas were right behind Archer. While sprinting toward the helicopter, a sanctuary only moments away, Thomas discarded the last rocket launcher and dashed.

McLeod was forty meters to the rear and closing. His eyes were on the men in the helicopter. But then he decelerated. Instincts warned him that something was wrong. He stared at the onboard gunners as the crew members lowered their weapons. Then, the unholy, unthinkable unfolded:

McLeod screamed, "GET DOWN! STOP! GET DOWN!" The noise from the thundering blades silenced his warnings.

The helicopter gunners opened fire. Focused on Archer, their machine gun rounds kicked up dirt in front and to his side. However, the final burst hit its mark. Archer was facing McLeod when the armor-piercing bullets spun him around like a suspended ragdoll until he fell to the ground, dead.

With the sound of earsplitting gunfire and the rocking of their unsteady platform, the onboard gunners struggled to vector their aim onto the moving targets of Dillon and Thomas. Finally, multiple bursts of bullets cut the two advancing Marines in half and quarters.

A stunned McLeod was frozen in place as if watching a nightmare unfold. Dillon shrieked as a dozen rounds pierced his chest and stomach, lifting him high. Thomas, in the face, died at once from a shotgun blast that blew his head from his body, followed by multiple hits of machine gun ammo that pummeled his dead torso. At Archer's moment of death, McLeod was staring directly into his eyes. With his M-14 rifle slung over the nape of his neck, in disoriented shock, McLeod collapsed to his knees, striving to discern what must be a lurid hallucination, and was stunned into inaction. The ambush was deadly. Team 33, so close to going home, was now, save one, all dead.

The helicopter rocked to and fro, striving to keep its support position on the steep hill. The gunners are now focused on McLeod; their bullets kicked up the dirt in every direction. Rounds danced all around him. Frozen by the unfolding, he did not move. Several pieces of rock kicked upward and pelted hard against his chest; dirt flew and enveloped his body from head to knees.

McLeod, in seconds, sobered to the situation, assessed, and instantly aligned his sights on the shooters. His "inner Marine" emerged; he fell into a prone position and returned accurate semi-automatic fire. Twenty rounds were fired, emptying one magazine. He quickly flipped to another fully loaded magazine taped upside down on the expended magazine. He disrupted the helo gunner's fire superiority by hitting the machine gunner and the helicopter with tracer rounds. McLeod's concentrated fire set the aircraft afire. The pilots panicked as smoke billowed out from the cabin. From his vantage point, he watched one pilot attempt to control the helicopter's wavering while the other sprayed the flames with a canister of fire retardant.

The remaining crewmember focused on the one remaining Marine who had discarded the shotgun in favor of the swivel-mounted machine gun. However, minutes of unrelenting rapid fire heated the machine gun's barrel and froze the operating system. He removed his trigger finger from the machine gun, unholstered his pistol, and continued firing.

McLeod fearlessly returned fire while cavalierly running at full speed directly toward the source of the incoming bullets. Accepting fate's resolve, he consciously challenged death to a duel. His concentration was on killing, not living. He daringly advanced, firing his M-14 with the stock of the rifle firmly placed under his armpit.

On McLeod's approaching side, the pilot opened the cockpit window, and with a pistol in hand, he began firing his semi-automatic 9mm (about 0.35 in) weapon. The helicopter continued to shake and sputter.

Tenaciously, McLeod returned fire and maneuvered his way out of the pilot's line of fire. The Gunner struggled to move his weapon into the new position; seconds passed.

McLeod knelt, snatched two M-2 fragmentary grenades from his war belt, pulled the pin on each, and tossed them one after another toward the helicopter. They found their mark.

The machine gunner saw the grenades and struggled to vacate the cabin, but it was too late. The grenades blasted, the helicopter shook, and pieces flung everywhere. Black smoke bellowed, and the giant blades slowed to a near standstill before a hellishly thunderous explosion.

McLeod rolled away from the most lethal effect, but the blast stunned him temporarily. Upon regaining his senses, the helicopter's smoking fragments spewed about; a human torso had landed a few yards before him. The torso lay face down, helmet on. He started to crawl towards the torso. As he crawled, he felt a flash of sharp pain in his left shoulder. Taking off his body armor, he investigated the wound. After wiping away the blood, a flesh wound appeared. A small shrapnel fragment forced its way between his shoulder and upper arm. Although the bone was untouched, a large segment of the shrapnel stood out from the skin.

He pulled a small, gray plastic box from his thigh pocket, opened the lid, grasped a syringe of morphine from the box, and then jabbed the needle into his thigh muscle. Not waiting for the morphine's dulling effect, McLeod reached with his right hand, pulled out the shrapnel, and fed gauze from his first aid kit into the wound.

Sensing the enemy's approach, he sped up his physical effort to reach the smoldering torso. McLeod grasped the torso's remains and turned it frontal. A dark-tinted sunglass guard attached to a green airman's helmet covered his eyes and nose. McLeod forced the face guard upward, revealing a broad mulatto face, round ebony eyes, and a gold tooth, which caught the sunlight and glittered brightly in the middle of his upper front teeth.

While searching the upper torso shirt pockets for identification, McLeod could hear the N.V.A. shouting and the barking dogs closing in. The helicopter explosion was their signal that the ambush had not gone as expected. Aware that time was running against him, McLeod scanned the pockets for identity clues. There was nothing: no emblems, no paper, nothing.

Then he noticed a new tattoo on the dead man's right forearm: a six-point gold star on a blood-red field, bordered by a thick, black-lined square above the star. The tattoo was also new, featuring the number "666" in black.

McLeod unsheathed his 10-inch Bowie knife and severed the forearm from the elbow in one proficient, fluid motion. He then stashed the bloodied arm in his pack, turned, and looked for the last time at the battlefield and his mangled comrades. The mangled bodies of Team 33, forever pictured in his mind's memory, their deaths and his guilt seared deep within his psyche.

Recovery – 1966

For two days, McLeod evaded the pursuit of N.V.A until he reached the safety of Camp Carroll. The camp was a last-resort rally point for patrols roaming in and around I-Corps. The Special Forces outpost is named after Marine Captain Carroll. A courageous former 2nd Force Recon officer was killed months earlier. Everyone in the mix had heard of Team 33 and its missing Team leader. Since his body was not with the other members of Team 33, they thought the NVA had captured him. McLeod's appearance in the S.F. Camp initiated relief, disbelief, and intriguing wonderment. Medics dealt with his wound at the camp's infirmary, and he was given food, water, a warm shower, and a very hasty physical. McLeod slept with the aid of a drug inducement for 12 hours. After two days of rest and recovery, the 1st Marine Division's legal officer requested the Army to fly McLeod to Da Nang. Upon arrival, McLeod was shown to his quarters and asked to draft a report of Team 33's patrol detailing the ambush. The SF camp's intelligence officer informed him that a search party had recovered Team 33 Marines in a shallow grave and the remnants of a stripped and badly charred CH-46 helicopter.

After showering and inhaling a cold C-ration can of beans & franks, McLeod, as ordered, wrote out his report on a white pad using a pencil with no eraser. Even though the process was emotionally agonizing, he documented the entire patrol from insertion to ambush. McLeod accurately made the tattoo drawing on the Cuban Gunner's forearm. He turned his report to the duty officer and walked away, thinking how eager he was to attend the scheduled morning debrief. At the very least, McLeod contemplated that the forthcoming questions and answers might help alleviate the guilt that was increasingly permeating his heart and mind.

He surveyed the area: the tent was large enough for thirty men to sleep comfortably; it was recently converted for the Team 33 debrief. A 3-foot-by-6-foot black chalkboard mounted on a large metal easel sat on the back wall. Two large wooden desks faced inward with a typewriter, a tape recorder, and a leather-bound bible. At the front of the room was a long green table with chairs behind it. A manila folder named "TEAM 33" in large black letters was on that table. Inside the door was a giant vat of coffee with paper cups, sugar, and powdered cream. McLeod poured black coffee, sat, sipped, and waited as instructed.

At precisely 7:30 a.m., two field-grade officers, one civilian and one female Captain, followed Colonel P.J. Sullivan into the tent. The Colonel broke the protocol to introduce himself and the two officers he described as adjudicators; the civilian was not introduced. The board of inquiry sat shoulder to shoulder in front, facing McLeod. The Colonel was off to the right in a cushioned chair. The uniform distinction was contrasting. McLeod wore his utilities and field boots, while the investigative committee, besides the one civilian, wore modified greens with decoration ribbons and spit-shined shoes.

The proceeding started with McLeod's left hand on the Bible as he swore to tell the assembly the truth. Next, he signed a one-page document affirming in writing what he had previously orally agreed to.

Captain Mary Jane Webster, one of the officers behind a table, sitting shoulder to shoulder across from McLeod, introduced herself and explained her role as the record inquisitor or investigator. For personal clarity, she informed McLeod that any member of the investigation committee could interrupt the proceedings at any time. The captain also mentioned that this pretrial investigation may be referred to as Article 32 proceedings. The captain reminded McLeod that he was answering under oath and that a polygraph may be a necessary follow-up.

McLeod went cold. The Marine Corps' fidelity to common purpose was decidedly absent. He realized at once that this debriefing was not a traditional one; it was, in fact, an adversarial precursor to a court-martial.

Captain Webster, the lowest rank of the ensemble of officers, guesses she worked extremely hard in her mid-to-late twenties to appear more aged than her years. With confidence in her voice and rank-induced pretense, she begins the inquiry with an insincere question: "Sergeant, before we start, would you like a glass of water?"

McLeod, sensing her insincerity, responded negatively. Captain Webster, as if in the middle of the ring receiving final instructions from the referee, touched Gloves, ignored McLeod's unmistakable tenor of indifference, and stated: "Sergeant McLeod, I have read your written report of Team 33's patrol. However, for the benefit of the committee, could you recall the noteworthy events of the patrol without the benefit of your report sequentially?" Webster pushed the button on the tape recorder and said, "Please begin." McLeod highlighted the patrol's activities, from insertion to ambush, including Gunny Hagerty's strong objection to Doc Marshall joining Team 33's patrol. Hampered by an emotionally weakened voice and watery eyes, he described the individual killing of team members. Detailing the firefight, how he blew up the helicopter, and why he knew the crew was Cuban.

Aside from Captain Webster, the committee members listened with eyes fixed on McLeod. Webster seemed uninterested in the story; unlike her fellow officers, she never took her eyes off McLeod.

After McLeod finished the retelling, Webster cleared her throat, poured a cup of water, and gulped it down. "Sergeant McLeod," Webster called out. Her eyes returned to him. "Captain Doss has adamantly denied ordering Team 33 to alter its extraction point." A cloud of disbelief registered its effect; knowing the assertion was an absurd lie, anger crept into his voice, "Captain, why would I put my Team at those extraction coordinates if not ordered there? Please explain why I would risk a midday extraction without on-call air support if I did not obey a direct order. Captain Doss is a liar. He makes a gross tactical mistake and covers it up with bullshit. My statement is correct."

Webster sat back in her chair. McLeod knew he was skating the line, calling a Marine Officer a liar. Nonetheless, for clarity of opinion, McLeod shouted, "Doss is a liar."

Captain Webster dropped her tone to an angry hiss, "Sergeant McLeod, let's be very clear about this. First, are you unequivocally saying that Captain Doss ordered you to risk the lives of your Team? Second, are you stating that Captain Doss knowingly changed your patrol's extraction coordinates, resulting in a North Vietnamese ambush supported by Cubans in a stolen CH-46 helicopter? Is this your statement? Are you certain, Sergeant McLeod?"

McLeod paused; the seconds between the question and answer lingered. McLeod felt a sense of convoluted bewilderment. A fellow Marine was questioning his honor, integrity, and competency. Bitterness and frustration momentarily turned off his means of expressing his utter disdain for such a damming implication.

"Sergeant," Webster called out, "do you wish me to restate the questions?"

"No, Captain. There is no need to restate. You are not only calling me a liar, but you're suggesting that I am a dishonorable idiot. Yes, Captain Doss gave the orders, and I obeyed. My obedience to such orders resulted in the death of Team 33, minus one. The fault for obeying a direct order was mine, but that order came from Captain Doss. My statement with certainty stands as written and delivered."

"Do you have any idea who, with deliberate forethought, planned the ambush of Team 33?" Webster asked while still staring directly into McLeod's eyes.

Emotional hell broke loose inside McLeod's mind. Images of Team 33's mangled bodies drift from port to starboard across the scope of his remembrance. The memory of Archer's eyes as they reflected death's acceptance, Dillon's body pummeled with so many bullets that the force of the bullets held his body in midair, blood gushing from the headless Thomas.

In a calm demeanor, McLeod responds. "Captain," he says, leaning forward and lowering his voice. Webster, in turn, shifted in her seat and centered her eyes on him. Standing in a physically threatening manner, McLeod says, "If I knew who plotted and planned the killing of my men, I assure you I would not be here sustaining your foolish, baseless nonsense. Instead, I would find and apprehend. I'd tie the culprit to a tree and slowly slice one extremity after another from his body; by artful slicing and dicing, blood-curdling screams would emit and warm my inners." Startled by the sincere horror of McLeod's deliverance, the setting hung in suspension like the smell of gunpowder in the aftermath of a firefight. McLeod was in a state of heightened anxiety. The officers clearly understood that Sergeant W.R. McLeod was traumatized.

The Colonel broke the tension. "Captain Webster, take thirty, Sergeant McLeod, shake a leg, and settle yourself."

Thirty minutes evolved into a welcoming hour before the board of inquiry was reseated. Colonel Sullivan asked, "Sergeant, are there more details of the gunship, crew, or any other lingering thoughts that this debriefing may have triggered?"

"There is one more thing: Check with Gunnery Sergeant Hagerty. He warned me before the mission that Captain Doss had taken an unusual interest in my patrol. He said he would investigate and get back to me. While in the bush, after receiving the change of orders, I tried to contact Gunnery Sergeant Hagerty but was unsuccessful. I am surprised he has not contacted me."

"Sergeant McLeod," the Colonel spoke with deadpan seriousness, "Hagerty is dead. A headshot at very close range, they found him hidden under his cot, covered in clothes."

"I'll be damned; the gunner is dead," McLeod whispered under his breath.

"Corporal Regan confirmed that your team did ask for Gunner Hagerty," the recovered Captain Webster continued with a non-prosecutorial tone. "I have some additional information that may be of interest. It is a bit of a mystery. Doctor Anh Li, stationed at the South Vietnamese Army sickbay in Dung Ha, vanished. However, we discovered a wealth of information on the doctor's social and professional connections. She knew and socialized with the ranked and influential within the South Vietnamese civilian authorities and U.S. military."

McLeod was puzzled and confused by Webster's revelation of Doctor Li's disappearance and the connection to his Team's ambush.

With a slight tone of empathy, Webster asks, "Sergeant McLeod, do you know the relationship between Captain Doss and Doctor Anh Li?"

McLeod knew about Anh Li's prior sexual encounter with Captain Doss but did not tattle.

Webster sensed that McLeod was sensitive to the question; she continued, "You see, Sergeant, the mystery is that Captain Doss disappeared at the same time as Doctor Li. We do not think this is a coincidence. I believe your intimate relationship with the doctor may shed some light on her disappearance. Could you please explain your relationship with Doctor Anh Li?"

"Other than admitting a sexual relationship with Anh Li, I have no information about her disappearance. "Frankly," McLeod answers, "I do not understand the link between my relationship with Anh Li, her disappearance, and the ambush of Team 33."

"Thank you, but to set the record straight, I deceived you, Sergeant McLeod: No one has interviewed Captain Doss."

With no hesitation, Webster continued. "In other words, the interrogation of Captain Doss has not happened. But, in the cause of seeking the truth, I deemed my deception necessary." While looking down upon her file of papers, Webster commented, "Sergeant McLeod, thank you for your contributions to this debriefing." She shuffled a few papers in the file, moving toward the last entry, and pulled out a crude drawing.

"Thank me for my contribution?" McLeod sarcastically repeats—thoroughly annoyed—McLeod responds. "You decided that deception was necessary?"

Stoically unaffected by McLeod's outburst, Webster asked a follow-up question. "Sergeant McLeod, as we informed you, the bodies of your team members near the helicopter wreckage were found; however, no Cuban soldiers or evidence thereof. My understanding is that you recovered a forearm with a tattoo on it. I have seen the drawing but not the forearm. Do you have the forearm?"

"Do I have the forearm?" McLeod snarkily repeats the question. "No, Captain," McLeod confirms. The flesh was rotting, and the tattoo became indistinguishable. So, I discarded the forearm, but I did draw it out in detail."

"So, Sergeant, considering that Gunny Hagerty is dead and Captain Doss unaccountable, we only have your word about Cuban soldiers and a forearm with a tattoo."

"Yes, Captain," McLeod said, standing and answering. Captain Webster, are you calling me a liar?" She stared into her eyes in a threatening manner. Noting McLeod's demeanor, Lt. Cornel Sullivan called a halt to the proceedings and ordered a ten-minute recess.

Captain Webster, notably frustrated, glanced again at the drawing, closed the file, gathered her case file, and left the room without further ado with the inquiry staff. The Colonel and his adjuncts remained. Colonel Sullivan walked over to McLeod.

"OK, Marine," the Colonel commanded. "Rest and recover. You have done an outstanding job in the bush and during this hearing. Arrangements are being made for you to rejoin your unit in Dong Ha."

Mesmerized by the proceedings, McLeod paid no attention to the Colonel's words. He stood beside his chair, assessing the debriefing until everyone was gone. His team members were dead. Then, along with Doss, Anh Li mysteriously vanished. The Gunner had taken one in the head. In a matter of days, his universe had turned upside down and inside out. Something deep inside had changed; he was no longer the same man, the same Marine. He felt betrayed by those who shared his ideals, which were encompassed in the uniform, anchor, globe, and eagle. He was no longer a believer, a member of the Semper Fi faithful. The Corps slapped him hard, and he would not turn the other cheek.

A month earlier, 1st Force Reconnaissance Company's base camp at Dong Ha in I
Corps Vietnam

Sergeant McLeod and Gunny Hagerty were sitting on a couple of spent ammo boxes scattered inside a half-bombed-out building. The Marines used the building to unwind with beer and music, playing tapes from a popular San Diego radio station. McLeod and Hagerty enjoyed each other's company while reviewing the tactical viability of integrating artillery and air support, agreeing that using Phantoms for close air support, other than dropping napalm, could not compare to the viability of Puff the Magic Dragon.

McLeod explained to Hagerty how important it was to meet personally with the 105-howitzer assigned gun team before insertion; McLeod emphasized that artillery support grid pre-plotting map coordination was an essential prelude to entering Comanche territory.

Gunny Hagerty knew McLeod took no chances. Before every patrol, McLeod would visit Cam Lo with tokens of appreciation for the assigned artillery personnel. He even gave the coveted trophy of an N.V.A. officer's belt buckle to a responsive gun crew that supported his Team during a notably tenuous firefight. McLeod and team members gave equal respect to the on-call air-ground support units.

Gunny eyed the mini recorder in McLeod's hands. "You're the only team leader who takes a mini-tape recorder on patrol?"

"I figure if the bad guys get too close, I plan on turning on my tape recorder, blasting out conversations of Marines in barracks while I boogied."

Hearing a noise outside the building, Gunny looked over McLeod's shoulder and abruptly stood up, leaving with a curse, "That's crazy." I've got to go. You stay in touch, Marine." Gunny grinned as he marched out of the building.

McLeod reflexively adjusted his government-issued Rolex by turning and twisting the jungle-worn wristband, checking the time. The Rolex distinguished rank, privilege, and time in service for those in Force Recon; Gunny Hagerty's quick exit was unexpected, but he soon understood why. Anh Li was in the doorway.

"My Sergeant McLeod," Anh Li declared, "Finally, I can steal a kiss."

"I was hoping you'd stop by," McLeod responded.

Anh Li outstretched her arms as McLeod came within range; she engulfed him, kissing him on his cheek and neck. McLeod squeezed her, lifted her body gently into the air, and caressed her as he lowered her back to the ground.

"Is everything alright?" McLeod asks.

"Tout va Bien. All I could think about was you. It was terrible. I could not concentrate on the patients. I need a kiss now and your body later this evening."

"In a couple of hours." McLeod smiled. They kissed. Ahn Li walked away, but not before turning back with the reassuring smile of a later rendezvous. McLeod watched her leave, hypnotized by the sway of her long, shiny black hair, which moved in rhythm with the action of her perfectly slender hips. The liaison has been three months of romance. If sex, their only shared relationship, was considered love, McLeod was in love.

Anh Li was an Orthopedic Surgeon working for the Red Cross and was assigned to the I Corps Sector of South Vietnam. She came from a multiracial family of Chinese, Vietnamese, and French descent and was raised and educated in Paris. Older than McLeod, Doctor Li was a pleasant contradiction in his otherwise stoic life.

Everything about Anh Li was overwhelming, particularly her professional status. Her ranking within the Red Cross included knowing and interacting with high-ranking military and political personalities. Anh Li never expressed any concern for after the war or immigrant sponsorship; her only interest was sex with Sergeant McLeod. At the beginning of their relationship, Anh Li recalled some family history. Her father, Louis Jadot, was educated at the University of Paris Descartes and was a distinguished medical doctor of French heritage. Louis's French father, Anh Li's grandfather, was the bearer of the Jadot family name. He loved his son. However, when Ah Li was only twelve, her father died. Upon his death, the Jadot family disinherited Louis's Vietnamese family and disavowed any obligation or acknowledgment of shared blood. Despite the Jadot family's behavior, Louis's wife, Anh Li's mother, created a loving home. She took back her Vietnamese Chinese traditions and her family name, Li. She pushed her daughter to mimic her father's academic excellence. Anh Li loved her father and decided to practice medicine out of that love and respect.

"Hey, Sarge, you want a beer?" a Marine asked. The query jolted McLeod out of his daydream. The Marine followed up with a distinction: "It's not cold, but not hot either."

"Sure," McLeod confirmed. The Marine tossed him a Bud. McLeod placed the beer on the makeshift table and laid out his topographic map for the next day's insert. The grid squares marked on the map are noted with references and reminders of past patrols, as well as reminders of Marines now on the other side of earthly madness.

Grid Delta was the code name for the jungle section between the radio relay station on Hill 158, Con Thien, and the North Vietnamese border. Laos was a few grid squares to the west. Although McLeod completed his overflight the day before and had worked on Delta Grid three months earlier, he still studied the map intensely, comparing his on-site traversing notes, recent aerial photos, and overflight briefings from other teams. In addition, he became familiar with the terrain and compared the orientation of contour lines on the map's topography and aerial photographs to prepare for the upcoming mission.

Team 33's radioman had wandered in earlier for a beer and caught McLeod's attention.

"Archer," McLeod shouted to his beer-guzzling radioman. Run down to S-2 and see if they got any new black-and-white on sections Delta and Foxtrot."

"Aye, aye as you command, my Sergeant! I didn't want any more of this warm beer anyway." A few minutes later, Archer returned with a handful of aerial photos and a message. "The Gunny wants to see you; something about tomorrow's mission. Maybe he thinks I'm too short for this last one."

Without responding responsively to Archer's hopeful remark that it was too short to go, McLeod grabbed his map and photos and left the building, shouting to Archer, "Short is when you're on the plane passing over the Golden Gate."

McLeod entered the company's S-2 office, where all intelligence and the Five-Paragraph Orders were verified and issued to recon teams pending insertion. Gunnery Sergeant Hagerty was bent down, scrutinizing the overlay; he didn't raise his head when McLeod walked in.

"Sergeant," the Gunny bellowed, "I was right; this new executive officer, Doss, has taken an unusual interest in your patrol tomorrow. I am suspicious. Why your patrol? Look at these notes on the overlay."

McLeod bent over and peered at Gunny's concern.

The Gunny continues, "See how the markings correspond to your Team and their movements? And here is the debriefing report from your last patrol in that sector. Now, why would Captain Doss be looking for this old information?"

Gunny finally looked up directly at McLeod and pressed on.

"Since his arrival two weeks ago, I've never seen this Doss guy give one hoot about the details of any of our recon teams. So, why Team 33's upcoming patrol? Do you have any ideas?"

McLeod shook his head. "As far as I know, this patrol is just another routine look-see. However, I had brought my debriefing notes from the earlier patrol in the same area a month ago.

McLeod searches his breast pocket and retrieves a green-colored notebook. "Here it is. During my visit to the area, we observed unusual activity, took photographs, and reported a group of suspicious individuals on the north side of the DMZ. "When viewed through the binoculars, it looked like a formal meeting. I could identify a uniformed N.V.A. officer, three uniformed South Vietnamese officers with what looked like a P.L.F. platoon, a CHICOM (Chinese PLA) uniformed officer, and two Caucasians, one in camouflage utilities, the other a female in civilian dress, taking pictures. The grouping was suspicious; my team was on the North Vietnamese side of the DMZ, but close enough to photograph the target. I turned in the film and briefed the report to S-2, who I assumed passed it on to G-2.

"Maybe you stumbled into something important," Hagerty suggested.

"I never saw the processed images; I don't know if the film was even developed. Hell, Gunner, that close to the North Vietnamese side of the DMZ, there's always bad guys wandering about; that's nothing new."

"Well, that briefing report caught my eye. I know the report went directly to the division, and I'm sure it ended up in Military Assistance Command, where some high-ranking intelligence officials decided on its importance. Interestingly, despite my inquiry, there was no follow-up, and now Naval Intel has requested a division G-2 order, specifically Team 33, to be deployed again. But more importantly, there's something wrong with this Doss guy. I've been investigating, and there are a few suspicious items. For example, I can't confirm his orders to 1st Force or secure his S.R.B."

McLeod hesitated, showing some confusion about the term.

"Service Record Book," said the Gunny.

"Oh, yes," said McLeod with a smirk.

With a concerned look, Gunny emphasized: "No one in Division knows him or of him; they don't even know where he came from or how he picked up this assignment with no recon background. He doesn't even smell like a Marine. He's too aloof, doesn't measure up, and lacks the intrinsic authority of a Marine officer. Anyway, two days ago, another one of this guy's strange recommendations was that Doc Marshall should go on your patrol. He insists it must be with your team. This patrol has more oddities outside of procedure and protocol. I can't wait until Major Rice returns from TTY; he's due a week from Monday."

"Dillon went to sickbay Today for some aspirin and noted how excited Doc was about the upcoming patrol. Dillon told him he was out of his mind. Late that afternoon, Doc came to my tent and formally asked if I had any objections. I told him the patrol members expected him to carry his weight and obey orders. As to this mysterious Captain Doss, if your radio contact is available while I'm in the bush and Captain Doss stays out of my field of fire, I'm ok with the Doc joining the patrol."

McLeod reached over and patted Gunny's shoulder.

"This guy is weird; something's not Kosher, as in him insisting on Doc Marshall joining your upcoming patrol," Gunner Hagerty's bitching continues. "

McLeod acknowledges, "By noting, he is the Exec, albeit non-Force Recon qualified." The Gunny grunted in token recognition. "Yes, the patrol is a go."

"Absolutely," McLeod confirms. "We have no choice. It's an order."

McLeod accepted the inevitable as he glanced down at his watch. Hagerty returned to the document, which was lying on his desk. McLeod turned away and raced out of the tent, shouting, "I'm running late." Heading for a cold shower, a shave, and a much-needed rendezvous with Anh Li.

It was well past six when McLeod arrived. As he walked in, he caught a glimpse of Anh Li in front of a full-length mirror, finger-combing her hair.

"That was a long two hours," Anh Li playfully chided while jumping on him panty-free with legs spread and knees on either side of his legs. "Please, lust me, take me as if this is our last. Take me anyway that pleases you; let's make love as if we will never see each other again."

Thinking of her words, as this is what I want, coaching with Anh Li's ass and midbody resting on his palms, he eased her into bed. Anh forcefully flipped her body on top, putting her mouth over his crotch. Eagerly, lustfully, she guided her hand between his legs, reaching for his rigid appendage, unzipped open his pants, and, with cock in hand, inhaled head and stem into her mouth. While insistently sucking on his cock she maneuvered her v over his mouth and tongue. Satisfying minutes passed. A guttural sound of bent-up relief signaled Anh Li's orgasm. McLeod, seeking penetration, placed his hands under her buttocks, lifting her thighs and resting them on his arm muscles. Gently, he lay her backward, carefully guiding her ass and hips atop a feathered pillow. She spread her legs, and he entered her. Both were presently exhausted after carnivorously enjoying the sensual transaction of their orgasmic yin and yang.

As they lay in each other's arms, they comforted each other with equal amounts of deception, each supporting the moment and the need to pretend. To pretend the now would never end.

In the sobriety of the killing and the dying, they understood that love was irrelevant; lust and sex were the now's tangible. They basked in their blatant giving and taking while enjoying the pretense of love.

As the night passed, lovemaking became a self-serving intoxicant, each striving to take more than they received—the fragrance of their lovemaking drugged each into a deep sleep. McLeod stirred while Anh Li lay asleep in his arms. He thought of how the fortune of convenience, circumstance, and dumb luck had aligned. Here, an East Washington High School dropout is having sex with the daughter of Louis Jadot from Paris in a Marine base camp in I Corps, Vietnam.

After a solid snooze, McLeod rose from bed before midnight and went to his area. He had a 5:30 AM insertion to catch a couple of hours of uninterrupted sleep before gathering his team and the final inspection.

The Insertion 0530 before the ambush

A soft mist had settled over the helipad as the four-man reconnaissance team verified its call signals and radio frequencies. The Team loaded NATO 7.2 armor-piercing ammo into their magazines and slammed it into the rifle's magazine well. Safety is locked, grenades are taped and secured. Doc Marshall was armed with a pistol, an exceptionally light carry. The Doc acknowledged the obvious and volunteered, or more, so insisted on humping the other radio and battery.

Three team members sat close, shoulder to shoulder, readying themselves for what was to come. It was only a matter of time before they were knee-deep in Indian country, where bullshit ends, and blood, guts, and fear begin. McLeod and Doc Marshall sat across from the Team; the silence was deafening.

"Team leader," the helicopter crew chief bellowed, "we've got to delay this insert, maybe for another thirty minutes. Our visuals are too low. So, hang tight; I'll get the word to you in time to prepare your equipment."

"A reprieve," McLeod muttered under his breath. "OK, men, you heard the man: thirty minutes. My merciful Catholic God has granted those gooks lurking in the jungle a few minutes of a reprieve."

"Remind me to light a candle in appreciation." Dillon cries out.

"Damn," Thomas gripped. "What the hell are we going to do with thirty minutes?"

"How about a Mary Davidson story?" Archer called out.

McLeod grinned.

Everyone but the Doc nodded in agreement. Doc looked from one team member to the next. He squinted and asked, "Mary Davidson?" The Doc had no idea what a Mary Davidson story meant, and no one volunteered to explain. The Team knew that Mary was a real character in McLeod's life. As McLeod described her, she was the absolute essence of a high-school sweetheart. Her blond hair and devilish blue eyes sparked a warning of naughty unpredictability. An athletic body, supporting firm and well-proportioned breasts, and a provocatively curved behind that a man could learn to appreciate. However, Mary was, by both popularity and demeanor, beyond McLeod's reach. He was a boy attracted to the unattainable and impossible; for Mary, unwittingly, McLeod did not exist.

McLeod had the memory of Mary filed and was ready to fictionalize. Mary was a classmate of his at East Washington High School. He left school in his junior year to join the Marines. He remembers the kindness of his homeroom teacher, Mrs. Swaney, and the ever-haunting failure of not making that makeable touchdown, as well as missing that tackle on defense. All stored away in his mind's library of diminishing self-esteem. Conversely, when seeking solace on long marches or lonely guard duty, McLeod would pull out the file and reminisce over his Mary make-believes. One night in the squad bay, everyone was talking of love lost. McLeod contributed a Mary Davidson story, knowing it was a white lie; regardless, the narrative was wondrously received. Everyone loved his Mary stories; to them, she was not a living, breathing person. She was, to each Marine, wishfully quintessential. The telling and retelling of the Mary Davidson stories were a distraction from the present.

"OK, Sarge, that's enough hesitating," Archer teased. "I'm ready for blond, blue-eyed Mary Davidson, the belle of East Washington High, homecoming queen, and head cheerleader."

"Hell, Archer, you remember more than I do. You should create some Mary stories so I can take a break."

"No dice, Sergeant McLeod; Mary is your woman."

"Oh yes," McLeod recalled, "there was that time in her father's garage after the German Town game...."

The Team leaned into the story with heightened anticipation, each thinking this might finally be the consummation. But long ago, McLeod sensed their true feelings about Mary. She was identifiable in terms of what could have been. Mary was the antithesis of their present: a haven, a wish, a wholesome desire; Mary Davidson was their altruistic ideal, of a moral unattainable. They sanitized their macho justification for the baneful deed of killing strangers as dutifully protecting the analogic Marys back home.

"Sergeant," the crew chief shouted, cutting off the Mary Davidson story. McLeod stood and moved toward the waiting helicopter. "We're going to light up the engines in five minutes. Stage your Marines for boarding. I'll give you the arm-in-hand when I'm ready."

The team heard the crew chief, and the signal to board was given. McLeod shouted, "OK, men, let's load up. It's time to earn that combat pay and rid the world of a few more commies."

In minutes, the Team was loaded. Grid Delta was the next stop. Despite the early morning delay and the sun just breaking the horizon, it was a windless, calm day; however, everyone knew the day would be another hot one in Vietnam. The swirling blades swooshed, and the engines roared. Marines had to lean on each other to communicate. The bird was a CH-46, loaded with C-rations, ammunition boxes, and cartons of body bags, ready for delivery after the 1st Force Recon Team 33 was inserted.

The crew chief was seated in his position, facing aft, under the pilot's upper control area. The machine gunner was a baby-faced young kid with the eyes of an old man. He had boldly printed "flower child" in black ink on his camouflaged helmet, next to a peace symbol known among Marines as the sign of the "great American chicken." He sat behind a mounted swivel-rigged M60 machine gun with a hundred-round load.

After extracting multiple dead and wounded the day before, the helo crew paid no attention to the recon team: no direct eye contact, no sign of concern, and no expressed empathy. It was all business. McLeod oriented his map against the physical distinct land features below. Then, he signaled to the crew chief that he wanted to communicate directly with the pilot. The chief passed his helmet, which had headphones encased within.

"Sir," McLeod loudly barked, "I want to orient myself in prominent terrain positions as we fly over them before the insertion. In the same grid, I'm looking at the wide bend from north to east on Grid Zone Bravo and the stand-alone mountain peak marked 257."

"You got it, Sergeant," the pilot responded, "I'll use those terrain markers on our approach to touchdown; is there anything else?"

"No, sir," McLeod signed off and returned the helmet.

Terrain features were sighted; the crew chief's hand signaled with five fingers, showing minutes to touchdown. McLeod faced his team members, looking each in the eye, and then gave a thumbs-up. The Team and the Corpsman masked their anxiousness by eagerly returning an alpha-ready thumbs-up. Four Marines were in a Force Reconnaissance team: a leader, assistant, radio operator, and scout. Each was cross-trained and prepared to supplement or assume the duties of the others.

George Dillon was the scout and, at twenty-seven (having left the Corps for three years as a civilian and reenlisted), the Team's oldest Marine. But then, George was born old. He was a confirmed, no-nonsense killer. George did not hesitate; he was comfortable with the present and did not plan for or expect any future. For George, the Corps and Vietnam ordained his deliverance as an errant warrior. The gods of violent conflict engendered the Vietnam War, and George rejoiced. His warrior mentality was to execute the required and, if lucky, die valiantly, never having to face the reality of the civilian world or his ex-wife once again.

The youngest, Edward Archer, was the radioman. He was good-looking, well-liked, gregarious, and intelligent. He came from the best families: a mother, a practicing doctor, and a father, a municipal judge. The parents loved each other and their only child very much. He joined the Corps after his girlfriend of two years left him for someone else. After nearly a thirteen-month tour of duty in Vietnam, Archer matured and came to terms with the consequences of his life-altering decision. He was a month away from reconciling with his family and the girl he left behind.

The assistant patrol leader was twenty-two-year-old Calvin Thomas, the epitome of the ideal Marine. Tall, wide-shouldered, with the physical features of a Greek god, he was a Marine Corps lifer, a faithful believer in the martial creed. Thomas's father was a Marine who was killed in action (KIA) while serving in General Puller's 1st Marine Division in Korea. For Thomas, as with his father, death was a professional consequence, a lethal possibility that he wore proudly as a badge of honor.

The helicopter flew at treetop level in a valley to obscure its presence. The pilot looked for a flat spot to drop off its load of Marines. The Team readied to exit. The helicopter descended to within eight feet of the ground. The Team jumped from the copter, rushed to cover and concealment, and formed a perimeter defense. With an ok sign, Archer affirmed radio contact, and McLeod acknowledged. The helicopter's roar and the violently displaced jungle grass gave way to silence.

Each man took a last glance at the only way home as the helicopter disappeared over the horizon. Frozen in place, the Team collectively spent fifteen minutes listening and scanning for unnatural sounds. Finally, sensory surveillance was completed. McLeod stood up, and Delta Grid's mission came to life.

The Patrol - 1966

By hand signaling, McLeod pointed Dillon in the patrol's direction, to the east, shirting a small waterfall on a path with large and small trees sprouting upwards, creating a green canopy spread over a natural trail. The patrol moved swiftly out from the landing site. Anxiety was high. It took time before the Team could settle down and claim their surroundings. After the first full day and night, the Team and terrain eventually grew tolerant of each other. The patrolling has been routine after three uneventful days; aside from aggressive bartering over C-rations and a brief but spirited competition coaxing burrowed leeches out with a lit cigarette, the patrol was uneventful.

Corpsman Doc Marshall shadowed, depending on the order of march, either Dillon or Thomas. Doc rarely spoke, which the Team found odd. Odder still, Archer pointed out to his teammates that Marshall was an E-7 outranking all the corpsmen in the I-Corps Sector, but he insisted on breaking protocol by going out on patrol. What's even crazier is that he received formal permission from Captain Doss.

However, in the 30 days (about four and a half weeks) since his arrival, he proved to his fellow corpsmen his expertise and knowledge. He was professionally respected. Nevertheless, the team members were still trying to understand that an E-7 Corpsman would ask for and much less be allowed to go out on a recon patrol.

The Team was two marching days away from their extraction site and half a day from where McLeod had taken the photos. Interestingly, the Team had not spotted any bad guys; this was highly unusual considering the sector. Everyone chalked it up to good luck. The Team was so close to going home; the mood was positive, and the men looked forward to their last few nights in the jungle. After setting camp for the night, McLeod escaped into a deep sleep, the type that afforded transit relief.

"Sergeant McLeod," Thomas called out as he prodded the Sergeant's right shoulder.

"OK, OK, I'm up." McLeod opened his eyes just before dawn.

"Captain Doss is on the phone," Thomas passed the receiver.

"Thirty-three Actual talk to me. McLeod was instantly alert and conscious of his situation.

The voice of Captain Doss crackled on the radio: "Thirty-three Actual; this is Alfa actual. Convert to secondary frequency and extract on Rally Point alternative instead of Station Blue. Any questions? over."

"Hold on, give me two minutes, Alfa actual." McLeod pulled out his maps and coordinates, briefly studying them. In five minutes, McLeod was back in voice communication with Alfa actual. "Sir, the suggested rally alternative is a discarded entry site beyond the range of artillery and many additional hours of traversing. I do not recommend utilizing that location as an extraction site."

"Sergeant McLeod, I am not interested in your opinion or recommendation. Instead, I am interested in you adhering to my direct order."

"I understand, Captain. Could you please confirm some on-site air support?"

"Yes, I'll call some in some fixed wing when you are near the extraction site."

"Captain," McLeod summons, "Sir, F-4 Phantoms are not the best air support. Instead, I prefer CH-46s with 'puff-the-magic-dragon capability.'

"I'll see that you get support," was the response, and then a click. McLeod put the receiver down and rechecked his map to establish a new route for the patrol.

"Archer, Dillon, huddle up. Where is Thomas? McLeod inquired.

Archer responded, "He's looking for Doc Marshall."

"The Doc lost?"

"Yes, it's dark, probably; stepping out for a number two is my guess."

"Well, OK, we'll fill him in later. The Exec changed our extraction site. Now, this is going to take a lot of work. It's a bit further, and the map's contour lines indicate that it's steeper terrain. However, we have foliage for cover and concealment for most of the way, but the final seven hundred meters to the extraction plateau are all uphill through what I assume will be elephant grass. Considering the time of year, it's shoulder-high and thick.

"Sarge, did I hear that right? No artillery support on the extraction site?" Archer swallowed nervously. "We'll be outside artillery support, and these deep chasms will hinder our communication."

"You heard correctly, Marine; the Exec did assure air. We need to be within Grid Tiger before nightfall. It does mean an extra day in the bush; hopefully, there won't be any more surprises."

"Sarge, ignore this order," Archer advised. "You know it's a tactical mistake. There's no sense in it. This new guy is non-recon. Does he know what he is asking?"

"Sergeant McLeod," Thomas returns, "the Doc is gone."

"Gone?"

McLeod paused. None of this felt right. "Thomas, I assume you have completed a thorough search and found no signs of this Corpsman."

"When you talked to Captain Doss, he just got up and moved into the jungle. I thought he was going to pee, but after 15 minutes." Thomas threw his hands up and shrugged.

McLeod replies, "I'll notify the captain." McLeod knows it is dark, and one can do nothing more than wait for daylight to erase the darkness.

"Archer, in the morning, notify Dung Ha of Doc Marshall's disappearance. Keep trying to reach Gunner Hagerty. We'll execute a 25-meter circular 15-minute search for the Doc at daybreak."

"OK, but please do not obey Captain Doss's order." Archer finalizes his plea, "I got a bad feeling about this."

McLeod knew the alternate extraction site's terrain was not conducive to positive communications. He understood the sensibility of Archer's concern. But in combat, disobeying an order was impossible. In the morning's light, the search was fruitless. They are all focused on moving to Grid Tiger.

The patrol moved forward with as much caution as the necessary pace allowed. Occasionally, Dillon would stop listening, and McLeod would check his compass and orient himself against the map. Still, considering the terrain and situation, the pace needed to be faster than tactically sensible. Nevertheless, McLeod knew they must reach the extraction point before darkness fell. So, the pace quickened, and the push was on.

In the evening, just before sunset, McLeod figured he was close enough and sent Dillon up a tree to confirm.

Dillon reported seeing the edge of the jungle and the elephant grass. The Team was there on time and intact.

McLeod picked a spot for the night, ordering no heat tabs or C-4 to heat the food. Everyone huddled in the thick underbrush of the jungle. Archer turned the radio to a zero-volume hiss and then horizontal for some one-eyed Shuteye.

Archer was, as usual, physically the closest to McLeod when the Team set in for the night. Though tired, Archer suffered from short-timer's anxiety and could not sleep. McLeod, sensing his radioman's concern, reminded Archer that soon, this patrol would be a distant memory.

The scent of the early morning and the rising sun woke the Team. They fought off the habitual inclination for a hot cup of coffee and settled for warm canteen water.

"All right; showers and hot food are hours away." McLeod softly forecasts, "Archer, be sure we establish radio contact before we head out to the extraction point."

"I'm on it," Archer says, putting in the extended antenna. I want to reach Gunny Hagerty instead of Captain Doss, but I'll speak with either of them. I also need the call signals for the extraction helicopter; we only have the frequency, site coordinates, and 1100 hours (about one and a half months) of pick-up time."

Thomas and Dillon were ready to move out. Archer gave the high sign to Sergeant McLeod, saying, "Corporal Regan, on the radio." He whispered to McLeod that he had asked for Gunny Hagerty. Regan told him that his instructions were to pass the information on the radio to Captain Doss and no one else. He'd sent a runner to find the captain and asked Archer to stand by. McLeod acknowledged and gestured to the receiver. Corporal Archer passed the receiver. Ten minutes passed; it seemed like an hour.

"This is Alfa actual; 33. Are you there?"

"Yes," McLeod answered.

"Are you in position?" Captain Doss asked.

"Yes, withstanding, Doc Marshall is wandering in the jungle. I have not received confirmation on supporting fire."

"Your support is on call. Air support has your call sign and radio frequency; the same applies to the extraction helicopter. They will communicate with you as soon as you reach the site. Good luck."

The radio snapped off on the receiving side before McLeod could talk with Gunny Hagerty. He doubted the alternative site's practicality and contemplated disobeying the order and calling Camp Carroll for help. McLeod knew those Special Forces guys would lend a helping hand.

His gut told him everything was wrong with the extraction. And for reasons unknown, Hagerty was unavailable. Thoughts of disobedience swirled around in his mind. But disobeying an order went against his Marine ethos, which was more potent than his common-sense inclination. Disobedience ran counter to some innate genetic traits that were instilled during the first week at Paris Island's boot camp.

The extraction location made no practical sense; nonetheless, he would obey his orders.

"Archer, any luck in reaching Gunny?" McLeod asked one last time.

"Not directly, but I did tell Regan to find Gunny and let him know the situation. He said he would."

Staying within the jungle's cover while searching for a natural path through the field of elephant grass, the team began their descent to the extraction site. Dillon chose a dry stream bed that flowed directly into the uphill climb, where the helicopter would most likely land.

"Sergeant McLeod," Archer signaled with a whisper while moving back to speak directly. "Regan just clicked me. He told me that he had personally told Gunny Hagerty of our change of extraction location and situation. Regan said a pissed-off Gunny was heading out to find Captain Doss. That was the last time anyone had seen Gunny Hagerty."

Unfortunately, we can't do otherwise at this point. "OK, Marines," McLeod barked, "get

back in formation. Dillion, you're on point!"

Dillon had reached the jungle's edge and halted the patrol. He signaled McLeod to come forward as he looked out at the open space they needed to cross. "Here we are, sir. There is no cover and only intermittent concealment until we reach the elephant grass, and it's all uphill."

"Well, let's double time up the hill. Thomas will follow you, so you must look back every few minutes. It's half to three-quarters of a click away, so plan to stop to catch your breath. Occasionally, stop the forward motion if you lose visual contact with me. Stop until you visually reconnect. Before proceeding, look for my arm in a hand signal for further instructions."

Dillon nodded his head to confirm his understanding. The patrol headed through the elephant grass to the extraction site. After a couple of hundred yards out of the jungle's concealment, the sounds of dive-bombing missiles ended thoughts of good luck. The first barrage exploded fifty meters short; the second, by the same distance, was long.

Post Vietnam-1969

After months of psychological treatments for guilt-induced distress and acute sleep disorder, McLeod's discharge from the Corps was inevitable. The doctors forecasted long-lasting social adjustment complications and initiated V.A. consultation treatments as a reliable remedy. Diagnosed with PTSD stress disorder, a career-disabling psychological review ended any possibility of retention in the Corps. He knew he was not well, but a deep, self-deprecating complex syndrome requiring restorative therapy was perplexing for McLeod to absorb and accept.

McLeod's guilt complex stirred into spontaneous anxiety attacks, including recurring flashbacks that induced dissociation issues that often synergistically fed one into the other. All of which resulted in an emotionally messed-up Marine.

For months, the guilt of Team 33's demise was emotionally debilitating, with crying being the usual result. Over time, however, the intensity and occurrence of spontaneous crying diminished; nonetheless, proportionately, McLeod's psyche convinced him that pleasure forbade and pain endured was an acceptable penalty. He was invigorated by the psyche-imposed flagellation (of pleasure proscribed and pain endured) as punishment for obeying Doss's foolish order and not dying with his team. McLeod had stumbled upon a medicinally holistic restoration of his malaise.

He bought a used Chevy truck, packed his earthly possessions into two nylon parachute bags, moved out of the Navy hospital, and executed an abrupt about-face from the only belief system he ever acknowledged.

He had no direction, purpose, or esprit de corps. For the first time, he circuitously wandered. He went nowhere. Then, one day, the phone rang. He immediately recognized the voice. It was Jay Navadel, an old Force Recon Buddy.

"How did you get my number?" McLeod sputtered.

"You haven't heard my voice since the days of Second Force, and all you can say is, 'How did you get my number?' That's great, McLeod," Navadel joked. "If you must know, you're registered with the 4th Marine Division. You're automatically placed in standby-reserve status. That's where I retrieved your address and phone number in Venice, California. Upon discharge, the standby reserve is automated, but as experienced, the left hand of the 4th Marine Division S-1 has no idea where they left the right."

"Indeed," McLeod recalled. "Well, what are you up to?"

"I am up to chasing you down. I have a mission for you".

"Mission?" McLeod perked up. "It has been a long time since I've had a mission. What is it?"

"The short story: I am in Vegas in the collecting markers business. I've been doing this gig for the last couple of years, doing pretty well, and now I need some help."

Jay paused, then asked. "Are you interested?"

"Hell, yes. When do I start?"

"As soon as you pack your bags and get here. Do you want to know how much it pays?"

"I couldn't care less. It pays what you give me. Where do I report?"

"Thunderbird Hotel, Las Vegas. When driving into Vegas," Navadel suggested, "stop at a gas station, payphone, call 702-779-0322, and I will meet you in the lobby."

"I will be there this Friday evening," McLeod assured Jay.

"Great!" Jay exclaimed.

Navadel's voice was a relief for McLeod, a positive, sentimental urging, a sorely needed life preserver for a drowning man, a directional reset.

With his two parachute bags, one in each hand, McLeod arrived in the hotel lobby as promised, and sure enough, there was Navadel, standing tall with his big, broad smile beaming, his identifiable front tooth gap visible. With arms wide open, he briskly walked up to McLeod and gave him a big, forceful hug, declaring how good it was to see an old-school Force Recon Marine. It was good to see his old friend. Blue skies and sunny days replaced his doldrums as if he had instantly recovered from a drunken fog.

"OK, buddy, let's get your stuff into your room. You're going to like this city and the work. I have checked you into the hotel. You are on the payroll, so you don't need to worry about room charges or expenses. I'll take care of everything. The valet will accept and deliver your bags; here's your room key. Let's go get a steak."

"You should know I have no idea what a marker is, much less collecting one," McLeod confesses.

"All in good time, McLeod," Navadel assures McLeod.

The steak dinner was at Jodie's Place, off Las Vegas Boulevard, on Paradise. After catching up, Jay tells McLeod he is marrying Barbra, his old high school girlfriend. The reminiscing continued, and after drinking a few, Jay asked McLeod about Team 33 and his medical discharge. Before McLeod could respond, "I thoroughly checked your status with former Colonel, now 4th Marine Division commander, General Sullivan. Presently, you are on inactive reserve status, and at your pleasure, the 4th Marine Division would love to have you on active reserve status. There is an infantry reserve unit here in Vegas."

"Unbelievable," McLeod responded, "the Corps wants me."

"Now tell me," Jay asks, "What happened to your team?" McLeod tells him of the ambush.

"By the N.V.A. or Viet Cong?" Jay inquired.

McLeod answered. "No, not directly; the N.V.A. aided and assisted, but a helicopter crew of Cubans ambushed us."

"Well," Jay suggested, "I assume you're going to find out who ordered the killing and retribute with the deadliest form of coerciveness?"

The straightforward assumption was like a bolt of lightning shooting through McLeod's brain. The quest for righteous revenge began to manifest, and from deep within, it inflamed his inner loins. Once burdened by relentless guilt, he has found magical relief in revenge. A simple question sparked the reason, a purpose that would ignite a redirection of McLeod's life. In minutes, he deduced that, satisfyingly, even if he died while striving to execute righteous revenge, his death was an acceptable consequence. From that moment on, McLeod vowed, as improbable as it seemed, to focus on finding and killing all associated with the slaying of Team 33.

McLeod adapted to chasing down gaming debt like a heated knife through cold butter. Within months, he learned that the work was a combination of reconnaissance and combat patrols. Measuring success was straightforward; either the funds were collected or not. Within a year, McLeod had become an expert in the business. He had gained Jay's confidence.

On the side, McLeod was networking his former Marine connections within the military's intelligence community, seeking information on the Cuban outfit that murdered Team 33. Unfortunately, the response from his limited contacts was not productive. No one wanted to delve into a time that most would rather forget. Hard evidence of a Cuban military contingent operating in Vietnam existed, but proof was not accessible to his low-level contacts. The Cubans inside that helicopter were proof enough for him and certainly sufficient to rile his revengeful instinct. But he needed a starting point to act on his quest, and he had no such entree.

Dumb Luck Shines

One fine day, while doing a collection job in Miami, chasing some monies owed to the Dunes Hotel, McLeod was put up as a guest at the Fontainebleau Hotel on Collins Avenue. He had completed his task, and the Las Vegas Dunes hotel comped a five-day vacation stay.

Then and there, the Great God of Circumstance & Serendipity shone on him. One of life's unexplainable, unanticipated events unfolded. As if conceived by a novelist stuck in the lethargic doldrums, a brilliant opportunity hit McLeod right between the ears.

On the first day of his vacation, not unlike many such March afternoons in Miami, it was sunny, hot, and windy, with bright blue skies. The hotel was bustling with people. Some eagerly engaged in conversation, while others circuited casually from pool to lounge, toweling off, adjusting their hats, and savoring their drinks. Couples assisted each other, generously spreading suntan lotion over their faces, chests, and shoulders.

McLeod was alone, sipping fresh-squeezed orange juice while enjoying a poolside parade of bikinis in motion. He relaxed on his pool chair, the incline adjusted to a 45-degree angle, and bath towels placed for comfort softened his backrest. A white terry-cloth bath towel was strung around his shoulders. As he adjusted his sunglasses from the top of his head to his eyes, a uniformed hotel waiter served a drink to the lady sitting directly in front of him and to his left. The waiter placed the drink on the table, exposing his right forearm.

The faded gold star against the black 666 on a field of red was clear; it was the same tattoo as the Cuban helicopter pilots. His adrenaline raced. McLeod's casual demeanor transformed him into a stalking hunter. Although his heart pounded as if he had just finished a hundred-meter dash, the sight of the tattooed Cuban ignited his innards. It was all he could do to keep from tackling the waiter. Prudently, he salvaged enough sobriety to preserve an opportunity for in-depth discovery.

Besides, the suddenness of the sight required a second look for validation. McLeod followed the waiter, seeking one more look to be sure. McLeod's heart pounded again as the waiter extended his arm, fully exposing the tattoo; it was the same design.

Assured that the lucky break was real, McLeod calmed down his inclination. Instead, he transformed himself from a tiger to a hawk. He hovered and stalked the prey.

It was mid-afternoon; the blinding sun hung in the center of the cloudless sky. Commonly, the adults barked and laughed too loudly. At the bar, patrons had to speak over the sound of the pool.

By late afternoon, Families had returned to their rooms. The pool area had degenerated into a joyful drunken melee. Indulgent behavior—grinding hips and exposed cleavage, buttocks pinched—the music's volume turned higher. But, regardless of the multiple enticements, McLeod's fixation was on one person. He followed him like a hungry lion, patiently waiting for the antelope to take just one more step.

Dumbfounded by the sheer luck of the situation, he contemplated the possibilities. The shock of the discovery gave rise to a plan of action. He stood, shook his towel, and hung it over his chair. Grabbing his utility bag, he walked casually but directly over to the bar where he'd noticed a USMC tattoo on the bartender's arm. McLeod wasted no time starting a conversation.

"Hey, U. S. Marine," McLeod called out. Your tattoo looks a little faded. You must be a real salt Marine, right?"

"Korea," the bartender responded to his brethren. "I got out in '52; joined in '44. It was so cold in Chosin that I swore I would never be cold again. So here I am in the Sunshine State. You look like a Marine. You were in Vietnam?"

"Absolutely," McLeod emphasizes, but he quickly changes the subject. "Say, this place sure has excellent pool service. So many people, all liquored up and rowdy. Incredible! How do you do it?"

"Good to be appreciated; the work is hard. Most guests expect quality service and are pleased to compliment the servers with excessive tipping," the bartender responded. "The secret is administrative control, solid professional staff, and managerial leadership. Guests have grand expectations that must be met or exceeded. Hotel management and staff understand that consistency of goods and services is the currency of guest retention. I am the resident insister. I graduated from the finest middle-management school in the world, the Corps."

"I can verify that my waiter, the one near the high board, was terrific there," McLeod said, pointing to the tattooed waiter.

"That's Rojo; he's not even one of my stables of regular Cubans—Rojo's Manny Zapata's cousin. Manny's my regular; his mother got sick, so he sent Rojo to fill in for him. I let them participate in this exchange program so I don't have to redo the paperwork, check their immigration status, obtain a W-2, or request permission from upper management. All these Latinos look alike to the bosses. At any rate, it's also easier for them; it's a no-cost, closed-mouth option, and they don't have to change names on the payroll scheme that benefits everyone and hurts no one. Surely, you can appreciate the beauty of that other than perfectly legal."

"So," McLeod noted, "when Manny is ready, he returns to work, and that's the end. Not a bad deal for all involved."

"Manny will be out for at least a month; that's my bet. Rojo keeps his head down and works hard. He earns generous tips that we all share, and he is always on time."

The two Marines shook hands, pledged allegiance with a "Semper Fi," and returned to their respective concerns. McLeod reached into his utility bag and pulled out his shorts, shirt, and sneakers. He then waited; after sunset, the pool was vacant. The cleanup began. Finishing with his work, Rojo motioned to his boss and disappeared to the employees' locker room. Shortly after, he returned in civilian clothes and, with a smile and a wave to his boss, vacated the premises.

Tracking The Prey

McLeod stealthily followed Rojo as he headed to a crowded bus stop across the street from the hotel. Several tourists and off-duty workers were waiting. McLeod blended in with the crowd and then boarded the bus, following a couple of passengers behind Rojo.

Twenty minutes later, Rojo stepped off the bus's front door. McLeod exited from the rear. He followed Rojo on the opposite side of the street for about half a block until Rojo turned right. Rojo then walked along the right side of a triplex apartment building and entered through a rear door. McLeod walked past the front of the apartment building, careful not to stop, look back, or show any hint of interest.

Before discovering Rojo, McLeod's thirst for revenge was hampered by the need for more information and access to the right connections. With Rojo's tattoo, the present is validated in real time and indirectly linked to the past.

McLeod dogged Rojo's leaving-work-to-home pattern for three days, learning that this Cuban was as predictable as a Swiss watch. Rojo lived alone; aside from work, there were no other movements, no visitors, nothing but work, and then he returned to his apartment. McLeod knew that searching Rojo's apartment and interviewing the Cuban was essential, so he decided to break into his apartment and wait till he returned. Monitoring revealed that 4:00 p.m. was the optimal time to enter. He would have three hours before Rojo returned from work and plenty of time to execute a convincing search and set up the ambush. McLeod knew that Cousin Manny would not be gone forever. He needed to act.

Wearing an oversized, long-sleeved shirt, McLeod pocketed a small Kodak, a fully loaded .45-caliber pistol with one round in the chamber, and a silencer tucked in his waistband. After putting on skin-tight pigskin gloves, he prepared to enter Rojo's apartment.

The door to the apartment was on the alley side, toward the back of the building. Potted palm trees concealed the entrance, spaced evenly in rows along the wooden walkway that connected the complex's front to the rear. The sun was setting. A giant shadow fell over the entire entrance as McLeod tried one key after another from the six possibilities matched to the serial code found on the lock. Finally, on the fourth attempt, the tumbler turned.

He slid the key blade out and opened the door only as far as necessary to slide through. He then gently shut and locked the door. He stuffed the keys in his pocket and stood motionless, listening to his heart return to its normal rhythm. The darkness required an adjustment to his vision; McLeod waited for his mind and body to acclimate to his new surroundings. He donned his cotton ski mask. The studio apartment was clean enough to pass an I.G. inspection. The white sheets, olive-green blanket, and white pillow stood out as bedding on the mattress in one corner of the room.

Before the in-depth inspection, McLeod fastened the silencer onto the pistol's barrel, returning the pistol between the belt and pants on the left front side of his belly button. He continued to explore, thinking this was an office, not a living space.

A Spanish-language TV guide and Bible rested on top of the Television. The clothes in the closet were organized and neatly hung, and the bathroom was no exception. The soap dish had a new bar, the clean hairbrush lay beside the comb, and the razor lay beside a can of Gillette shaving cream.

Inside the medicine cabinet was an orderly arrangement of sized bandages, a whole roll of white tape, Hydrogen Peroxide, a bottle of Bayer Aspirin, Iodine, and a Red Cross-labeled anti-bacterial gel. He curiously scanned the clothes, newspapers, sports, and girly magazines.

The creaking sound of wood on wood violated the quiet. McLeod shifted his gaze from the latest cover of Hustler toward his back, reached for his pistol, and attached the silencer. A flood of light spilled in from an opening where only a wall had been moments ago.

Suddenly, a slight sound of wood-on-wood friction separated part of the wall between the bed and the small writing desk. An opening as wide as a door appeared. For McLeod, the contrasting light from the opening was like a flash of lightning. Facing him in the foreground of the opening, a surprised man stood frozen. The figure hesitated, trying to make out the shadowy image before him as his right hand held down a rope cord that had triggered the door's opening. When McLeod came into view, the man was shocked. He had already begun to step in. Off guard and temporarily frozen in place, precious seconds passed.

The man recouped and started to step back, but in his rush, tripped and faltered. He instinctively held onto the rope as he tried to recover, but fell to his knees. The door opened wide. With the pistol in hand, McLeod charged forward and caught sight of two other male figures in the hidden room. A Uzi and three revolvers were now on a table in the back room. The two inside the room reached for their weapons. McLeod's index finger automated the trigger squeeze. The first round blasted, hitting the seated man squarely in the chest. The speed and caliber of the bullet blew the guy off the stool. At the same time, the man on the floor, with his free hand, reached up and pulled hard on McLeod's waist belt while the other hand released the cord, fully opening the door. McLeod smashed the man on the top of the head with his pistol butt.

At the far end of the back room, the third man pointed a 9mm (about 0.35 in) Uzi at McLeod and pulled the trigger: nothing, no discharge. He reinserted the magazine and slapped it upwards from the bottom with his right palm. A secure metal-to-metal sound assured the shooter of the proper union.

Too late: McLeod moved his pistol into position as a sharp pain shot up in his left thigh. He ignored the pain and concentrated on the man with the Uzi. McLeod squeezed the trigger; the round fired lower than intended and hit the gunman's groin, causing him to bend and spin backward, screaming in agony. McLeod's second round hit the center of the bent-over gunman's head, smashing it like a melon. Blood and bone splattered in all directions.

McLeod now addressed the pain in his thigh and found a stiletto jabbed into his upper thigh. The now fully conscious assailant released the handle of the blade and struggled successfully to enter the back room. He reached the UZI. Absorbing incredible pain, McLeod calmly aligned the front sight to the struggling man's body and squeezed the trigger.

McLeod considered the possibility that the noise could have compromised his position. That was his thought until he noticed the extensive handmade soundproofing.

The embedded stiletto stopped most of the bleeding. Raiding the medicine cabinet, McLeod found a container of hydrogen peroxide, a tube of antibacterial substance, and a small bottle of iodine. Before pulling out the knife, he took off his shoes and shirt, stepped into the shower, ran the water, and gently pulled the blade out. Blood rushed from the wound, the shower floor, and the drainage area. Pressing down on the wound with the rag in his hand stopped the bleeding enough so that he could take off his pants. Sitting on the side of the shower tub, he applied the peroxide. After a few minutes, he poured the iodine over the one-inch gash, followed by some antibacterial first aid, and then bandaged and taped his wound securely. He washed the blood spattering off his face. Taking sheets of toilet paper, he wiped the entryway of blood spots at the sink, deposited them, and flushed. He stuck the bloodied washcloth in his pocket and looked down at his watch. Two more hours before Rojo would be home.

McLeod searched the closet until he found a suitable change of clothing. Putting his bloody clothes and knife into a paper grocery bag, he checked his watch and continued the search.

He found an extensive list of Spanish surnames within the soundproof room, including Miami addresses, telephone numbers, and photos of family members, with names and birth dates noted on the back. The evidence showed that the Cuban team's mission was to monitor, extort, and terrorize exiled Miami Cubans, using family and friends as leverage. Proving that Miami was not beyond the reach of Fidel Castro

As expected, the sound of a key inserted into the lock, the waiting over, like clockwork, Rojo had returned. Unaware and vulnerable, Rojo entered his apartment and reached for the light switch. McLeod smashed him on the back of the head with a Uzi. Rojo stumbled back and fell face forward. Dazed but conscious, he tried to gather himself, but McLeod leaped on him and bound his wrists with riggers tape, then shoved a washcloth in his mouth. McLeod whispered in Rojo's ear. "Let me catch you up on the new situation. Your buddies are all dead. I'm here to get some specific information." Rojo's head nodded up and down, affirming he understood.

"Okay," McLeod continued, "I'll pull out this wet washcloth in a moment. However, I want you to understand that I am aware of your involvement with Uncle Fidel, and I am not interested in it. I am only interested in your tattoo. So, the deal is this: Cooperate and answer my questions, and I will leave you alive. Don't answer my questions, and I will kill you."

Still wearing his ski mask, McLeod pulled the wet gag out of his mouth. Rojo stared at him.

"Who is the current commander of Triple-Six Battalion?" McLeod demanded.

"I am not aware," Rojo pleads, "of a Triple-Six Battalion. I served in a special unit that forced us to tattoo Triple-Six on our right forearm."

Rojo's answer was satisfactory. However, the next question was not as easy.

"Who is the commanding officer of these special hombres?"

"I don't know," Rojo answered defiantly.

"Don't know; imagine that. You don't know; mi amigo, tú dices 'no sé.'" McLeod smirked sarcastically after displaying his far less-than-perfect Spanish. "Rojo, this information is not secret. There's no betrayal. McCleod shoved the cloth back into Rojo's mouth. As McLeod reached inside his pocket for his butane lighter, Rojo's eyes opened wide, glimmering with terror. McLeod flipped the lever, and a robust flame ignited. He placed the flame three inches under Rojo's left ear, and the Cuban's skin turned roasted red. The smell of burning flesh permeated the air for ten seconds. Rojo struggled. Sweat poured down his forehead. He whimpered in pain, eyes watering, smearing his face. McLeod withdrew the lighter, pulled the wet cloth, and applied it to Rojo's smothering ear.

Rojo gasps, "Ochoa General Arnoldo Marcus Ochoa. Since the beginning, Marcus Ochoa has been the commander," Rojo's voice quivered. "He is the man. But, please, I am only a soldier. I know little. I do what they tell me."

"Does this Ochoa ever leave Cuba?"

"Yes, he vacations every Christmas in the Canary Islands as a guest of the Russian ambassador to Spain. They have been friends for many years. Moreover, Ochoa's daughter is married to the ambassador's son."

"What are the dates of this vacation?"

"At Christmas, from December 15 to December 28," Rojo confidently replies.

McLeod asked, "How do you know these dates so well?"

"Because I was once on his family's security detail, there is much careful planning."

Rojo's eyes reflected a truthfulness, followed by, "I swear this is the truth. These dates in Cuba are common knowledge and have been the same for many years."

"One more question: What is the significance of 666 under the tattoo?"

"Before my transfer into counterintelligence, I was, for less than a year, a member of a highly decorated team from special units; they considered themselves fiendish devils. The original unit members created the "Triple Six" as their designation, and over time, the creation was officially adopted.

McLeod put the cloth back into his mouth. "I am going to leave you here tied up. I am going to call the police. They will turn you over to the FBI, eventually deporting you back to Cuba. Castro is disappointed in your unit's discovery. However, if you tell them of my Ochoa Christmas vacation questions, they will kill you. So, let's let this hostile interface be our secret. More than likely, this intrusion will be blamed on a stateside Cuban family member whose family your comrades extorted. If I were you, I would support that story."

After pouring hydrogen peroxide over Rojo's ear, a search was conducted to ensure nothing pointed to his person. McLeod left the apartment. Forty minutes later, from a payphone, McLeod called the police.

Opportunity Knocks – 1974

Upon returning to Las Vegas, Navadel sat him down to discuss an ongoing development: " Barbra's father, as a precondition for his blessings, wants me entirely out of Vegas. So, if you agree, pass on to me this year's receivables and your commissions, less your salary, and the business is yours." An overwhelmed McLeod accepted Navadel's generosity and the giant step forward it represented.

Jay Navadel was off to his hometown in Buffalo, New York. He had accepted a job working for his in-laws' family business and left Vegas in three days. The company was McLeod's, lock, stock, and all the barrels.

McLeod had been discharged from the Corps for over five years and spent the last 30 months (about two and a half years) working in Navadel's collection business. With Navadel's assistance in operational nuances, statutory particulars, and, most importantly, the numerous casino connections, the assumption of ownership was seamless.

With Rojo's input, the plan to avenge had developed a specific mission; the first step in the puzzle was coming together. McLeod had a target and a December timeline to prepare. His target was General Marcus Ochoa, the Commanding Officer of Tropas Especiales, Barralión 20270, and the leader of the super-elite Commando 43 members. They will all be with their family in the Canary Islands. Now, McLeod has the independence to act and the financial wherewithal to fund his revenge.

In the meantime, McLeod took to his business with the intensity of a thousand worker bees. He drove his collection percentages upward until the company's performance competed directly with the older, more established firms.

Although McLeod's passion for the business was essential, he quickly learned how vital an outstanding accountant or administrator was to its effectiveness.

One late afternoon, McLeod had just left his office when a car approached him. He recognized the driver as one of Sam Diamond's veteran Silver Slipper Casino employees.

"Mr. McLeod, the boss, would like to see you at your earliest availability. Would now be an imposition?"

McLeod was familiar with Sam Diamond but was still surprised by the invitation. Intrigued, McLeod stepped into the backseat, and the driver immediately started babbling about how management was so pleased with McLeod's collection work. Moreover, the driver was overly optimistic about McLeod's future. "Mr. Sam Diamond is a man of respect."

Remaining silent, McLeod was curious about Mr. Diamond's invite. He recalled a confidential personal favor he had completed for Mr. Diamond weeks earlier. Maybe this was the reason for the summons. He shrugged off the driver's flattery as gibberish. They were minutes away from the Silver Slipper Casino.

Sam Diamond was seventy-five years old. He moved to Vegas in 1961 when

Cohen was convicted of tax evasion for the second time. In 1946, Benjamin (Bugsy) Segal tried to hire him as a floor man at the Flamingo, but Cohen talked him out of the opportunity. In 1971, Sam was five feet seven inches tall, slightly built, with white hair, gentle manners, and was well-liked. He was a dapper dresser— Sam fronted ownership of the Silver Slipper, a grandfathered-in casino with no hotel.

Sam had two sons: a schoolteacher, the 'good' son; the other was a gambling drug addict who stole from his mother's jewelry box to meet his insistence on "doing stupid." The 'bad' son had run up a gaming marker at one of Reno's casinos and run off with the cash from forged checks.

McLeod understood it would be an embarrassment for the Diamond family and worse if the Reno casino people got to him first. McLeod received his assignment through a well-known intermediary and had yet to meet Mr. Diamond. With absolute discretion, McLeod completed the assignment in three days. McLeod had not heard from Mr. Diamond, nor did he expect him to; it was nothing more than a job. He refused, as a strategically solid move after the cashed checks were repaid, to accept payment.

The driver pulled up to the back of the casino. An attendant opened McLeod's door and ushered him through the casino's rear door entrance. Once inside, Mr. Diamond's secretary greeted McLeod: "Mr. Diamond is so pleased you could meet him on such short notice. It's appreciated. Follow me, please."

McLeod nodded. Curious, he followed her into the casino coffee shop, where Sam sat with his wife, Marion.

Sam spotted him halfway. Marion rose, gave Sam a little peck, and then excused herself. But before she regressed, Marion asked, "Mr. McLeod, would you like some coffee?"

Still standing, McLeod gave an affirmative, "Yes, ma'am."

"Thanks for coming; it was time we met," Sam said. Please have a seat. Marion and I valued that personal favor you so discreetly executed. Now, I need to address a business issue I've been contemplating. I've had my eye on you for a while. I admire your consistently diligent business practices, general business acumen, and reputation for discretion. All these positives generate respect."

Sam paused as the waiter delivered the coffee.

"Mr. Diamond," McLeod started to speak. Sam's hand, palm facing outward, cautioned him to stop talking and listen.

"McLeod, I have been on this gaming racket for 50 years and have seen many changes. I know that slot machine technology is evolving from mechanical to a software-based system. This billionaire, Howard Hughes, will dramatically change this once morally unacceptable business, making it acceptable to have families as customers. Public traded corporations' acceptance of gambling as a legitimate enterprise is at the forefront of Wall Street's and Main Street's interests. And frankly, I am unprepared for this change; I need your help."

Sam then divulged a secret: "I'm selling the Silver Slipper to Howard Hughes, presently living with his Mormon overseers at the Desert Inn. I also own the Aladdin Hotel. It currently lacks a gaming license, but it is expected to obtain one soon. I've got some partners from St. Louis and Detroit; they've secured seventy-seven million in Union pension funding. They will receive super-majority equity in the joint, and as a secure base, the pension fund will earn two points above the U.S. Wells Fargo bank interest rate on their investment. I negotiated a seven-year first right of refusal on buying out their ownership at a 10% discount on the market price.

Sam paused as the server refreshed his coffee. He then explained that this meeting was a job offer that would evolve into his second-in-command position in six months. He would collaborate with the existing team to facilitate the sale of the Silver Slipper to Hughes Corporation and repurpose the Aladdin Hotel. Finally, McLeod confessed, "Sam, I never finished high school. The only degrees I ever dealt with were the windage and sight alignment on my M-14."

Smiling broadly, "McLeod, I left school in the eighth grade. Formal education is important, but it is not the deciding factor. I have measured your accomplishments and know you are the man I want for my particulars. You will be accepting responsibilities, but these responsibilities will be proportionate to your authority. I have five in-house attorneys, an accounting department, and dozens of consulting MBAs at your disposal. We will initiate the system's integration process within the next six months. Your organizational placement will require a gaming license, and you will act operationally as my right hand and manage the hotel's international marketing. "I need you to say yes because you start immediately," Sam earnestly continued.

"Yes," McLeod answered. "May I ask why we are having this discussion in a coffee shop?"

"Because!" Sam exclaimed. Howard's Mormons have bugged my office, home, and casino office and have paid informants to canvas the casino. They seem a bit paranoid; this Hughes fellow is strange."

Regarding your collection business, pass the purchase price to my accountant, and I'll buy and merge it. I suppose you have an employee who can run it, and, of course, its biggest eventual client, the Aladdin Hotel, will guarantee increased revenue.

The two parted with a confirming handshake. McLeod's hiring spread expeditiously from Diamond's property to the gaming community. The anonymous businessperson instantly became a budding luminary. Suddenly, without any substantive evidence other than Mr. Diamond's endorsement, he gleaned respect. However, McLeod proved his worth within six months, validating Sam Diamond's wise decision.

Sam Diamond, a Vegas Legend 1975

A common expression is that the challenge defines the man; that adage went double for McLeod. As evidenced by associates, fellow employees, and competitors, McLeod gained the reputation of being a resourceful, determined, and dependable day-to-day manager.

Sam and his partners accepted the Teamsters' Financing and operating terms. As Sam's trusted assistant, McLeod's power and prestige grew. Within a year, McLeod caught the eye of the growing dominance of the Hughes Corporation. However, the employment offered by Mr. Hughes had no persuasive possibility. He stayed with the Aladdin Hotel to protect Sam and to prevent any conflicts with his partners. McLeod's loyalty to Sam and his enterprise was unquestioned.

At the end of his second year, with the Aladdin Hotel business firmly in place, General Ochoa's Christmas in the Canary Islands was nearing, and he was fortunate to have hired Delores Cheng to assist in his professional responsibilities. By chance, McLeod recognized Cheng's administrative abilities when cross-purposed with her boss, Mike Evans, on mutually beneficial matters. It was evident to everyone that Delores took a personal sense of ownership and pride in her work. For a decade, she served as the personal assistant to Evans, one of the pioneers of the Vegas Strip. McLeod only met Evans by chance; the encounter was brief but disappointing.

Although Evans was aloof, to the point of hostile arrogance, McLeod respected what Evans had accomplished. That lucky encounter with Evans led to his meeting with Delores. McLeod and Delores hit it off immediately. Thoughts of Delores working for him one day were never far from his mind.

However, after six months, McLeod felt that Delores' fate had dealt him a fatal blow: she had quit her job with Evans to pursue marriage and the possibility of a family. But fate had affected quite the contrary. Her marriage, sadly for Delores, lasted less than a year. When she returned to Evans, he reminded her one time too many of his advice not to marry, emphasizing with a recurring pithy of "I told you so." One day, she'd had enough; Delores took offense and quit. Wasting no time, McLeod made her an offer. She accepted, and again, the sky parted in favor of the ex-Marine.

Without a doubt, Delores was the best, most positive business resource ever directed at the benefit of W.R. McLeod. She was discreet, confident, intelligent, and faithful. Even in the most pressing of circumstances, Delores reigned with absolute control. She oversaw her area and McLeod's workspace. Everyone respected her domain; Delores was honest, forthright, and consistent. The most profitable segment of the casino's gaming action came from the international department, which rated five secretaries; Delores hired them all and managed their functions. She never forgot anything. However, her most significant contribution was managing McLeod's schedule. Aware of Team 33 but unaware of his revenge scheme, Delores instinctively knew that such details were not within her purview. Therefore, she never asked questions unless the answers served her boss's interests.

"McLeod," Delores, like most, loved to call her boss by his last name. There is a Mr. Sepúlveda on his way up from the lobby."

"Oh, yes. It's on Thursday. Give me five minutes and send Mr. Sepúlveda into the conference room."

Delores nodded and returned to her outer office.

For convenience, McLeod had lived in Aladdin since he began working for Mr. Diamond. McLeod realized that staying in hotels all these years suited him.

"Señor Sepúlveda, please come in," McLeod gestured warmly. It is gratifying to meet you in person after all these weeks of correspondence." Delores gently closed the door behind him. Raymond Sepúlveda, a favorite son of Colón, Panama, his hometown, was known as a gentleman of contacts, discretion, and impeccable manners; his business reputation was one of respect.

He set up lucrative international business transactions in the Free Trade Zone. For example, after arranging a discreet initial introduction to Cuban General Martinez Vasquez, American goods, despite the explicit embargo, flowed unabated from Colón to Cuba. Sepúlveda took full advantage of the Boland Amendment (that restricted and even prohibited the sale of U.S. arms to the contras) in consort with U.S. Southern Command. He traded Panamanian bananas and sugar for Czechoslovakian and East German small arms. Sepúlveda arranged a transaction with the Central Intelligence Agency surrogates for distribution to Colonel Bermudez, known as Comandante 380 in Honduras.

Sepúlveda was a Harvard graduate, an honorable man who had learned to fly above the chaos. His information was accurate and, most importantly, timely. It was common knowledge that the Drug Enforcement Agency and the Central Intelligence Agency had offered him a blank check to work for them. He politely refused. Sepúlveda walked confidently towards McLeod, right hand outstretched, anticipating a hardy handshake. He found satisfaction.

McLeod informed Sepúlveda that the Sepúlveda bloodline was traced to Castile and Aragon's royalty. He knew that his ancestors were the original people who populated, built, and defended Porto Plata, the first city of Panama.

"I am impressed, Mr. McLeod; you have done your research," Sepúlveda complimented.

Sepúlveda was sixty-two, fair-skinned, with light brown hair and a slightly receding hairline combed right to the left. He had big, happy, blue eyes that reflected sincerity benignly. Dressed in a cream-colored, perfectly tailored silk suit, he wore no tie but sported giant Colombian emeralds on each cuff.

"Puerto Rican rum, light, with lime and ice," said McLeod, handing his guest a large round glass.

Sepúlveda accepted the drink and smiled, pleased that McLeod had done his homework.

"Please," McLeod gestured for them to sit. "Your affection for fine rum and other such epicurean delights is no secret. But, then again, you are a man whose business is in the knowing."

Sepúlveda nodded appreciatively and cut to the chase. "Since our mutual friend suggested I could be of benefit to you. He briefed me on your specific interests. Of course, as I mentioned on our most recent phone call, I have personally arranged my travels to coincide with this timely intelligence."

"Excellent!" McLeod barked with satisfaction.

Sepúlveda continued. "Your interest is in General Marcus Ochoa, who commanded a hand-picked special unit Raul Castro chose for foreign deployment. I have researched this Cuban Army outfit; their archives have been cross-referenced, and I can confirm the information."

"Here are those files. Accessed at some risk by my Cuban connection." Sepúlveda set his drink down and, with his right hand, reached into his left inside jacket pocket and passed McLeod a mailer-sized, thick white envelope.

"You will find the General's biography, schedule, family, and some collateral details that you will find beneficial. Everyone in Cuba is familiar with the Ochoa family's Christmas vacation, but the enclosed details are more difficult to obtain. Additionally, I have identified a former senior-level member of this unit who served under the General in Vietnam. He is a frequent Vegas visitor."

"And this individual is your welcoming surprise? Is he presently in Vegas?"

"Yes, you may rendezvous at the Dunes Hotel after the evening show lets out," Sepúlveda confirmed. "Anticipating the possibilities, I was finalizing some inquiries and did hit a rich vein of golden information. What phone number will I call, let's say, within the next 4 to 5 hours, to convey the when and where?"

McLeod handed over a note with two numbers to call, one to Billy Lamb and one to Jodie's Place; Sepúlveda paused briefly, observing McLeod. "Have I met your expectations, Mr. McLeod?"

"Indeed, sir, you have." McLeod declared. McLeod removed a manila envelope with $10,000 in cash from a nearby desk drawer and handed it over. Then, with both men gratified, McLeod walked Sepúlveda to the elevator and asked him a parting question. "The planning of your visit happened when you knew this very senior person would be in Vegas—nice touch," McLeod compliments. Back at his office, he took the private elevator up to his apartment. Once inside, he dimmed the lights, set the air conditioning to 68 degrees, and played soft music.

Although successful, McLeod had more acquaintances than friends and no confidants. Of course, dysfunctional personal issues mattered less in the grand scheme of material day-to-day functionality.

McLeod closed the door behind him. The smell of lilac permeated the air; the bi-monthly therapy session was about to begin. It always started with music to relax and clear his mind from interfering thoughts. Concentrating on his breathing, he began to relax mentally.

It was time for his weekly therapy session. McLeod enjoyed the sessions, even though he thought the therapy itself was nothing more than a form of self-hypnosis. Aside from that opinion, McLeod, playing the contrarian, understood that his deeply rooted and well-deserved guilt had its advantages. After over a year of professional help, he finally accepted the reality that he did not want to be cured. He did not want to forget and forgive. Revenge is a willful, uncontestably focused driving force—his raison d'être.

As the therapists waited inside his apartment, he was determined that today would be his last session and wasted no time in sharing his decision with them.

"Good evening, Doctors," McLeod greeted the doctors. Typically, McLeod spent thirty minutes in conversation with psychologist Dr. Joyce Mathews and her sensitivity therapist, Debra Manning, before beginning treatment. This time, however, upon McLeod's disclosure, the doctors tried to counter McLeod's unwillingness. They confirmed that his deeply embedded guilt would, unless mitigated, continue to trigger acts of physical and psychological flagellation and societal isolation and, in combination, influence suicidal tendencies.

The psychiatrists attributed McLeod's difficulty in experiencing emotional or physical pleasure to his belief that he followed an order he knew was tactically unsound and incorrect. This obedience resulted in the death of Team 33's members. Doctor Mathews suggested that continued treatment could help McLeod manage the emotional distress without self-recrimination.

Finally, to end the conversation, McLeod stood from his seated position, blatantly interrupting Doctor Mathews by thanking the doctors for their efforts and straightforwardly dismissing their services without further explanation.

The stunned doctors were surprised into silence. McLeod looked at them directly and said he no longer needed their services. He escorted the doctors to the door and politely bid them farewell from his suite, gently closing the door behind them.

After years of repressing the underlying treatment for his illness, McLeod had reached a diagnosis. The remedy was simple: the satisfaction of revenge. McLeod restrained his rage over the years because he lacked the material means to act. Now, he has the financial means and can finally act. So, with the aid of Sepulveda's forthcoming, McLeod formally starts his quest to kill all those responsible for the butchery of Team 33.

The phone rang; McLeod answered it. "Hello," the caller announced. "McLeod!"

"Yes, go on, Billy; I'm listening." McLeod recognized the voice. Billy Lamb always did the job; most importantly, McLeod trusted him.

"Updating," Billy explains. "Mr. Sepúlveda's man will call you at Jodi's Place on or before 10:15. By the way, I've checked Mr. Sepúlveda's man of interest. In craps, he is renowned for betting on the field to achieve higher win percentages while reducing favorable odds for the player. On roulette, he bets spontaneously; there is no rhyme or reason to a particular color or number. His Mexican girlfriend, now a resident of Vegas, always bets red. Senior Gomez from Guadalajara, Mexico, is a premier comped guest of The Dunes Hotel. Go to Dunes Casino after the dinner show lets out; you can't miss him.

McLeod acknowledged, hung up the phone, and dressed for a drink and steak at Jodie's. The restaurant Navadel took him to on his first night in Vegas.

McLeod arrived at Jodie's Place, a private saloon and restaurant club, at half past nine rather than his usual 7:30 dinner hour. He entered from the private entrance. Barbra, a stunning woman of Teutonic descent, greeted him within a minute of his arrival. A neat Johnny Walker Blue was delivered, complemented by Barbra's flashing deep blue eyes, and a smile would encourage the bashful.

From the beginning, Barbara had had a crush on McLeod. She was fifteen, and he was twenty-six, and over the years, the crush had outlasted many boyfriends, lovers, and serious hopefuls. Barbara was a beauty. Her long legs, perfect curves, and flowing strawberry-blond hair were, at the very least, sensually compelling. However, Barbara's finest qualities were her ever-present smile and winning disposition. For Barbara, the crush on McLeod had matured into a loving regard. Jodie, the owner of Jodie's Place, enthusiastically endorsed and encouraged her desire to be in love with McLeod. But such love was never to be. McLeod looked upon Barbara as sweet and innocent. A woman who deserved a man to father her children, someone to grow old with, a man who could love her the way she deserved. McLeod knew that he was not that man.

"Ms. Barbara," McLeod greeted her, sweetly kissing her on each cheek. "Here are the Sinatra tickets and four backstage passes."

"You're the best," Barbara smiled as she took the tickets, kissed him gently, and offered him a new menu.

Thank goodness McLeod thought she did not know him. He enjoyed her willingness to treat him with loving respect, but he knew that her affection would diminish if she were to learn about his pledged mission of revenge.

The menu had a glossy photo of Jake, Jodie's late husband. Jake's picture and the whiskey prompted McLeod to reminisce. The idea of Jodie's Place went back many years before the physical location served its first meal or drink. It started one jam-packed night while Jake "The Dice Man" Lewis worked as the shift boss at the El Cortez. Jake watched the play on the blackjack and craps tables, trying to catch a cheating dealer overpaying his winners. As he scanned the floor, he saw Jodie, a new cocktail waitress, and fell instantly in love.

He romanced the twenty-eight-year-old Jodie for two weeks, proposed to her, and married her on the third Saturday after their meeting. Jake was a forthright and honorable man. That was Jake's only marriage. He was forty or so, and his only love; as Jake said, "My love for Jodie is a mortal lock on a winner." He was a devoted husband who never lied, deceived, or asked questions that might force a lie or embarrassment. Jake was an exceptional man who passed near his 85th birthday.

On the day of Jake's death, Jodie said her only regret was not kissing and holding him as he passed. Jake was vibrant until a week before his death. His stomach cancer was fourth-stage terminal before the diagnosis. When he was bedridden and death was on the verge, Jake agreed with Jodie that he would not die until all those who loved him were at his side. Cruelly, Jake died in the middle of the night with Jodie asleep on a bedside sofa. It was the only time the Dice Man ever let anyone down.

The burial was a sad event attended by scores of mourners. McLeod, of course, was there. McLeod revered Jake's friendship. They met one night at Jodie's Place. Jake, for an unknown reason, abruptly approached and befriended McLeod. The attraction for Jake was simply the identification of a fellow hard charger with pain in his eyes. Jake never had a brother or a son. McLeod served in a combination of both roles.

After his death, Jodie developed a motherly concern for McLeod, while a mutual love for Jake drove them closer. It was Jodie's way of inspiring joy in all those around her; she was all heart, but with Jake's passing, her heart grew heavy and selective.

Jodie's Place was a restaurant where one could have faith in the consistently high quality of the food and drink, combined with an old Vegas presentation. Most of the staff started with Jake and Jodie 20 Years earlier. Over the years, Jodie collected many oddly exciting characters. They seemed bonded into a special uniqueness, a time warp wherein they could not exist as a group in any other setting. Each character emitted a sense of belonging. From Mr. Biggest, the 275-pound, 6'5, official greeter and keeper of the peace (he allowed no profanity). To Harry Wham, the piano player, a vintage character of extraordinary diversity who always kept a shot of Kentucky sipping whiskey nearby, to the former kinsmen of Bugsy Segal's Flamingo Hotel, they all found a home at Jodie's Place.

McLeod sat while Barbara went to the bar to get another whiskey. The phone rang. "Mr. McLeod, it's a local call for you," the bartender informed him. He would not give me his name, but he's confident you are here."

"Thanks; please put him through."

"Señor McLeod," began the caller with a heavy Spanish accent. I speak for my patron, Señor Sepúlveda. Our man will enter the casino floor after the Dunes Follies show tonight at midnight. He will be with his Mexican American girlfriend. His bodyguard will meet them as they leave the showroom. You cannot miss our target; he is a massive man."

"Is there anything else?" McLeod inquired.

"Yes, if you go to the front desk of the Dunes under your name, a package will be waiting for you."

Before McLeod could say thank you, the caller hung up. He signaled to Barbara that he was ready to order dinner. McLeod enjoyed his meal, kissed Barbara, waved goodbye, and headed to the Dunes Hotel.

Dunes Hotel Mr. Vargas, I Presume-1978

The casino was packed with people leaving the show, colliding with those who wanted to get in. People pushed, elbowed, and yanked their way, turning side to side, all determined to slip, pass, and get through the crowd.

McLeod had picked up the package and read the three pages of double-spaced typed research content on Gomez. He then positioned himself on an elevated area, looking down with a clear view of the vortex below. In two minutes, Gomez was sighted; the caller was correct. Gomez was a whale of a man to whom the crowd willingly gave access. The description matched perfectly: the girlfriend in a pink dress with a black purse, a burly bodyguard, and Gomez, a massive man in Milan-tailored clothes. McLeod knew he had his man: the Cuban link to Vietnam. He felt a slight rush.

"So, this is Gomez," McLeod said to himself. "An extraordinary, a member of Cuba's diplomatic corps, a wealthy businessman, and noted casino high roller."

Of course, McLeod was not interested in Gomez, the high-roller Mexican businessman. Sepúlveda's report informed McLeod that the Las Vegas tourist cutting a swath through the casino was Arturo Vargas, a Cuban national, not Federico Gomez. From 1966 to 1970, Arturo Vargas served as the liaison officer at the Cuban Embassy in North Vietnam.

Meanwhile, "Gomez," the subject of interest, shuffled and waddled through the casino, leading the trio, and finally arrived and settled at the roulette wheel. With some effort, he managed to get the cushioned chair saddled. The floor man acknowledged Gomez's three-finger sign, asking the floor man to authorize placing $3,000 worth of gaming chips in his front. Gomez's smile and polite nod confirmed the transaction. He pulled out a cigar and passed it to his girlfriend. She gently placed the cigar between her red-lipsticked lips and slowly, sensually gyrated it in and out. The girlfriend sucked on the cigar, first from one side and then from the other. The oral exercise left little to anyone's imagination. She took the cutter and cut off the puffing end, then inserted the cigar and lit it, inhaling and exhaling a couple of puffs before handing it back to Gomez.

Gomez lifted two stacks of black chips, his entire amount, as if in slow motion. He placed one stack on the square red, the other on red thirty-two. Disregarding the ball's rotation, puffing on his cigar while keeping an unconcerned cavalier demeanor, he barely paid attention as the dealer called out: "Red 32." With the pretense of the anticipation of a win assured, he calmly exhaled smoke from his cigar.

All eyes were on Gomez. He presented a calm, confident gambler; however, his girl was animated, wildly throwing her arms in the air while clumsily grabbing Gomez's clothing. She shouted, "Ganamos! Ganabamos!" While looking at the dealer, Gomez gestured his withdrawal from future play. He had won; for the sake of the onlookers more than his own, he was leaving a winner.

The dealer counted Gomez's chips, voided his marker, loaded the winning balance onto a chip tray, and, with an insincere smile, said, "Good luck." His fellow players, in unison, silently acknowledged the wisdom of his decision to quit. Gomez threw down two black chips for propina and withdrew from the table. The roulette crew responded with a chorus of "Thank you, Mr. G."

McLeod intercepted him as Gomez sent his girlfriend with his bodyguard to the cage and headed for a place to sit. "Mr. Gomez, my name is McLeod. I oversee the operations at the Aladdin Hotel. Could I buy you a drink?"

"You have me at a disadvantage. Have we ever met?" asks Gomez.

"No, we have not; certainly, I have the advantage. Would you allow me to correct this misfortune?"

"Of course," Gomez assured McLeod with a smile. "But you should know I am pleased with my relationship with the Dunes. They have always treated me with the utmost care and consideration."

Sensing a casino recruiting conversation, Gomez waved off his girlfriend, telling her to take the cash and play the slots. "She's so easily pleased," Gomez commented.

McLeod and Gomez slowly made their way to a seating area in front of Le Dome restaurant. They took seats opposite each other and ordered drinks.

Gomez ended the casual atmosphere with accent-free questions. "What is it you want? Is this a case of one casino trying to market a competitor's player? Since we have never met, you're not here on a social call?"

"You are correct, Mr. Vargas, so I'll cut out the pleasantries." McLeod's use of Vargas instead of Gomez startled and alerted Gomez. Aware of the shock, McLeod continued, "I know of your former diplomatic status, and you're other than diplomatic business or tax-free importer status. I am also aware of your agreement with Raúl Castro and the Mexican government. However, I must ask you...."

With a stern, slightly raised voice, "Please stop!" Gomez stood indignantly. "The direction of this conversation is ridiculous."

"I surprised you," McLeod calmly asserted, staying seated, "but I should caution you, sir: I know your Panamanian intermediaries. Shall I reveal one name?"

A nervous Gomez sat back down. McLeod leaned over and uttered, "Manuel Noriega, Chief of Panamanian Army intelligence, a very powerful hombre."

Gomez motioned the bodyguard, who had stepped closer, to step back. This encounter has evolved into a private conversation. McLeod could see the sweat over and under the wrinkles on Gomez's broad forehead. His eyes narrowed, and his manner was apprehensive.

"Mr. McLeod, you agree we have never met. You have me at a significant disadvantage, and the timing is inconvenient. Nonetheless, you have my attention."

McLeod continued: "I know you have an ongoing, multi-million-dollar commercial-product smuggling operation. Colonel Noriega provides intelligence and border-crossing connections, and Carlos Eleta, your partner, is the banking source for all your multi-currency transactions. I also understand that this venture does not deal with illicit drugs. I also know that you are strictly engaged in avoiding duties, taxes, and tariffs; such avoidance of government fees is one of your pluses. This business of yours is not of interest to me. God bless your capitalistic heart. What does interest me is Operation White Light."

Gomez stared at McLeod, stunned by the mention of decades plus a secret operation. Then, putting on his best look of confusion and puzzlement, he recited, "Operation White Light...Yes, I faintly remember. It was a long time ago, and I had neither files nor a lot of memory; however, if I could help in any way, I would. Where and when shall we continue this interrogation? It is interrogation, is it not, Mr. McLeod? For whom do you work?"

"I am not with any intelligence agency or authoring a tell-all book, nor an instrument of any government. The information I'm looking for is strictly personal."

"Mr. McLeod, Vietnam was long ago. McLeod slid a business card in front of Gomez. "You may need a day or so to retrieve this information. Here is how you may reach me. I will leave the time and date up to you. I will pick you up at your hotel when you're ready." Not waiting for a reply, McLeod stood up, smiled, and warmly said, "Mr. Vargas, it was a pleasure meeting you." Satisfied that the meeting was substantive, McLeod retraced his steps toward the exit and disappeared into the crowd. He was enjoying the hunt.

The Rats Come Out to Play

McLeod was not a man who befriended others. However, the whims of chance provoked an exception. Billy Lamb was the exception. He was the youngest son of a Mormon family of seven boys and the most mischievous of them all. He drank and smoked; at fifteen, he impregnated a thirteen-year-old when he turned seventeen, but found a way to abort the child. The youthful Billy was both unlucky and an undisciplined fool. If Billy had roamed about during the Wild West era, his behavior would have found him hogtied in jail or dangling from a large oak tree. However, Billy did have one genuine "get-out-of-jail" card: his oldest brother was Sheriff Lamb, a very connected and sympathetic enabler of Billy Lamb's nonsense.

One night outside the Aladdin, near the booth where people stood to pass their parking tickets to the valet, a helmeted motorcyclist with a passenger straddling behind drove onto the throughway lane; the straddling passenger, thirty-five feet away, aimed at a target standing in the valet line. At that very moment, unaware of what was happening, McLeod walked from his car into the hotel.

As fate would have it, Billy was directly in the line of fire, walking from the hotel to his car. Billy unknowingly walked to the side closest to the shooter. The two men were like ships passing in the night, unaware of the other's presence. When the shooter opened fire, he hit Billy, who fell against McLeod. The shooter had fired twice, hitting Billy with the first shot and harmlessly high with the last.

The bullet hit Billy in the shoulder. The bullet fragmented into two pieces of shrapnel and penetrated his neck and shoulder blade. There was blood everywhere. Long story made short, McLeod felt that wittingly or not, Billy had saved his life, and for the next six months, with the best professionals' help, he nursed Billy to a full recovery.

The shooting was a blessing for Billy and the Lamb family. McLeod's concern and friendship snapped Billy out of his old persona, and the incident profoundly benefited Billy Lamb, catalyzing him into an entirely new, different, and better person.

"Mr. McLeod," Billy's voice on the other end of the phone started. It's just as you suspected. This Gomez guy, flying alone, ordered a plane from Vegas Charter. The flight plan names Belize City as the destination via Houston for refueling and international clearance, departing from Vegas tomorrow at 1:30 a.m.

"Thanks, Billy," McLeod continued. "Did you receive a transcript of his call?

"Yes, boss. He made three calls: one to Vegas Charter, the other to Belize City to arrange pick-up."

"And the third call?" McLeod interrupted.

"To an Arlington, Virginia, area code," Billy replied, "Traced to a Michael Cornfield at 722 Military Road."

"Interesting. What does the transcript say?

"I have a faxed copy coming over to your place as we speak. The conversation was from Gomez to the receiving party, whom Gomez called Mongoose. The guy sounded mature and familiar with Gomez. They did speak of Operation White Light, but only as the subject of your interest."

"The assumption is that Mongoose and Cornfield are the same," Billy concluded.

"That would be my guess," McLeod agreed. "I did request background on Cornfield from the casino's investigating department. We know this Confield/Mongoose is a private pilot flying his single-engine to Houston, which will need explaining. Why would this fellow respond so promptly to Gomez's panicked request?

"Get a hold of Franklin over at Vegas Charter and replace their chartered pilot with one of mine—use Pat Chartreuse. Ensure the flight plan, charter agreement, and service payment are with me as my counterparty. Gomez will pay in cash, so destroying any evidence of that transaction is important. Billy, I would like you, identified on the flight manifest as navigator, to sit in the jump seat up front with the pilot and co-pilot."

"No problem, sir."

"Tell Chartreuse to fly to Houston, making sure we pick up Mr. Cornfield. Once they land in Houston, time will work against us, so coordinate your arrival with Cornfield's. Once airborne, with Cornfield on board, change the flight plan: Instead of Belize City, fly them back to Vegas-Nelles. It will be an early morning flight, so there should not be a noticeable orientation issue after consuming sedative-induced mixed drinks. Pat knows the landing spot; it is the abandoned Army barracks facility we used in Operation Red Flag. I will secure the right to land from my buddy over at Information Management. The runway is long, wide, and in decent shape."

"Call Marge," McLeod ordered, "the dispenser of special drinks, our favorite nurse, and limit the briefing to what is needed. And Billy: make sure she brings the stun gun, just in case."

"Yes, sir, I am on it."

"Once you leave Houston, let me know your ETA. I will monitor your radio frequency and wait at the landing field."

The Interview

A platoon-size tent is pitched over the permanent concrete flooring, which remains ready for occupancy. Part of the tent's interior features thick synthetic-grass carpeting and kerosene lamps that provide adequate lighting for the entire area. A folding aluminum and wood dining room table held coffee, hot water for tea, and various canned sodas and fruit juices, all tossed into a large ice bucket. In addition, there were six comfortable leather seats, several foldable director's chairs, and two portable toilets just outside the tent.

The landing zone was lit, and Chartreuse glided the plane for a smooth landing. The crew left the plane without disturbing the sleeping passengers, and Billy escorted them to the motor home to freshen up, eat, and drink. Billy and three others in McLeod's crew entered the plane to wake up Gomez and Cornfield with ammonia inhalants.

Within minutes, Gomez and Cornfield, startled and confused, awoke. Both felt the stupefying effects of the drug-laced drinks. They stood, glanced at each other, and walked off the plane. Disorientation was plain; McLeod said above the normal tone, "You're perfectly safe; plenty of coffee in the tent." Gomez and Cornfield entered the tent, poured coffee, and then took advantage of the soft-leathered chairs.

Benumbed by the new situation and circumstances, the two quietly sipped their coffees, sensing their weakness and needing time to analyze. McLeod was understandably eager to hear what Gomez had to say. Nevertheless, he disciplined himself to wait, allowing his captors time to familiarize themselves and adapt to their new surroundings.

"Gentlemen," McLeod broke the ice, "please enjoy your coffee. A clear head is the starting point for this morning's discussion. I have plenty of time; I assume you do not. I can respect your discomfort; nonetheless, you have the required information.

I must express my disappointment with Mr. Gomez's initial acceptance of discussing my interest in his life as Arturo Vargas. Regrettably, Mr. Gomez, your attempt to flee forced my hand and put Mr. Cornfield in danger.

McLeod paused and poured a cup of java. He positioned himself ten feet across from Gomez and Cornfield as they quietly sipped their coffee.

"Senior Gomez, as stated, I have zero interest in interfering in your business; however, if you do not cooperate, and once again, I assure you I do not work for a government agency or newspaper or have any political affiliation. And I have no interest in drafting a book. The information I seek is purely personal and will remain confidential. My Panamanian-sourced information is dated; however, I now understand that Colonel Noriega is a General, and his chief of staff, Colonel Justines, is your direct contact. Your business partner, Carlos Eleta, has enabled the same steady revenue, so there is no significant business change for you. I only want information about the past; I have no interest in your present circumstances or situation.

Senior Gomez, you have had connections with high-ranking military personnel in Fort Sherman for a considerable time. Your network influence is profound; I assume the profits are substantial, and you want to continue this business without disruption. If you doubt my veracity or ability to act, I will call Justines and Eleta to confirm. You can forewarn them of the forthcoming impairment to your robust enterprise."

McLeod picked up the phone; Gomez signaled, "This is unnecessary; you have my cooperation." McLeod puts down the phone.

While authenticating his Panamanian connections, McLeod observed Cornfield's demeanor. The man was distinguished, in his early sixties, with a full head of gray-white hair cropped short. He was Anglo, tall, slender, taut-skinned, and tanned, with a physical frame suggesting exercise, a well-regulated diet, and an internal, well-honed military discipline. Cornfield appeared intellectually inclined, reflective, and academic, contrasting with McLeod's brusque manner.

His attire was a bland, brown-wool sport jacket with sewn leather-padded elbows, a buttoned-down collar, no tie, and cuffed cotton trousers belted by a WWII-era navy uniform belt. On the fourth finger of his left hand was a visibly worn US Naval Academy ring, class of fifty-nine. A nylon-banded, black-faced Rolex watch was around his wrist, but what caught McLeod's eye was the primitive copper bracelet on Cornfield's right wrist. McLeod knew them as tribal ordinations given to special friends by the Montagnard and Nung peoples of Vietnam. The bracelets had no visible latch; instead, they were molded shut. The bracelets were, as tradition, permanently affixed. McLeod concluded that Cornfield was a Vietnam War veteran but a desktop warrior with connections to combatants. The Montagnard bracelet might be a gift from a combatant, and the Commander is pretending to have had combat experience with the indigenous people.

Seeing that his guests had recovered and were comfortable and alert, McLeod introduced the discussion. "Gentlemen, I want to clarify that you are my guests. Yes, I agree the invitation was compulsory, certainly illegal, and, at best, an encumbrance. This approach was not my first choice. Nevertheless, why don't we all agree to make the most of it so we can go our separate ways as soon as possible? I am interested in Mr. Vargas's experiences in Vietnam. I am seeking informational details about a Cuban unit in which Mr. Vargas was a member; that is all. This meeting is an event that has been forced upon all of us. Convey the information and answer my questions. Your cooperation will abruptly end the meeting. Both delivered to your destination of choice, the safe, sound body and mind."

"Please refer to me as Gomez; Vargas no longer exists."

"Of course, Mr. Gomez," McLeod consents.

Gomez motioned as if to speak, but was gently held back by Cornfield's right hand. Simultaneously, with the calmness of a man addressing a gathering of his peers, Cornfield delivered an introduction that emphasized his rank and naval intelligence experience. Then, as if summoned to speak at an interview or seminar, Cornfield robotically started, "Mr. McLeod, I endorse your polite conversational approach. I am retired Commander Michael Harrison Cornfield. In 1970, a Cuban alerted the FBI to his interest in defecting to the United States. A senior Cuban official, Arturo Vargas Mendez, worked within the Miami consulate. Arturo received this "golden" assignment because of his excellent English and his mother's influence. Arturo's appointment as director of public relations for the Cuban Consulate in Miami was an opportunistic blessing.

It took a month of persuasion to convince Arturo to stay on and advance his position instead of defecting. Since 1957, Cuba's primary concern has been maintaining a positive cash flow. A weak Marxist-Lenin economy devolved into a barter system. After turning away from the U.S. trading relationship, dependence on Russian goodwill meant losing sovereignty. The Soviets consistently secured the best outcome in every transaction. U.S. Dollars, attained legally, extralegally, or otherwise, were Castro's primary necessity. The incursion of Cuban soldiers into Vietnam and Angola was related directly to cash income for Cuba."

"It sounds like the U.S. had the Castros exactly where they wanted them," McLeod suggested.

President Carter decided it was better to help rather than hurt the Cuban economy—a generous and thoughtful gesture. Carter insisted on continuing this policy, but the CIA thought otherwise. Eventually, with the Cuban government's approval, we at the Agency created Gomez, a wheeler-dealer businessperson. He fed millions of U.S dollars into the Cuban economy."

"Why in the world would America do such a thing?" McLeod asks.

"Influence, intel-gathering, day-to-day control of who, when, and where, and a timely understanding not only of Cuban command and control systems, but we had an intelligence peek into all countries south of the Rio Grande."

"In other words," McLeod emphasizes, the United States taxpayer-subsidized the Cuban economy."

"Yes," Cornfield replies. Consequently, Fred and I have formed a personal friendship over the Years."

"So, you are his handler?" McLeod injects.

Cornfield ignores the remark and infers, "Mr. McLeod, it is my understanding that your interest in my friend concerns the Cuban unit functioning in Vietnam under the auspices of Operation White Light."

"Exactly!"

My friend's business operates within the black economy; any complaint would involve legal discovery. I am interested in helping my friend, and you agree that once the information is divulged, that will be the last we hear from you. We agree with this gentleman's understanding. So, please let's start this discussion, as you call it, knowing that we will speak directly and honestly."

Gomez's eagerness to speak gushes out, "Mr. McLeod, I apologize. My anxiety induced me to call my good friend. Now, with regret, I have involved him in this affair.

My mother, who was educated in the United States, used English at home, so I learned the language from an early age. I have always enjoyed American culture, music, and films- well, everything American. I love America."

"I think caffeine has spun around and turned you into a Yankee. It's wonderful that you, since childhood, have loved America and everything American," McLeod applauds the sentiment."

Then Gomez butts in, saying, "But you are interested in my life as a Cuban soldier serving in Vietnam, not necessarily my love of America."

"I could not have said that better," McLeod confirms.

Gomez continued, "I served two long Years in Hanoi, Vietnam. I was never directly involved in the details of the heroin business; Colonel Calvo was my operational commander. I was a desk-bound facilitator of White Light Operations. I served as an administrative and logistical assistant to Colonel Calvo. I made no decisions; I was not a combat soldier; you would consider me a paperwork manager."

McLeod looked directly at Gomez and exclaimed, "Heroin trade! So, Operation White Light was a heroin buy, sell, business arrangement?"

Gomez nodded his head and added a smirk.

McLeod contemplated, the ambush of Team 33 might have been because, unknowingly, the Team photographed heroin principals engaged in a covert meeting, and that's the reason for the ambush?

Without an invitation, Cornfield broke into the conversation. "In the beginning, in the opinion of our government's intel agencies, the initial motivation for Cuban military intervention in Vietnam was a fraternal reaction in alignment with fellow communists. Or, as the Cuban military suspected, the Russians ordered, and the Castros obeyed."

"So, you're saying the Cubans were eventually led into or persuaded by some means into dealing heroin?"

"All I'm saying is that there were Cuban advisors in Vietnam a month before any heroin trade engagement," Cornfield insisted. "Cuba's trade was Soviet oil and technical services for sugar and bananas, which was nothing more than a barter agreement. The exchange was essential, but it did not address Cuba's need for the Yankee dollar.

Gomez tried to interject. Cornfield stopped him with a hand gesture and continued. Initially, the Cuban government's engagement in Vietnam was fraternal. However, once on the ground, soldiers and support units reported the cash the Russians and Chinese pocketed in poppy harvesting and distribution; Castro lost his innocence and insisted on participation."

Gomez insisted on injecting: "Despite Castro's intent on keeping his eyes and fingertips on the day-to-day operational activities of Cuban forces deployed, however, for practical reasons, he lost direct control to the local in-field commander. Besides, the Cuban military operating in Vietnam was very hush-hush; of course, though adamantly denied, the secret, within a year, became undeniable."

"My good friend Gomez painted a picture groomed for export to the West," Cornfield rebutted. "At no time did Castro act for ideological reasons. Initially, Cubans were in Vietnam because Cuban intelligence learned of the richness of heroin trafficking. The decision to engage in the Vietnam heroin trade was a deal hatched between the Russian GRU and the Cuban DGI, a joint venture."

"Who was this, Colonel Calvo?" asked McLeod.

"Colonel Eduardo Calvo Aragon was the last commander of Cuban soldiers in Vietnam; he created the operation named White Light."

"White Light Ops was all about heroin," explained Gomez. Indigenous people, North Vietnamese, South Vietnamese, China, and to a lesser extent, the Viet Cong, acting as the gangsters of Southeast Asia. Everyone was in on this deal. It was because of this heroin operation," Gomez stopped talking to sip his coffee, "that I first met him."

"Met who?" McLeod raised an eyebrow.

"The Russian," Gomez declared, "The guy, the hombre that ran the show; he was a dangerous, no-nonsense Glavnoye Razedyvatel'noye Upravleniye or simplified GRU agent, sanctioned by the elite operating with the blessings of Moscow's cadre of the powerful. This agent became independent of the GRU, while the GRU cadre became more dependent on his enterprising abilities. Or, more pointedly, he ignored the less powerful GRU members and paid off senior leadership handsomely. He advantaged, enabled, and clandestinely created a sovereign, sophisticated, wholesale, multi-million-dollar business that buys the poppy, creates the heroin, and sells this illicit drug to proven distributors. His unhindered gathering and distribution system enriched the GRU's most potent assets, as well as the Cubans, but not the domestic security forces. The subsequent failure to share the GRU bounty earned the wrath of the KGB. Like Al Capone's gangsters in Chicago, the two intel agencies were fighting over the pieces, parts, and spoils.

Fidel ordered an in-depth vetting of this GRU operative before agreeing to the joint venture. Cuban findings suggested that the Russian agent was a highly disciplined sociopath. Possesses an exceedingly high IQ coupled with a narcissistic personality, swirled within a reactive attachment disorder. In other words, Fidel thought, a perfect fit for Colonel Calvo."

"Hold on, Fred. The GRU membership may be incidental; we do not know for sure," Cornfield cautioned. We know extraordinarily little about this Russian. We don't even know his name. For internal identification, we referred to him as Ivan. It is somewhat exaggerated, considering Ivan the Terrible's history, but it is typical American coinage. Admittedly, Langley conducted an intensive but stymied for lack of resources investigation on this Ivan fellow to discover his external connections."

"And!" McLeod injects.

"Because the war ended so abruptly," Cornfield continued, "and the investigation's sensitivity required a slow-moving bureaucratic need to know, evidence was inconclusive. Mindfully, when a CIA investigation is described as intensive but limited, it sounds half-hearted in scope. The intel bureaucracy did its best to redirect the required research material into the abyss of the great void. Simultaneously, there was evidence that less than honest USAID senior officials facilitated the Bank for Foreign Trade as the transactional and funding source."

"That's a mouthful," McLeod remarks with a tinge of skepticism.

"So essentially, by means, variable, and corrupt by funding the war, the United States created the means to financé Ivan's heroin enterprise?"

"But it was an incomplete investigation. One that is inconclusive and therefore invalid," the Commander proclaims.

"My dear friend," Gomez injects. "I say this with deep respect. We have known each other for decades and never discussed these topics among the hundreds of shared conversations. There is no doubt that the Russian was a GRU agent. And, of course, U.S. war funding motivated the corruptible to put dollars in their pockets."

"Frankly, I had no idea of your innocence," Cornfield confesses.

"I see. I have offered a therapy session to old friends," McLeod muses.

Startlingly, Cornfield stood up. Disregarding Gomez's recent comments, his eyes widened. "Wait a minute," he said, with his right hand pointing to McLeod. I know who you are. By God, you are the leader of that recon team that Cubans from the special battalion gunned down back in sixty-five, or was it sixty-six? Now I understand your interest. I remember the incident report."

Gomez looked befuddled. "My friend," Cornfield enlightens Gomez. "Our interrogator is Sergeant McLeod, the leader of Force Recon Team 33. His team was ambushed and shot dead, save one. Division G-2 ordered a month-long investigation into this incident. Yes, Force Recon Team 33, I remember reading the report: Ambushed by an unmarked, Cuban-manned U.S. Army C-46 helicopter.

Captain Doss, whom I was told about much later, was not Captain Doss but, at the very least, a communist spy. He, according to McLeod, guided the team into the ambush. Doss disappeared into the hinterland after team leader McLeod arrived at the Special Forces camp. I was posted at naval intelligence then, and my staff and I surmised that Doss spent about ten days as the Exec Officer of 1st Force Recon Company."

"Did you ever figure out why Doss did what he did?" McLeod questioned.

"I am guessing it had something to do with Ivan and North Vietnamese intelligence because of Doss's coordination with Dr. Anh Li. As I recall," Cornfield sniped, "she was someone our sergeant knew well. Then, as if discounting the importance of the conversation without skipping a beat, Cornfield directly addressed his friend, "Fred, our abductor, is a man seeking revenge."

Gomez smiled at the revelation and, with a slight smirk, commented, "Since it was two decades ago, there must be a deep-seated something to feed the beast for so long."

McLeod replied, "There's no statutory limitation for killing my Marines."

Cornfield responded, "Sergeant McLeod, Lady Luck has served you well. I believe we can fill in some dead space between us."

McLeod nodded, adding, "I would appreciate the help."

Cornfield continued, "Many in the community, including myself, thought Captain Doss was Ivan the Russian. That theory abruptly dropped when the Army CID police in Da Nang found the real, dead Captain Doss in Da Nang. As I investigated the person posing as Doss, I learned that this guy could never be Ivan."

McLeod injected, "And why is that?"

"Because the man you know as Captain Doss disappeared when you arrived at Camp Carroll. Regardless of our efforts, he escaped, and we lost all contact with him. We never heard from him again. The high probability was that he is dead."

McLeod asked Cornfield, "Your known activities of Ivan were little to none. To conclude that Doss was not Ivan was evidenced by some other means."

With the raise of his hand, McLeod says, "No need to comment."

Immediately changing the subject, McLeod asks, "What led you to believe Anh Li and Doss headed to Hanoi?"

Cornfield replied, "By interviewing Indigenous people, one-month-old, retraced by a reliable informant source who tracked their pathway, saw Doctor Anh Li and two white-faced men with an entourage of armed men, we assume one is Doss, the other the GRU agent heading north. Evidenced by the CIA, Navy counterintelligence confirmed her as a French communist, a Viet Cong sympathizer, and a spy for the North Vietnamese."

McLeod's insides turned over at the confirmation that Anh Li was a North Vietnamese spy. McLeod held his composure, but now understood why Doss could not be Ivan.

Nonetheless, unanswered questions bandied about inside his head. Noting McLeod's discomfort, Cornfield paused.

McLeod asked: "When did you confirm this intelligence?"

"Sergeant, do you mind me addressing you by your rank?" "As you please," McLeod affirmed.

"Because the war ended abruptly with the swift invasion from the North and the abdication of American engagement, there was no final determination. However, my staff did assemble a working hypothesis; indeed, the hypothesis was part of our final quarterly and annual internal summary. There were no charges or interviews, but she was under surveillance by Army counterintelligence, as were hundreds of Indigenous people working within our ranks. No one thought she was a trained operational spy on a mission. You seem shaken by this information. Is there something you would like to share?"

Without responding to Cornfield's invite and question, McLeod suggested, "Let's get back to this Russian agent."

Gomez jumped into the conversation, "General Ochoa called a week before the Colonel's deployment to Vietnam for a meeting. Although Ochoa was his superior, Colonel Calvo declined to attend and sent me in his stead. The General's aggravation was clear; he, along with many field grade officers, detested Calvo; Fidel's brother Raul, more of a pragmatist, saved him from God knows what."

"Can we please get back to this GRU agent, Ivan?" McLeod insists.

Gomez continued, "At our first meeting, Ivan told me that Calvo and the Cuban contingent were critical to the heroin operation. The Cubans would make the playoffs and distribute all the varied non-cash considerations." Calvo's troops serve as mediators and enforcers amongst all parties.

"Considerations..." McLeod inquired.

"I mean, other than cash, weapons, or processed heroin; a combination or one over another; whatever they wished to compensate for their cut of the profits," Gomez explained. "But back to this first encounter. As with General Ochoa, Ivan was annoyed by Colonel Calvo's absence, knowing I could not speak for the Colonel. It was understood that Calvo's presence was a mandate. My inability to devise a credible excuse for the Colonel created a goaded sense of disappointment.

Notably, throughout my entire time with this GRU operative, also known as Ivan to the Americans, he consistently maintained a threatening demeanor of willful disrespect; factually, I've never seen or heard him behave otherwise. I felt he could, at his whim, slap me across the face with his rifle butt or shoot me. I left the meeting with the impression that this man was an errant combatant. And that confrontation was his natural state of being."

"Quite a dastardly fellow," McLeod snickers with a slight smirk.

"One more important point," Gomez rushed to complete his statement. It is impossible, or should I say impossible, for this GRU agent to even ask Colonel Calvo for a meeting without Father Castro's approval. There would never be a meeting without Castro's tacit approval.

"Just to be clear," McLeod inquires, "Moscow insisted on the deployment of the Cuban military to Vietnam. Who oversaw the Cuban troops in Vietnam?"

"There is only one man," Gomez responds, "General Ochoa. Because of his relationship with Raúl Castro, only he had the gravitas to secure that assignment. Within three days of returning to Hanoi from my first meeting with Ivan, which originated in the DMZ, a radio transmission from division headquarters in Cuba announced another scheduled meeting with him in five days. Colonel Calvo and I attended that meeting. That was the last time I saw him, but, more so, all information or meetings related to the GRU Russian agent never again reached my desk."

"What did this Russian look like?" McLeod asked.

"He was more than six feet and inches tall, I would say in the late twenties, muscular, with blond hair and cold, Sinatra blue eyes. As you Americans say, he had wide shoulders and an attitude of 'my way or the highway.' He had a fluent understanding of Vietnamese, Laotian, English, and Spanish, and I overheard him on a radio call. He certainly had a communicable understanding of the American vernacular. He had a platoon-sized unit of heavily armed Laotian and Chinese mercenaries."

McLeod asked, "This role that the Russian had for the Cuban forces was significant. How did Calvo take to this role?"

"Like a duck to water," Gomez said, "Calvo's function was to provide assurance that the harvesting, transporting, and the multiple buy-sell transactions occurred as designed and agreed. This function was the perfect match for Colonel Calvo. This assignment satisfied his desire for operational independence and, most importantly, placed him in a highlighted form back in favor with the Castros."

"This Calvo guy sure knew how to make enemies," McLeod commented.

"Yes, however, he had a rare resource, the ability to satisfy Castro's need for cash. The Communists and their socialistic ideology aggravated Calvo. He was the ultimate capitalist, an entrepreneur extraordinaire," said Gomez. "Early on, Calvo deduced that Castro and the Cuban economy desperately needed U.S. Dollars. Castro had the need, and Calvo found the satisfaction. To the rescue, Bell Telephone implemented the means. For a price, Miami Cubans can maintain contact with their families back home. This unknown legal income source enriched the Cuban government just in time.

Raul loosened his rein for services given to Colonel Calvo, thinking he could yank his chain at will.

"If he was so connected," McLeod questioned, "why was he expelled to Vietnam?" Then, continuing, "I can't imagine he had the forethought of exporting U.S. dollars from those jungle enclaves."

"Exactly," Gomez agreed. "Everyone thought the same. Since Calvo was an arrogant, apolitical, non-believer, everyone thought he had finally pissed off his protector. The rumors were that Calvo was very depressed upon receiving his orders for Vietnam. He could not secure a meeting when he tried to use his previously well-established sway with Fidel. Calvo felt that his ranking superior, Marcus Ochoa, a man he had successfully ignored, persuaded Castro to rid Cuba of this belligerent non-believer. At one staff meeting, Colonel Calvo decided not to attend. General Ochoa's response echoed the thoughts of every Cuban field grade officer: "This Calvo hombre is an Aragon-bred noblesse obliges pretentious counter-revolutionary ass."

"That's a mouthful," McLeod suggested. "Tell me more about this, General Ochoa."

"Please allow me," Cornfield said. "In every measurable degree, these two men, Ochoa and the Calvo, were opposites. Ochoa was of medium height, with large hands, rolled shoulders, a barrel-shaped chest, and a slight build, reflecting distinctive Negroid-Indian heredities. Conversely, Calvo was tall, slender, and white-skinned, with a pedigree of Aragon blood ancestors, including Philip I, as the Colonel insisted. Calvo considered his fellow Cubans, indigenous Indians, and African migrants far below his bloodline ranking. Born before Castro took power into an upper-middle-class family, his father, an attorney, joined the revolution early and died defending Cuba at the Bay of Pigs. Calvo spent most of his youth in Spain and Peru, attending military school and training for a career in the military. His mother lived with his father's sister. A mother whom he rarely spoke to or visited.

For reasons of hubris and certainly unmerited, even as a young Lieutenant Calvo before his glorious handlebar mustache, swaggered about as if he were the Conquistador de Cuba."

"And this Cuban General Ochoa?" McLeod inquired.

"General Ochoa received his military training in Cuba and Russia. He was a Marxist ideologue, a doctrinaire, and a true believer in the revolution. Although I know the General received his cash cut from Calvo's success, he despised the Colonel."

"Did the Commander leave out any material description?" McLeod turned to Gomez.

"Nothing material," Gomez confirmed. "I would like to emphasize that he was a man lost within his narcissism. I should note that I did find some personal consolation in knowing that the only one Calvo was deathly fearful of was the Russian. After the first meeting, the Colonel did his best to work through intermediaries. Please note that this information is based on third-party rumors and subjective deductions. I believe Calvo always obeyed every nuance of what Ivan ordered. In other words, as you Americans say, he didn't give the Russian any lip."

"So, the invulnerable Calvo had a sharp, deep dent in his armor," said McLeod.

Cornfield gave the nod. "Therefore, as the story of Calvo unfolds," McLeod adds, "aside from what the man thought of himself, we know he was no more than a tool, a knife, and a fork that Castro used to serve his interest."

"So, this dance between Ivan the Russian and the Colonel continued until the music stopped?"

"Yes," Cornfield affirmed. "Until the war abruptly ended."

Fresh coffee was poured, McLeod took a sip, and Billy changed the tape in the recorder. McLeod's inquiries comforted Gomez and Cornfield, leading them to conjecture that they would soon be on their way.

"There must have been a ton of money in that enterprise," McLeod surmised. "Castro must have been pleased."

"The necessity of third- and fourth-party engagement is complicated. Yes, it was due to the ton of money, but the task." Cornfield continued. "We believe that the heroin for cash exchange took place at many locations, all of which required local cooperation from officials who, for a fee, looked the other way. Calvo's duty, one he thoroughly enjoyed, was physically transporting the cash to the banking facility in Singapore for distribution and allocation.

"If I understand this properly," said McLeod, "White Light Operations were about the harvesting and selling of unprocessed heroin; the Russian was in charge, the Cuban soldiers were the enforcement, and Calvo was the bag man.

So, what does any of this have to do with the killing of my men? And how do Doss and Anh Li fit in?”

“The conjecture is,” Cornfield continued, “the connection flows from the Russian GRU agent to North Vietnamese intelligence, to the unknown connections of Tran Thien Khiem, to Viet Cong agents, to Anh Li, to Doss, and, for reasons still murky, to the killing of Team 33. A Canadian, Stephen Henry Knox, portrayed himself as Marine Captain Doss. The orders from the 1st Maine Division were fraudulent. He did not just wander in as the 1st Force Recon executive officer at Dong Ha; there was a connection along the chain of command.”

“You mean a communist sympathizer?” McLeod injects, a spy, a dirty rat within senior command?”

“I’m as perplexed as you are about the exactness of the person's motivation,” Cornfield responds. However, I doubt that it is a senior officer; more than likely, someone within the staff had access.

“Ok, please continue,” McLeod requests.

"Knox knew that his stint was tenuous; he would be discovered. His direct contact was likely Anh Li. She met all the distinguishing marks of a communist informant, so we presume the relationship predated his appearance, so Doss must have known her as a member of the Red Team."

"You're saying this Doss insertion validated the existence of a high-ranking communist sympathizer with the command structure," McLeod deduces.

"I hypothesize that it is probable that Doc Marshall's story about being lost in the jungle should change to a planned rendezvous. With Doss's help, he inserted himself into the patrol as an escort to meet up with the GRU agent. Marshall, a KGB agent working as a Corpsman, was reassigned to engage Ivan, who insisted the meeting occur at his base camp, a grid zone off the Ho Chi Minh Trail in Southeastern Laos. I guess that the KGB wanted their cut of the heroin business and sent their already inserted agent to negotiate the deal."

"This heroin business must have had incredible cash flow. Imagine sacrificing a deep-cover KGB agent to take part in the heroin business. Cash triumphs over ideology; obviously, there was enough cash to convert a communist into a capitalist," McLeod suggested. "Calvo must be sitting pretty somewhere, sipping his gin and tonic and waxing his mustache."

"No," Gomez readied himself to rebut McLeod's assumption. "Calvo

He was killed a week after Saigon fell."

"What?" McLeod exclaimed.

"Yes, that's what I heard," Gomez confirmed. "Calvo knew that the war's end meant going back to Cuba. He was a spoiled bourgeois; he could not return to Castro's Cuba."

"But this guy was in the business of deception; surely, he knew the drill," McLeod suggested. "He must have anticipated the war's end and planned accordingly."

Cornfield interceded. "Think about it. He, the Russian, also expected the war's end.

With Castro's help, the GRU agent was a few steps ahead of Calvo.

"What does that mean? McLeod barked, looking perplexed. He started to ask a follow-up question when Cornfield, sensing the need for more information, raised his hand to continue.

"We know Fidel Castro was in league with the Russian GRU, sent Calvo to Vietnam. Fidel manipulated General Ochoa's hatred for Calvo by duping the General into thinking that he was effectively banishing the disagreeable Colonel. Instead, at GRU's invitation, Castro sent his prized entrepreneur to Vietnam to secure Cuba's cut in the lucrative heroin trade. Fidel presumed that this venture could significantly enrich the Castro family's off-Cuba bank accounts and fund Cuba's balance of payments. Deniability as to any participation in the drug trade was critical. Therefore, except for those stationed in Vietnam, only Castro, the GRU agent referred to as Ivan, and senior members of the GRU were aware of the scheme.

"Smooth," McLeod remitted. "Upon receiving his orders to Vietnam, the Colonel must have felt ostracized; General Ochoa loved putting the Colonel's face in the mud, and Castro, the puppeteer, loved the deception."

That is the story as I see it," Gomez conceded.

"Now, about Doc Marshall," an irritated Cornfield exclaimed. "He was a KGB agent repurposed to negotiate the participation in Ivan's heroin business. These two intelligence agencies frequently got in each other's way. Usually, the disagreements were over budgetary issues; this time, the dispute was fueled by excessive greed in a no-rules, illicit business thousands of miles away. The Moscow KGB officers had no idea of the GRU's viciousness. Ivan killed Doc Marshall and placed Doc's bullet-ridden body in plain sight in the I-Corps sector between 'The Rock' and the river's edge. The body placement led the finder to suppose that NVA troops killed him. Of course, the photo of the bullet-ridden body of Doc Marshall was a warning to the KGB in Moscow. Stay clear of GRU operations.

"So, once again, you can confirm that White Light operations were a multimillion-dollar opium poppy harvesting and processing enterprise?"

"Indeed," Cornfield agreed.

"General Ochoa was taking the money, so he must have known something?" McLeod asked.

"He knew that Castro sent the Colonel there, and he may have known bits of the Russian's heroin trade, but never timely and always in arrears," Gomez confirmed. "Remember, Ochoa was never in Vietnam, and a survival-oriented Cuban General knows when it's best not to inquire into the departmentalized need-to-know tradition of the army."

"Hmm..." McLeod responds. "So, Ochoa and Calvo worked for Castro, ok, but it was the GRU agent who ordered the hit that involved Cuban special ops on American Marines, and this Russian did so unilaterally. This bold act confirms his operational independence, but more importantly, this Russian agent had deep connections in Moscow, the U.S., and Cuban intelligence.

"Well," Gomez tries to respond. Cornfield's abrupt interference cut Gomez off.

"Though possible,' Cornfield continues, "I, too, believe that the Russian had to clear the ambush with General Ochoa."

"Maybe, maybe not, but without Calvo's involvement, there would be no Cuban soldiers on that helicopter shooting at my team," McLeod interjected.

"It is my impression, looking back, that Colonel Calvo was the go-to guy for anything involving Cuban troops." Frankly, I do not know how Calvo managed to keep so many different-sized and colored balls in the air simultaneously. The guy had a superhuman ability to departmentalize."

"Calvo, I agree, must have been one smart hombre," McLeod concluded. "How in the world could a person with all his special talents and access allow anyone close enough to kill him?"

"His reflection beguiled him," Gomez continued, "I think his narcissism neutralized what should have been cautious skepticism. Calvo was a target in waiting; Castro would never allow someone with his informational access to live. He thought otherwise. No one could have been more surprised at the ambush than Calvo. Reported as shot and thrown into the sea."

McLeod stared at Cornfield and said, "I bet no one found his body."

Gomez seemed perplexed by McLeod's statement, "His body! What do you mean?"

Cornfield answered. "You're right; I assume you can guess the rest. The Colonel's backup was his CIA Counterintelligence contact in Singapore. He had specific and embarrassing information on Cuba's involvement in the heroin trade. So, he became an informant and took advantage of the CIA's offerings. "And!" Cornfield queried McLeod by pointing with an index finger in his direction.

"And the CIA faked his death," McLeod guessed. "And whisked off to Langley."

"You are good. Mr. McLeod, outstandingly good."

"My God," lamented Gomez. "And all these many years believed the rumor. So now I find out he was a spy for the CIA and working for my good friend."

"I'm sorry, Fred." Cornfield turned to Gomez. "It was company business that did not affect you."

Gomez nodded positive.

Cornfield continued, "The CIA thought that Colonel Calvo was an excellent source for internal information on the workings of Cuba's military in Vietnam. He was not. Naming counterparts in Vietnam was of zero value. He did help build a limited profile on the Russian Ivan. However, his most significant contribution was informing the CIA of European, Canadian, and particularly Spanish investment and investors in Cuba."

"So, where is Colonel Calvo?" asked McLeod.

"For the first year, the company, via multiple interrogations, gained, or better said, supposed they gained some insight into the Cuban engagement in Vietnam. In turn, the Colonel milked us for all he could get. In short, his usefulness proved inadequate; besides, nobody wanted to work with such a pretentious ass. Last I heard, he moved to Spain. He found work as a consultant for a group of Spanish companies investing in Cuba. I have his file, but the information in it is outdated by ten years. Calvo knew nothing about Team 33, so you need not put him on your most-wanted list. Before my retirement, I introduced the Colonel to former Commander Harper, the Vice President of Information Management, Inc., a private company based in Las Vegas, Nevada. I have no idea if he took the job offer or not."

"Yes, I understand you emphasize that Calvo did not order my team's killing; nonetheless, I'd like to scan over the file, "McLeod said with a snarky delivery. Is there anything else you can tell me about this Superman-like Russian GRU operative?

"You have exhausted my Ivan stories," Cornfield answered.

"I think the Russian is no longer a Russian," Gomez guessed. "No longer a Russian?" McLeod inquired.

Gomez smugly replied, "If I were looking at the world in the near present, I would seek out a domicile that appreciated my services. So, I would choose a country without an extradition treaty agreement with the United States. An approachable and amenable governing leadership that would need my services."

"Well," McLeod asserts, the Russian is out somewhere."

Gomez motions meekly, "Yes, and there is a sanctuary, a place that could use his services, a protectorate that benefits from his residence."

Senior Gomez, speaking of protection," McLeod asks, 'How have you survived so well all these years?"

"I never confront; I never compete. I strive to satisfy everyone's interests. I always share. I'm never greedy. You now have my secret to a long and prosperous life."

McLeod acknowledged the affable tact with a nod, adding, "When possible, I assume, is the only caveat. For the last time: Colonel Calvo, was he aware of the killing of Team 33?"

"The Colonel may have heard something of the killings." Gomez contributes, "That is the fare of war and warriors. But this is purely speculative."

Cornfield quickly cut in, "It was Arnaldo T. Ochoa Sanchez, not Colonel Calvo, who ordered the killing of these Marines."

McLeod promptly inquired, "So you must know the reason why?"

Cornfield calmly responded, "I do not. However, I could speculate."

"Well," McLeod comments. "If nothing else, your speculation is at least entertaining."

"At Naval intelligence," Cornfield noted, "we hypothesized that Cuba's Giron Brigade worked hard to secure the Ho Chi Minh trail thoroughfare, also known as the Annamite Range. As a result, despite the bombings, valuable resources flowed from North to South; it was on this trail that unscheduled logistics-related meetings took place. I suggest that the probability is high that Team 33's photos documented and visually sighted a high-level meeting called into session by Raul Valdes-Vivo, a DGI operator with Russian, South Vietnamese, and North Vietnamese accomplices in attendance. A Cuban war correspondent named Marta Rojas was also present. I know this is a possibility because I read it in her newspaper. She innocently published the day and time of the meeting in a respected Cuban newspaper. With an arrogant slant under the nose of U.S. Forces. Unfortunately, the article had wide distribution; Maximillian, Ochoa, and Castro were alerted to what they considered a damaging possibility."

"How did the Russian GRU agent discover these photos and distinguish Team 33 as the information provider? Imagine the depth of intelligence coordination needed," McLeod asked and noted.

"Please, Sergeant Cornfield demands, answer your question: how in the world did the Russians attain such classified information?"

"A high-ranking U.S. traitor handed it to the Russians," McLeod confidently answers. There is an insider, an in-the-know field-grade military officer, a collaborator."

"Sergeant, you have guessed upon a wide berth of perchance. Who knows these things? It happened twelve months ago. So, was the Colonel culpable? Could he have ordered the attack? I would advise that Calvo knew nothing about your team's ambush. Are we done?" an intensified, obviously irritated Cornfield questioned.

"I have just one more question," McLeod injects. "Senior Gomez, other than immigrating to Peru, what do you think happened to the Russian?"

"His only other location option," Gomez responds, "is Cuba. It's the only safe place where he can safeguard his money and person. Not only was Castro's Cuba a steadfast ally of Russia, but the Castros also had continuing employment needs for this wetted GRU agent."

Cornfield snappishly inserts himself into the conversation, changes the subject, and reveals a revelation. "Gomez, our host's interest is revenge for anyone associated with killing the Marines of Team 33."

McLeod did not expect the Commander's dead-on-target exclamation. Nor the reference to Team 33.

Cornfield recommends that revenge is never sweet. After 25 Years of service, I was passed over for promotion and asked to retire. Then, one day, out of the clear blue sky, an up-and-coming Navy Commander, stationed in Washington and attached to the CIA, orchestrated the demise of my naval career. I could have sought revenge during my last 90 days (about 3 months), but I passed on the opportunity and just moved on."

McLeod interjected, "Commander, if you are suggesting some backdoor pathos. Stop! You're squandering words and time."

McLeod stood and positioned himself directly in front of the Commander. "I appreciate the information submitted thus far, but please keep your psychotherapy suggestions to yourself."

With that statement, McLeod left the tent.

Billy took over. "Gentlemen, the plane is ready for boarding. Mr. McLeod wants to assure you that you will never see or hear from him again." Billy advised, "Mr. McLeod expects confidentiality."

Canary Islands – 1980

It was October; back in Vegas to manage some Aladdin Hotel business, McLeod had been integrating the information provided by Gomez and Cornfield into a reference summary, noting how Cornfield suspiciously insisted that Colonel Calvo had nothing to do with the killing of Team 33. Why was he so adamantly sure? The relationship with Sepúlveda had matured. McLeod thought of Sepúlveda as a valuable business connection, so he offered a junket representative contract, noting that he is one of fifteen Latin reps for The Aladdin Hotel. Initially, McLeod attempted to conceal his actual, revengeful aim. However, with all the hovering-around questions and background interest, McLeod thought it best to come clean on his plot and goal of killing Ochoa and the Russian.

Six months ago, McLeod asked Sepúlveda to use his Cuban connections to gather specific info on the Ochoa family's Christmas vacation. Sepúlveda complied but noted that the Ochoa family vacation was open to public information. Indeed, La Revista Hola planned a photo spread for this upcoming Liar's vacation.

Armed with the Ochoa family's information, McLeod left Vegas. This time, his absence will last a month, during which he will be on a working vacation to market fresh players, visit travel agencies and tour operators, and encourage player harvesting. His primary goal was to kill General Marcus Ochoa.

McLeod confidently contemplated the operation as the plane's wheels touched down on the Island of San Jose in the Canary Islands. The long-anticipated mission had continued as planned; nonetheless, a mix of eagerness and doubt permeated his senses. Negative probabilities plagued his mind and sometimes got the best of his positive outlook.

He reminded himself that two independent sources, each segregated from the other, confirmed the same information on the general's security procedures. He affirmed that Ochoa's travel details were faithfully followed; every detail, including the family's logistical information and general vacationing habits, as well as the restaurants and bars the General liked to eat and drink at, was never altered.

The jolt of the plane stopping at its off-ramp snapped McLeod from his contemplation and into the present.

Dressed in all the trappings of an amateur photographer of oceanic landscapes, wearing a New York Yankee baseball cap and behaving with the curiosity of a first-time tourist, McLeod readied his equipment for departure. As everyone readied to disembark, the plane's cabin was filled with anticipation and excitement.

Acting out the role of a slightly anal traveler, McLeod asked the flight attendant how far the town was from the airport and if the taxi service was a dependable transportation mode. The attendant was an island local. Her response was as if she were offended. She gave a bland assurance that the island has all the modern conveniences of New York, with no crime.

McLeod disembarked and started walking to the beginning of his long-awaited destination. Immigration and customs were now the only obstacles preventing him from successfully inserting himself into the killing zone of revenge.

Because of the arrival time, three plane passengers were trying to get through the same customs and immigration portals. It was a madhouse. McLeod looked like a naturally apprehensive first-timer to the islands, with hands and shoulders bearing baggage, a passport, and a tourist visa.

After thirty minutes of patient waiting, the line progressed ten yards with an equal amount still in place. Tension crept into McLeod's psyche as several 'what ifs' returned to sprint across his mind. He successfully fought them off by acknowledging the virtues of planning, patience, and adaptability to ever-changing terrain and situations.

Eventually, McLeod was in a taxi to Casa de Rosanna. This comfortable, 15-room, rent-by-the-week apartment building included, for a rental fee, the use of an old but functional pick-up truck.

The plan was to arrive a week in advance and become familiar with the island environment while developing the specifics of a plan that ultimately led to the death of General Marcus Ochoa. Years of vengefulness could now evolve into meaningful preparedness.

Knowing that observation was the first requirement when preparing an ambush, McLeod studied the area in detail. He was determined to develop a plan founded on surprise. The not-so-extensively guarded Ochoa family did not negate the need for McLeod to remain vigilant. A change of pattern or circumstance could easily alter any well-conceived plot.

Years have passed since the killing of Team 33, and revenge seemed the only viable antidote to the weight of guilt's persistence. The killing of General Ochoa was a win-win solution. If he succeeded, the antidote of satisfaction would deliver relief. If he died in the process, death would provide relief.

McLeod's quest for retribution had destroyed any appreciation for life's offerings; his craving for revenge, now a behavioral dysfunction, a willful compulsion, pervaded his entirety. Since the killing of Team 33, his life had been a long, drawn-out flagellation of mind, body, and spirit. The life of W.R. McLeod had been nothing less than a slow, eventual horizontal slicing of the wrist. Guilt and revenge, a deadly, poisonous symbiosis, were competing for satisfaction. One feeds upon the other, eating and devouring the host's natural interest in survival. Finally, as he did most evenings, waiting for the night's passing, his only escape was drug-induced.

Last year, Hola magazine, a weekly publication for the Spanish-speaking world, published an excellent article on the Ochoa family. The article highlighted the Cuban family's enduring affection for the island. Replicating the Ochoa vacationing to-do highlights was a favorite of many of the island's tourists. The government of the Canary Islands loved the all-positive exposé. Hola had planned a follow-up article for the following year.

The interviews in last year's article revealed some previously unknown personal details that put a human face on the General and his wife, along with the never-changing itinerary, providing valuable insights into scheduling for an assassin.

Extensive research has revealed the following information: The Ochoa family's Christmas vacations have never deviated in patterns or events. Peter, the husband of Ochoa's daughter Elena, always arrives during the last week of the six-week holiday hiatus.

For Maria Ochoa, the Canaries' Christmas holiday was an extraordinary blessing for a notable Cuban General's wife. She could openly practice her Catholic faith. Unfortunately, it was only at that time that she could, with permission, meet and greet her exiled Americanized family, who left Cuba after Castro's successful revolution.

McLeod had been on the island long enough to secure familiarity with the surrounding community and several observation sites. He had his photos developed in town, presenting clear topographic images to help build his professional narrative. After a few days of the pretense of viewing geographic locations, he eagerly awaited the General's arrival.

McLeod noted that the soon-to-be-occupied vacation house was on the southern leeward shore of the island, an area famous for fishing and boating. For half a mile on either side, there were only clumps of thick, willow-green thickets, sand, and water. Even the road to the house was a private ingress from the main highway that encircled the island.

The floor plans of the Victorian-style house revealed three living levels topped with an A-frame attic. The porch was irregular in design, except that the front and rear entrances wrapped around the whole house. There is a short but adequate wooden pier. Colossal tractor tires hung, chained in suspension, to cushion hulls from the pilings. Two black, broad steel ladders were positioned on the tie-down sides between the tractor tires, providing a safe approach for boarding or disembarking.

A 1970 Owen, a 35-foot, diesel-powered fishing boat with a fiberglass-over-wood open deck, is tied to the dock. According to island sources, Ochoa understood there were better fishing boats but insisted on using the old one, which he refers to as "Buena Suerte."

With binoculars, McLeod positioned an excellent observation point on an elevated vegetated knoll that looked directly over the beach house—the day had finally arrived. McLeod saw servants run about the property, finishing the last assigned tasks. The site had an excellent view of the Ochoa house and veranda. He noted that the male servants and gardeners wore white shirts and khaki pants. He acknowledged that after the elimination of General Ochoa, his chance of escape from the island, much less the house, was slim. Dressing as a servant might confuse the guards enough to get him to his parked vehicle.

A black SUV, followed by a small bus and a large van, pulled up; the Ochoa family arrived on schedule. The servants greeted the General and his family. Everyone looked joyful; in no time, the family was out on the veranda enjoying the ocean view.

McLeod felt overwhelmed by the unfolding reality of the moment. For three days, he observed the Ochoa household's activities and the dedication of the support staff to their routine. Their fishing day started at 5:30 a.m., and they returned without fail at 1:00 p.m. The General would then disembark and head directly for the house while the guards, wearing shoulder-holstered pistols, and servants cleaned the gear and gutted the catch.

The General returned to view at 6:30 to 7:00 p.m. when family and staff surrounded him. Finally, at 11:00 p.m., he retired to the veranda, usually alone but sometimes with one or two men puffing on a cigar with a brandy snifter. Whether sitting or meandering about, he appeared relaxed and satisfied. His routine so far is predictable.

Founded on the routine, McLeod contemplated the outline of a plan. At 10:00 a.m., the servants, except for the cook, always went to town with the General's wife and daughter. Every day, the cook and servants left the house at 12:30 p.m., carrying empty cloth bags, and returned in two hours with the bags full of fresh fruits and vegetables from the market.

He saw that the back door was always open. The wife and family habitually left within an hour of their 9:00 a.m. breakfast. At 1:00 p.m., the General, after fishing, went directly to his room to shower. His pattern confirmed that he was unguarded in his toilette.

McLeod imagined that the General, seduced by the comfort of a prolonged hot shower, would never suspect a violation of his personal space. Precious time would pass before anyone would knock on the bathroom door. Dinner was always after 8:00 PM; McLeod made his decision. The daily market run would signal when to enter the house. The place to hide must be somewhere within the General's bedroom; that could be tricky, but under the bed was as good a place as any.

McLeod decided: Tomorrow was the day that made the night's passing a crucible of pending vengefulness. While cleaning his military-issued .45 and silencer, he contemplated, finally, after so many years, Team 33 would execute its first "life for a life." His mind raced with the diverse ways to kill General Ochoa. For this up-close and personal killing, the Bowie knife was used. "Yes," McLeod thought to himself. The Bowie would be perfect: silent, with no ballistics, painful, and deadly.

What were the odds," pleasingly thought McLeod, that I would find the outfit's leader? Until now, an invulnerable and unassailable leader of Cuban forces in Vietnam.

Over and over, he outlined the plan, emphasizing within his mind the look of surprise and terror on the General's face. First, the stun gun; second, rig the mouth with rigger tape; then, with his bowie knife, the first stab would be to the stomach for Dillon, the second to his left shoulder for Thomas, and the finale, the point and body of the blade into his throat.

Blood would be everywhere; as an act of bravado, McLeod would shower, change his clothes to mimic the servants, and, with a pistol in hand, exit the house. Or, if discovered, pledging never to be captured, kill as many of the General's bodyguards, and die a warrior's death.

The time arrived, but the family prepared the porch for guests instead of leaving at or before 10:00. Silver domes covered the food set on white linen placed on the table, and then, with wine bottles in hand, servants hurried to complete the offerings.

McLeod caught sight of an approaching motor vessel in the distance. It was one of the island's charter boats. The charter pulled up along the other side of the pier where the General's fishing boat docked. He saw them wave and heard the mutual honking of foghorns that embellished their greetings. As the ship cautiously approached the dock, a crew member jumped from the bow onto the pier with tie-downs. The Ochoa family ran down from their house, cheering. McLeod was curious, baffled, and disappointed; adjusting his binoculars to the distance, he saw two people who looked like passengers on the aft deck and two more parts of the crew on the boat's bow. This deviation from the schedule discombobulated the plan. McLeod could make out that two people were disembarking. He put down his binoculars, grabbed his camera, adjusted the lens, and began to snap pictures.

The first was a tall, frail-looking Caucasian male dressed in a Stetson cowboy-style hat, sunglasses, loose-fitting jeans, and a light-blue denim jacket, and walking with a cane. The other was a woman; she had her back facing McLeod while instructing the crew on what to take ashore. Black hair trailed down her back; she was casually dressed in white pants, a light black sweater, and deck shoes. She ordered and pointed; the crew responded obediently. She had a commanding manner; finally, turning to greet her host, her arms outstretched, she was enveloped in a warm embrace by the entire family. He still could not see her face. "The plan is dead," thought McLeod as he stared into the binoculars at the woman. McLeod switched his binoculars for the camera and snapped many frames. The woman turned to face the crew again. However, she was indistinguishable from the entourage that unwittingly hid her. She was shorter than everyone around her and a bit on the slight of frame," McLeod observed. General Ochoa focused on the woman, whose back was facing McLeod. He snapped frames as a crew member handed the woman a wide-brimmed straw hat and sunglasses; she put both on. Then, they all moved in a gregariously slow stop-and-go manner toward the veranda.

The crew unloaded behind the entourage and carried luggage, including four garment bags and three metal-framed trunks, to the house. The crew then returned to the yacht and abruptly motored off.

"So much for the plot and plan," McLeod murmured.

The arrival of guests voided the original ensnarement. Nevertheless, McLeod assured himself that the General was still on the island. While that fact held, he acknowledged that the opportunity to kill the General was still within reach, and he was determined to seize it.

It was 8:30 a.m. the next day. McLeod predicted that the hospitable Cuban family would maintain their traditional Christmas vacation pattern and take their guests to town for sightseeing and shopping. McLeod parked and sat in his truck between the main road to town and

the vacation villa. McLeod had been staring into his rearview mirror, impatiently awaiting some sign that his guess had proven correct. He was frustrated that he had to start from zero on planning, but he knew a new opportunity would arise.

Surprise Plus, Plus

McLeod drank his hour-old thermoset hot coffee and glanced at the stillness behind him. But then, sure enough, at 11:30 a.m., the same black SUV that had delivered the family from the airport to the beach house showed up in front of the residence.

The driver opened the doors on the right side, and everyone entered. "I was right," McLeod grinned. The SUV passed by McLeod on the way to town. After assuring him there was no security chase vehicle, he followed at a respectable distance. The limousine headed directly down Calle Marina and towards the town center. Once in the shopping and restaurant sector center, the limousine pulled over to unload its passengers.

The General's wife and the female guest began a slow, arm-in-arm procession as they walked, talked, pointed, and peered. Two bodyguards followed the procession in a relaxed, inattentive manner.

Instead of passing by all the shops, the ladies ventured into a few while the men waited outside. No one seemed concerned about time or destination; the goal was simply the enjoyment of a stroll and the compatibility of each other's company. McLeod followed the group across the street while pretending to read a newspaper. He went unnoticed.

They strolled for almost two hours, crossing the street and re-crossing until they reached Plaza del Arte de Oro y Plata, a small but luxurious hotel with a legendary restaurant and a renowned chef. It seemed clear that this was their destination. McLeod hurried back to his pick-up and drove to the hotel's restaurant. He positioned himself opposite the target. Eager to get a clean, close-up look at the guests, he adjusted his smaller binoculars on the female guest. The slightly built woman with long, straight black hair turned her head inexplicably directly into his line of sight. Finally, a clear view of her features came into focus. The revealing image shocked McLeod: his fingers lost grip, and the binoculars dropped from his hands. He picked them up, placed them, and adjusted them.

It was her, he verified. Anh Li!

He was staring at a woman he had not seen since Dung Ha. It was her. There was no doubt. Anh Li was alive and in the company of General Ochoa. Stupefied by the visual, a myriad of questions erupted in his mind.

Cornfield was right. Anh Li was a spy. The question raced across his mind. Was she? Did she? Did she share responsibility for the killing of Team 33? Fighting off the temptation to walk into their gathering and demand answers—or ask no questions and kill them all—prompted his hands to tremble. He could not stop shaking or keep his binoculars steady.

McLeod contemplated: "How could I have been so dumb? I was humping her while she and her brethren were killing Americans. She and Doss disappeared when they found out I survived the ambush. I never suspected her betrayal; how naïve and stupid of me."

Finally, sickened by the reality, McLeod pulled the truck over and got out. He stood for a moment, then bent over, retching everything from his insides.

McLeod incarcerated himself within the confines of his room. Over time, the disappointment of General Ochoa's pattern change evolved into a new, highly personal, and valuable target of opportunity. The murderous bitch was now within his grasp. Once again, dumb luck has proven its viability. The omnipotent gods of circumstance and serendipity have presented an advantageous situation. Yesterday's concerns evolved into a sense of wonder and opportunity. Anh Li was now the focus of McLeod's interest, with General Ochoa running a distant second.

McLeod watched from his concealed post the following day as activity on the veranda de-escalated into relaxed contentment. The gentlemen sat in a circle, drinking champagne and puffing cigars. The ladies abruptly stood and walked down to the beach in McLeod's direction, holding hands. McLeod casually moved into a position of deeper concealment behind overgrown beach vegetation.

There was just enough light to be concerned about discovery.

However, the ladies were too engrossed in conversation to look in McLeod's direction. McLeod was able to view Anh Li up close. Her beautiful hair and shapely body were just as alluring. It had been years since he had been so close that he could almost smell her. He realized the opportunistic scale of his dumb luck on the walk to the truck; the sky parted, and Anh Li had fallen within his reach. She had answers to essential questions. McLeod realized his inclination to slit her throat needed suppression. Killing her would not reveal the truth; information took precedence.

That night, McLeod's nightmarish cries stirred him to wake; the last moments of Team 33 had played out. A detailed, intact dream left him unable to go back to sleep. Armed with black coffee, he awaited the sunrise to rescue him from his melancholy.

The morning unfolded on his observation site; McLeod saw the unidentified male guest with Anh Li outside the house. An attendant hurried from behind with luggage in tow. The male guest walked with Anh Li, with the Ochoa family leading the way. The limousine pulled up, and the two exchanged goodbyes; the unknown man then left.

A local group of musicians entertained on the porch, and the afternoon passed. McLeod watched and waited. Just before daylight defeated darkness, a limousine pulled up to the house. A tall, well-proportioned man stepped out in his late thirties or early forties. The door opened before he could knock, and out flew Elena, screaming with joy and arms outstretched. Elena, the General's daughter, pulled Peter, her husband, inside. McLeod knew he had less than two weeks before the vacation was over, and, as they did every year during their holiday, they would fly to Paris for shopping. The question is whether to act now or forestall.

Anh Li, his new target, was never alone. Five more days passed with no opportunity to act. Finally, on the sixth day, the airport limousine pulled up in front of the house.

McLeod was terrified that the Paris trip was the reason for the airport limousine. He stayed calm and reassured himself: "I know the name of the Parisian hotel. I could seek her there."

Moments later, the family, including Anh Li, headed for the airport in the limo. McLeod followed, thinking of what he would need to arrange and what he should or should not do. Then, like a thunderbolt, he recognized that Anh Li was unlike the others, who were carrying clothes suited for wintry weather. Could it be? Was this the opportunity?

The limo pulled up in front of the departure gates. Everyone was kissing Anh Li. Under his breath, McLeod murmured, "Yes, it must be so!"

Anh Li re-entered the limo; unbelievable, McLeod reflected. The Hail Mary pass was completed from the worst to the best.

McLeod followed Anh Li back to the house; he could afford no more surprises. He knew that he must confront Anh Li, regardless of the consequences. All the years of contemplation seeking revenge had evolved in this time and place.

Following Anh Li's limo from a safe distance back to the house, he thought of Dong Ha, the war lost, Team 33, and those patrols. He discussed patrols with her, never considering that the doctor could be a spy. She was a heart-throbbing delight, and now I want to kill her. How could a perspective change so dramatically? How could I have been with the woman who had a hand in killing my team? He drove past the beach house and headed home for his last night on the island.

Packing all his essentials, McLeod cleared his mind and focused on his self-imposed duty. First, answer questions, ensure she is discovered in the morning, and then exit the island. He drove to the film developer's shop, picked up the photo package, and thanked the developer for his work while casually mentioning that he would be leaving the next day.

It was 6:00 p.m.; the sun had set. The evening was calm.

A slight wind cooled off a warm day. Anh Li sat on the porch chair, peacefully rocking. He saw the servants leaving for the day. She was alone. Like a stalking tiger at a popular waterhole, McLeod eyeballed his prey. Lastly, Anh Li stood and walked into the house.

McLeod entered through the back door, locked it behind him, and carefully placed his utility bag on the floor. The living room light was on; McLeod moved toward it and turned the light off. McLeod found a position just outside the kitchen where there was a scurrying noise. He sat in the darkness on a cushioned chair. Seconds later, Anh Li walked out holding a plate of food in one hand and a glass of milk in the other. McLeod grasped the lamp string. He pulled it, and the darkness turned abruptly to light. McLeod stood.

The effect shocked and froze Anh Li, who was in place. She screamed and dropped the plate and glass.

"It's you!" exclaimed Anh while backing away. "McLeod didn't reply.

"I feared someday..." Anh gasps in disbelief.

"Yes, you knew that someday... the scattered pieces would mend, and the truth revealed."

Like a rodent caught in the light, Anh ran into the kitchen, a dead end. McLeod approached. Reaching for the first available weapon, a paring knife held in her right hand, she slashed the blade back and forth. She tossed dishes, pots, and pans at McLeod with her free hand, but every defensive effort failed. McLeod gripped her hair and threw her to the ground. Anh Li was flung into the living area. On her knees, she started to stand. McLeod rotated her on her back and straddled her. For seconds, they stared at one another. Helpless, Anh tried a different approach.

"Sergeant McLeod," she said with a persuasive, calming demeanor, "I know you are angry. But please release me; your grip is too tight. It's hurting me. Please, let's talk."

McLeod did not respond; everything seemed to be in slow motion. Again, Li Anh asked for a release, but McLeod did not respond. Again, the reality of her being under his weight had frozen his response. Finally, as if splashed on by a bucket of freezing water, he snapped out of his trance; McLeod lessened the tension of his grip.

McLeod climbed off her without speaking while holding tight to her right wrist as he dragged the five-foot-two-inch, 115-pound woman into the living area toward his utility bag. He pulled out one of the three-foot-three-quarter-inch nylon lines and tied her hands behind her back. She protested, appealing to his empathy. Instead, McLeod reached back into his bag, removed another line, and tied her feet together. Then he attached the end of that line, by a snap link, to Anh Li's tied hands.

McLeod grabbed a roll of the rigger's tape and sealed her mouth, then picked her up over his shoulder and carried her upstairs. He investigated the three bedrooms, looking for the one that still had the appearance of her things. Finding her room, he leaned forward and slid her off his back onto the bed.

He sat on a chair directly facing Anh Li and stared at her. Scattered thoughts crossed his mind, each competing with the other for prominence. McLeod knows that memory is a disordered, truth-fragile, anagrammatic, and distorted sense of unreliability. After twenty years of separation, the Marines based in Dung Ha, Vietnam, and Dr. Anh Li were not the same individuals who had confronted each other in the Canary Islands. He accepts that the relationship happened. But for the two people gazing upon each other, Father Time has hermetically sealed the emotional present from the past.

Like a rat with one foot firmly snared, Anh Li was bound and held; her physical position was degrading and uncomfortable. But on the other hand, Anh Li realized she was still alive. Therefore, there was something left to be decided. There must be some unresolved consideration; hopefulness calmed her as she concentrated on escaping this deranged situation.

Aware that the intrusion was a spontaneous opportunity and that anything could happen at any time, McLeod hurriedly searched for her belongings, starting with her purse, then a small blue canvas pack with numerous zippers and pockets. Anh Li muffled outcries of defiance; her eyes begged McLeod to stop and rip the tape from her mouth. Ignoring her, he went ahead to open her handbag. Inside was a wallet containing several American and French credit cards, as well as French, Panamanian, and Cuban passports, all bearing Anh Li Jadot's name. Additionally, there were several color pictures: two old black-and-white photos of Anh Li and one with her father and mother holding a diapered baby.

There were also six color pictures back-to-back in three separate plastic liners. One was Anh Li, as McLeod remembered her, holding a toddler. The photographer's interest was the child; the little one looked Eurasian, with a sharp-pointed nose, round eyes, and beautiful, thick black hair. Anh Li, the proud mother, looked pleased and satisfied. The picture directly behind that one was of a tall, slim white male wearing a Leopards baseball cap and dark glasses. McLeod showed the picture to Anh Li, wondering if that was the child's father, but received a blank stare in response.

"So, this is Doss," McLeod said with a raised, threatening voice. "He fathered your child. You were with this traitorous bastard all these years?"

McLeod reached his right hand down to his left inside calf and pulled his Marine Corps-issued K-Bar blade from its sheath. Anh Li quivered. Then, concentrating on Anh Li's exposed neck, he traced the point of the blade across her neck. Anh Li urinated; the smell permeated the room. McLeod snapped back the nylon line, pinning her legs to her wrist. He ripped the rigger's tape from her mouth and cut through her clothes and the rope that bound her ankles together.

Carrying her to the nearby shower, with her hands tied behind her back, he turned on the water, adjusted for temperature, and continued to tear at her clothes until she was naked. The warm water, with McLeod applying soap to her skin, washed away her urine; her body quivered. McLeod dried her with a bath towel. Put a bathrobe over her shoulders. He walked her back to the bedroom. McLeod took two rope lines, made a loop on one side of the line, and looped it over the bedpost. With the other, he tied a secure knot over her left wrist and repeated the procedure on her other wrist and the bedpost. He then cut the binding, holding her wrist behind her back. Although spread-eagled on the bed, Anh Li was relieved to have her arms freed from her back. The tape was removed; she said nothing. Her quivering stopped. A calmness overcame her.

"I have some questions," McLeod declared. But McLeod could not follow up before Anh Li's verbal assault: "What are you doing? Please, talk to me. Ask your questions. Let me explain. I promise you the truth; you were surprised to find me here. You're hurt; I can help. I will tell you all you want to know."

Halfway listening while holding two four-by-five black and white photographs in hand, McLeod asks, "Who is the man in this photograph?"

"That man in the baseball cap is a GRU operative. The other is the man you know as Doss. Please, we need to talk. I realize that the surprise is overwhelming.

"Yes, we need to talk," McLeod replied. "I do have questions. Doss is your man. I am surprised; I did not recognize him; aging has done no favors. After I saw you, I was stupefied, catatonic, and then enraged. The idea that Captain Doss is with you should have been obvious; you both left Vietnam together. I have only one real question. Why! Why would you participate in the murder of Team 33?"

"You must believe me," she pleaded. "I knew only a small part of the operation. I was not aware of Team 33's situation until after the fact. I would have done something; I don't know what, but I would have done something. I would not let you get on that helicopter. I enjoyed you very much; you were so innocent and virile. I had feelings for you. But there was a war. And I was working for your enemy."

"Listen carefully," McLeod emphasizes. "I am not interested in a long, drawn-out story."

Anh Li asks, "What specifically would you like to know?"

"Specifically," said McLeod, "I would like to know why in hell, Team 33? Why such an elaborate ruse to kill four Marines? And what role did Doss play in the plot?"

"I cannot confirm, however," answered Anh. "I heard that Max, the Russian...

"Max the Russian?" McLeod queried.

"Max is short for Maximilian." Anh replies, "It was your team in the area weeks earlier that crept in very close. You were on the North Vietnamese side of the DMZ and succeeded in taking photos, which were subsequently passed to the G-2 Division intelligence. Unless intercepted, the images would eventually be presented to the CIA and Naval Intelligence. Somehow, Max received a report that one or more photos revealed a picture of him, his officers, and his South Vietnamese spies. He feared that your team could physically identify everyone photographed within binocular range. Once the photo's value is decided, intel officers call in Team 33 for an identifying debrief.

"This Russian, Max; how well do you know him?"

"I know him very well. As I have said, he is the man in the baseball cap. I kept the photo because, although aged, that is the only image of his person."

"You know where he is now?" pressed McLeod.

"He is in Cuba," Anh answered. "Max is well-guarded. I have not seen or directly communicated with him in years."

"His full name, and what about Doss? From where did he originate? Where is he now?"

"McLeod, you're scaring me. Will you untie me? I promise to answer everything. The war is over. There is no need for this."

"What is the Russian's name?" McLeod ignored her pleas.

"His name is Maximilian Orlov Ivanov."

"And what about that asshole Doss?" McLeod abruptly snaps in rapid succession. "The real Captain Doss was a naval counterintelligence officer on temporary duty assignment to the 1st Marine Division at Da Nang. Someone high-ranking officer in Naval intelligence must have made the placement substitution, exchanging the real Captain Doss for the fake."

"All of this to murder Team 33?"

"As I said, I do not know the details, but Max was determined to snag the KGB agent posing as a corpsman and shoot up Team 33. That's why Captain Doss, under orders from Max, enabled the Corpsman Marshal to go with Team 33. I only learned of this after the fact. If it is Max that you want, I can help find him."

"So, you're going to help me find and kill Max? So much for a spy-to-spy loyalty." McLeod continued the questioning, "So Max, the Russian, decides to have Team 33 drag out this corpsman KGB agent so he could arrange the killing of my Marines? Sorry, I have a hard time with that one."

"I did not know the details. I am offering pieces and parts of twenty-year-old memories gathered after the fact. Doss told me after the fact that the corpsman was to kill your team and then manage his way to a rallying point to hook up with Max."

"You were a spy planted deep in the mix of U.S. military operations. Do you want me to believe you only knew bits and pieces after the fact? You were a covert operator. The operator obeyed and dispatched the given orders, leading to Gunny Hagerty's death and three members of Team 33."

"There was a war." Anh Li explains, "I was a young believer in Ho Chi Minh's version of a united Vietnam. Today, I have regrets. But that was then; this is now. Can't we act civilly and cordially and discuss your issues and concerns? Sergeant McLeod, the war is over."

"Hmm," McLeod considers, "with malicious heart and murderous intent, of course, that was then; now, the North Vietnamese spy that abetted the killing of Gunner Hagerty and three Marines of Team 33 is offering a truce, an understanding. Offering the sensibility of a kumbaya transference of actions that led to the death of four Marines was a forgivable indulgence."

"Yes, why not?" Anh Li confirms. "The conflict is over."

"It must be nice to departmentalize, set the past aside, and move on; if I were that person, I would not be here."

"I cannot feel your pain, but I realize your suffering. Let me help you."

"You're twenty years late on that offer," McLeod snapped. But please clarify if you can; the dual-missioned KGB corpsman did not obey one part of a two-part order. Not killing the Marines of Team 33 and Doc's middle-of-the-night disappearance were linked to Doss's change of extraction site."

"All I remember," Anh replied, "is that Doss received his instructions indirectly from Max, who was connected to a high-ranking American in Naval intelligence."

"The corpsman had a fully functioning radio to communicate with Doss and, I assume, the Russian. Doc disobeyed an order for a reason, and that reason was predicated on unknown information to me. Or was it when Doss changed the extraction point? Marshall feared something was wrong. So, he left the patrol one day earlier. Once he left my patrol, no one knew what had happened to him; the Russian knew because we assumed the Doc dialed him up."

"What happened to Gunnery Sergeant Hagerty?"

"I do know, Anh Li volunteers, "that Doss was particularly concerned about Gunnery Sergeant Hagerty's pending investigation."

"The killing of Hagerty was an impulsive act taken out of extreme caution. There was no predetermination to do so," Anh Li replied. "Doss panicked over Hagerty's investigation of his posting, so he sent word to have Hagerty meet him near the ammo depot and had one of our infiltrators, the Vietnamese you knew as Sam. The local barber, a Viet Cong operative, shoots Hagerty. I was aware after the fact."

"Well, I was so naïve," McLeod admitted. "While you were spying for the enemy, I openly discussed missions and patrol events. I let pussy, shut down common discretion. I am so ashamed. Unknowingly, I was a valuable character in your melodrama. I wonder, between you, Sam the barber, Doss, and who knows how many more, we Marines were lucky to have made it through the night with our throats intact."

"If it helps," Ahn informs McLeod, "I was not interested in any information you arbitrarily passed me."

"Well, Doss, your compatriot was the man who gave the orders that ended the lives of my Marines."

"I swear, the only person who had such authority was Max. His forces managed the heroin trade; the cash from that enterprise was shared and proved an asset to the profiteers. I am confident he ordered and controlled all operations regarding the assault on Team 33. Of course, because he used Cuban soldiers under the command of Colonel Calvo. Max could not have executed the ambush without the Colonel's complicity."

"You sound very sure of yourself. What about Doss and his complicity in the ambush of my team?"

"Yes, I am certain. Doss was a dutiful Marxist, an anti-war zealot who, like Jane Fonda, was overwhelmed by the theoretical while paying no attention to the real terms and conditions. Doss is today what was then, and ever since, tethered and manipulated. I used his authority to leave the compound at Dung Ha rapidly. He was no more than a piece of furniture to move about in the interest of the cause."

"How did the orders to change the extraction place evolve?" McLeod questioned.

"Please let me explain."

"Well, explain," McLeod says.

"One day after, Team 33 left Dung Ha for the bush. I received a message from my NVA sources that ordered Doss to change the place of extraction. Neither Doss nor I knew anything about the Cuban helicopter or the reason for the change in extraction. You understand the need-to-know principle; Doss and I did not need to know. Neither of us did any of the thinking. I presume Max wrote the orders to ambush Team 33. Gunnery Sergeant Hagerty was too interested in Doss, which prompted his assassination."

McLeod sharply changed the subject with a raised voice, "You sure did get out of Dodge City in a hurry."

"I thought I was a well-placed, high-value asset. I never thought my superiors would out my cover in such a cavalier manner."

"You should know a high-placed spy within Naval Counterintelligence informed your superiors that your arrest was pending. He, whoever he is, outed you," McLeod suggested.

"I had felt for a while that my luck had run its course. Invites to the right places and certain people dried up. It was Doss who approached me with the order to leave. Oddly, if compromised, my orders were to inoculate Doss with an overdose of morphine. Fortunately for Doss, I did not obey that order."

"Why Hanoi?" McLeod inquired.

"I had arranged with my mother for a safe house a few miles outside Bangkok. I knew that if things went wrong, I couldn't necessarily rely on help from within my command structure. I understood that I was on my own. However, upon rendezvousing with Max at the designated rally point inside the DMZ, he and his entourage of mercenaries accompanied Doss and me to an airport deep inside the countryside. Five days later, we flew to Hanoi.

"So, Doss grew on you and has been a part of your life from then to now. The little rat has had a good shot at life."

"He is a weak person with many regrets," Anh Li implored.

The description of Doss riled McLeod. "Well, where is this weakling?

With many regrets? Or are you his protector as well as his lover?"

"If I told you of his past, his reasons..."

"You want to explain the life story of a traitor? McLeod thundered with a raised voice, "Is this some excuse for his sins? If so, keep all these reasons to yourself. Where do I find Doss?"

"He is back in Cuba," a nervous Anh Li responded. "He will leave Cuba if I ask him to meet me somewhere."

"I see, you are going to help me kill your man?"

"Well, I am tied up, and as you know, when restrained, saying and doing are not always compatible," Anh Li clarified.

"Honest answer," McLeod concurs.

"I am thirsty. Could you please hand me the water bottle behind you on the dresser?"

McLeod reached back and grasped the water bottle. He held it, uncapped it, and placed the drinking end onto Anh's lips. She drank several gulps.

"OK, what's next?" Anh Li confidently asked.

"Are you going to help me kill your man, Doss, your friend General Ochoa, and this Max guy?"

"Doss is not my man. I am tied up and frightened out of my wits. So why would you believe anything I said? Surely, I would say anything to get out of this predicament."

"So, say it," McLeod commanded.

"Yes, I will help you."

"Great! See how easy that was? I am interested in reading the files you brought with you."

"I intended to do some work while I was on vacation. The files have nothing to do with the past. There is nothing there about the Russian."

"These files could have collateral communication, informational specifics, such as dates, places, addresses, and phone numbers."

"Well, all right. I am not stopping you. It is a waste of time, but it is your time." Sensing the opportunity, Anh Li asks, "So what about my life? What will keep me alive after all this information has been extracted to your satisfaction?"

With a calming tone, McLeod asks, "I assume the child in the picture is yours?"

While looking intently at McLeod, Anh Li responded with a firm "Yes."

With the first sign of sympathy, "The child will need a mother. I'm seeking your cooperation. This information is essential to me.

"Fine," Anh agreed. "Doss's real name is Stephen Henry Knox. He now uses the name Henry Knox. After Hanoi, I helped him get into Canada to reunite with his retired parents. His parents, who were resolute Marxists and heavy smokers all their lives, were ill and died within days of each other, six months after Henry's return. Their deaths devastated an already emotionally weak man. Nevertheless, he always kept in contact with me. I helped him enter Mexico, and through a Cuban connection, he obtained Mexican citizenship. In time, I got him to Cuba. He taught English and became friends with the Ochoa family's children. Although disenchanted by the reality of Cuba's Marxism, his life, though full of regrets, was serviceable."

"Where and how did you recruit him into service?"

"I did not recruit him. However, he revealed to me that he received an advanced degree in political science in Canada. He was following in his parents' footsteps in the teaching profession. He, as well as his parents, was a member of the League for Socialist Action. At the university, Russian operatives interviewed and offered Knox a scholarship to attend the Marx-Engels-Lenin Institute in Moscow. That is where his training as a covert agent took place. Henry was born in the United States, so he has dual citizenship. I know he entered the U.S. Navy as an Ensign in 1963. After schooling, because he spoke fluent Russian, he served as an intel officer to a command posting at Quantico, Virginia."

"Did he ever serve under an officer named Cornfield?"

"I never had reason to ask him about my duty assignments," Anh Li responds. "I know Henry was in Da Nang, receiving his orders. A well-placed high-ranking officer fabricated orders for the posting to 1st Force Recon in Dung Ha. Someone with power but not staffed within the 1st Marine Division. I knew a man posing as Captain Doss was coming to complete a difficult mission. My assignment did not require further details."

"That's a flat-out lie," McLeod shouted. "I remember you telling of meeting Doss in Da Nang and having a one-nighter with him."

A shivering Anh Li responded. "Yes, I told you that, but it never happened. I cannot remember my motivation for telling you that...."

"But it does prove," McLeod emphasizes, "you know much more than you're telling me. You conspired with Henry Knox in Da Nang before he reported to Dung Ha as Captain Doss."

"Yes," was the reply. However, after the reporting of your survival, Henry lost it. Reality hit him right between the eyes. From then on, the academic who envisioned acting for a Marxist cause ran smack into reality. After a successful escape from Vietnam, I could not abandon him. I took him into my home and made him a part of my life. I did not and could never love such a man. I have never had a sexual relationship with him. We are not friends; Henry, formerly known as Doss, is an adult child under my care. He is my adult dependent. A shell of a man, racked with guilt and disbelief in Marxism, the belief that prompted his part in the killings of Team 33."

"Who is the well-placed, high-ranking officer who fabricated the Doss orders?"

"Only a few would know who issued the order. Max knew enough to execute the mission and nothing more."

"Finally," McLeod sighs, "a half-truth. You were the conduit between the Russian and the Russian mole."

"Ok, after the escape and evasion from Dung Ha, you worked initially in Hanoi and eventually in Cuba," McLeod continued to access information.

"Yes, Anh Li confirmed. "There are many details I am omitting; nevertheless, I needed the work. I no longer practice medicine. Instead, I managed a business and stabilized my financial and professional status."

"Imagine," snapped McLeod, "the communist spy has embraced the spirit of capitalism. It's a little late for my team! Now, those who were killed in the name of Marxism benefit from the persuasion of J.P. Morgan and caveat emptor; it is, indeed, a disingenuous world."

Ignoring his words but watching his eyes gazing at her mostly naked body, she dared to believe that she could sexually arouse McLeod. If so, she might have the power to redirect his hostility. Acting on her assumption, she shifted her robe to expose a bit more of her naked thigh. McLeod's eyes tracked the motion and followed the contours of her skin before forcing himself to look away.

"Hey, Marine," Anh Li cooed, "Do you remember us? We were so good together. I have had thoughts of you for years. I see how you look at me; it is as it used to be. Do you remember?"

McLeod sensed the play. It felt blasphemous, but blood was rushing to his penis.

Anh Li smiled and demanded, "McLeod... untie me."

McLeod ignored her request but loosened the tie-down. He separated her bathrobe, exposing her breasts and waist. She stared at him and sensually angled the spread of her legs. Her body was sensuously positioned, legs spread just as they had been so long ago.

"Please," Anh Li begged. "You must take me. Please!"

McLeod leaned over her: "Where is dear maligned Henry now?"

"After, I will tell you everything, after. But, for now, let us forget and pretend. Pretend that nothing has changed. Come on. I know you feel the same. You want what I want. And I want you in me."

Though tied by a nylon line, Anh's right hand had enough slack to reach between her legs. Concentrating on McLeod's body language, she started to masturbate and then offered up her fingers to McLeod's mouth.

McLeod regressed to their last night together. He sucked on her fingers and unzipped his pants, exposing his hard-on. She reached with her hand, gently inserting him, and sighed with the insertion. McLeod shoved and forced his penis into her; it felt so good. Thinking of her duplicity, her years of spy-whoring her way through scores of men perversely stimulated McLeod within minutes; he was ready to ejaculate, but instead withdrew.

From somewhere deep inside, the guilt of having sex with this North Vietnamese spy, the woman he once trusted, the one complicit in the killing of Team 33, instantly eliminated all lust or sympathy. Remembering that deceptiveness was her trade, McLeod looked down upon her.

Anh Li stopped all physical movement. A look of terror raced across her face. Her seduction had failed. It was too late. With both hands, McLeod reached for her throat, gripping and squeezing. Anh Li fought, but it was impossible; she could not counter his weight and strength. Staring into her eyes, McLeod tightens his grip. Beneath him, Anh Li shakes, quivers, and shivers until her resistance ends. Then, as if forced to wake so the nightmare would end, McLeod released his grip and stood up and off. He dashes outside to inhale the fresh air and recover. On reentering, he sees the limp body, the object of his wrath.

The satisfaction of revenge waned as the intoxication from the kill had its effect. Hands shaking, a cold chill permeated McLeod, sitting on a chair facing Anh's body. Unlike his beginning-to-end thought process of killing General Ochoa, the strangling of Anh Li was spontaneous. A trembling McLeod stared at the body. He knows the killing was murder, and no moral reconciliation is possible. In this instance, revenge was not sweet; it was remorseful. The act had no satisfactory recourse; it branded him a murderer. His hands continued to shake, and his body trembled.

It was midday. The upheaval within McLeod's mind had subsided, realizing that conclusions drawn by investigators midday tomorrow necessitate today's actions. The authorities will seek out the perpetrator. It was reasonable to believe that he could be a suspect simply because he was a loner who left the island, coincidingly with the police finding the body. Counting on the viability of his false identity and alias passport, he knew he had to leave that night. He took Anh Li's jewelry, cash, and some personal items, wrapped them in a plastic bag from the kitchen, and buried them far from the house, using his gloves.

All evidence would point to a hostile entry, a confrontation, dialogue, a struggle, rape, and death by strangulation after walking around and scanning the scene of the murder. McLeod readied to leave and gathered all relevant documents, accepting that such material tied him directly to the scene; he took the risk. Glancing at Anh Li's body for the last time, McLeod retraced his entry path to the exit. He gathered his utility bag full of information and vacated the premises.

The Retrograde

After five days of traveling, McLeod returned to Vegas. As he walked into his office, Ms. Delores commented, " Well. "The 'sailor home from the sea and the hunter home from the hills' has finally returned to port. There are pressing issues, and I put them in order of priority on your desk. Remember, we have an obligatory invitation to Mr. Diamond and his party this afternoon. Billy Lamb will join us."

Sam Diamond and his wife have lived at the Las Vegas Country Club for over 25 Years. Sam would say they lived in three rooms and rarely visited the other ten.

Sam and Marion were naturally gregarious people and loved to entertain. But this night was special for Sam. He had decided to use the occasion to pitch McLeod on a brand-new opportunity. Sam called away on the phone when McLeod and company arrived. So, in addition to waiting for Sam's return, everyone gathered in The Sunrise Room. Guests milled about, conversing and enjoying the food and drinks. Finally, Sam finished his call and returned to the event. Seeing McLeod and catching his eye, Sam beckoned him over.

With a drink in hand, McLeod followed Sam into the library. The library at the back of the house was private and wonderfully comfortable.

"Welcome home; it is so good to have you here right before me. It has been too long."

Sam continued without waiting for a response from McLeod: "I have some news. Remember your idea about the concept of a hotel-casino confederation? Where all hotel-casino properties would share certain information, such as the cost of insurance, goods, services, even labor, and then assimilate the real-time data into a reporting format?"

"So that each confederation member got the data, initiating a standard operating cost," McLeod added.

"You commented that it made too much sense for all our competitors not to contemplate the idea. They have contemplated the idea and have unanimously nominated you as the managing director. Using your words, members have given you the authority commensurate with the responsibility."

With a big smile on his face, McLeod could see that Sam was excited about the confederation coming into existence. "Sam, I know you understand the confederation's positive ramifications, and of course, I agree. However, accepting the position would mean leaving you and everyone at the hotel. How could I do that? Besides, I thought the person running the confederation should be an accountant, an attorney, or both. It never dawned on me that I would be selected."

"McLeod," Sam replied, "you know that gravity could not pull you away from me. But, my dear friend, you need to know something else: I am selling my majority in the hotel. I want to get out of this business. I want the buyer to be someone who will accept and protect my middle management people and all employees who have been with the property for over five years. Divide five percent of the sale price among all employees who have been with me for over seven years. In other words, the buyer must have a vision that complements my operational sensibility, a lot of money, and compassion. It is not a common combination here in Vegas. So, you see, you're about to become quite rich, and the Director of the Confederation position is a perfect perch from which you can plan your next big move."

"I swear, Sam," McLeod confessed, "I never thought of anyone but Sam Diamond owning the hotel. The property and town will never be the same."

"The same was said when Siegel was gunned down. Cohen went to jail, and Lansky wanted nothing to do with the Los Angeles mob. Frankly, I am an old man wanting to enjoy the present while suffering through the debilitating effects of aging and waiting for death's knock on my door. The hotel-casino operation is demanding. As with all living things, my optimum operating time has passed. I am tired.

Now, shall we make the most of the moment? Remember, a lifetime is no more than a consecutive string of moments; moments are all there is. Therefore, one of the more meaningful ideas is to find the means to enjoy the moments while one is above the ground. Oh, and, good friend, one should not enjoy these precious moments alone."

McLeod put his arm around Sam as they entered the crowded dining room.

It was common knowledge that Sam Diamond's Aladdin Hotel was a quality property. Unsurprisingly, the buyer was found to be qualified and affirmed in record time. Escrow closed within ninety days, and an era had passed.

The confederation was established, and Delores followed McLeod, even though leaving Aladdin was as difficult for her as it was for him. In confidence, McLeod had informed her that he would leave the position to pursue other interests within six months if she entered the confederation as assistant executive director. She would be his replacement, pleased with the news but not with the change of venue, which some people call progress. The aging Delores preferred it as it once was. It was Wednesday evening, and McLeod was preparing for bed after another strenuous day at the office when a call from his office phone rang in his apartment.

"Is this McLeod, Sergeant McLeod of 1st Force Recon Company, Vietnam?" a male voice asked.

"Who's asking?" McLeod responded.

Stephen Henry Knox. You would know me as Captain Doss."

"So, you're willingly walking into the valley of death," said McLeod. "Anh Li told me you were a weak, debilitating mess. Where are you?"

"I am in town, Sergeant, Doss replies. When would you like to meet?"

"Tomorrow," McLeod said emphatically.

"Tomorrow, it is," Doss confirmed. "Three in the afternoon, on the south corner of Spring Mountain Road and Las Vegas Boulevard, I'll stand directly outside the shopping mall's Spring Mountain entrance. I have things to say. It will not take much time."

The phone clicked. McLeod held the phone briefly, then slowly lowered it to its cradle. McLeod called Billy and told him about the pending Doss rendezvous. Considering that Doss openly declared himself, avowing the advantage of surprise, the odds were that he wanted to talk.

After the call, McLeod rushed to the office, expecting he could trace Doss's call. The trace showed that the call came from a payphone at the Stardust Casino; McLeod returned home, denying himself a keen desire to go directly to the Stardust Hotel.

Sleep came quickly and easily for McLeod. Usually, he could not sleep without some chemical inducement; however, that night, he slept like a carefree baby, knowing He would be face-to-face with Doss tomorrow.

At 11:00 a.m., Billy was in McLeod's office explaining the setup and presenting the regular veterans' positioning and stations.

"Boss," said Billy, "I have positioned a monitoring team in the area. Additionally, I have the most beautiful ninja bodyguard posing as a tourist shopping. Believe me, boss, she's good."

"If you say so," McLeod affirmed. He must know I want him alive. Doss has eluded the authorities for decades, and out of nowhere, amazingly, he calls me for a meeting."

"This is a felo-de-se, purposed as an assassination run to take you with him. I think life has run its course for this fellow. The man's purpose has lost all meaningfulness with Dr. Li's passing."

"Interesting analysis, Doctor Billy. I had no idea you spoke Latin," McLeod grinned. "You may have missed your calling."

"Billy quickly responded, "I picked up that Latin phrase in a book titled The Death of Marcus Antonius and Cleopatra; I have just used up the extent of my Latin."

"The probability of this outcome favors your prediction. Doss is not running away. He is running to this meeting. And I am impressed by your erudition."

"What's an erudition?" McLeod ignores the question.

Billy positioned himself three blocks from the rendezvous corner and moved his people into the meeting site. It was 2:30 p.m. McLeod arrived at exactly 3:00 p.m. From McLeod's right, a voice called out calmly.

"Sergeant McLeod, I am Henry Knox or Doss, as you might refer." McLeod slowly turned. On a wooden bench decorated with merchant advertising sat Doss. Thin-faced with a three-day beard sporting light brown sunglasses rim, a crumpled hat, tieless, and a half a size too large light grey suit. Worn and filthy, his eyeballs were reddening, cheeks sucked in, and the man looked like death still standing.

"Please sit down, Sergeant," Doss requested as he moved to the far end of the bench. McLeod hesitated.

"Please," with a hand beckoning, Doss pleaded; McLeod obliged.

"I know you want me dead; nevertheless, if you would grant me some patience, my death is yours to witness. For a bit of forbearance, I will present a bonus prize."

"You have a prize for me?" McLeod questions.

"Yes, Max, the Russian; I have time-sensitive details on his whereabouts and vulnerabilities."

"Lovely of you," McLeod comments, "but if you came to trade, I am uninterested."

"No trade. I would never put myself in such a position with you," Doss assures.

"So, what is your reason for...?"

"Hmm," Knox interrupts. There is no reason; the rationale of evidentiary deduction has eluded me for over a decade. Sargent, I have direct, unencumbered culpability in destroying my person, my spiritual self. Remorse for such is my millstone. It has worn me down and crippled me. But she gave me a purpose when Anh Li was near and around me. I loved that woman. After all this time, it magically picked from the past and was placed in the present. You killed the only person of value in my life." While intensely staring at McLeod, Knox charges, "The police report was garbage. I know it was you."

McLeod queried, "The two of you had no issue killing my team. So, now, after all these years, you have remorse; such a sad, pathetic story."

"I agree it is a sad, pathetic story. Anh Li knew that you were alive. One evening, she casually mentioned Rojo's run-in with you in Miami. After Anh Li passed, I was unsure why seeing you became such an all-important event. One might say this meet with you is the crowning glory of my sad, pathetic self."

"Ok, sad and pathetic. Now what?" McLeod asks.

"Please stay on point; don't babble," McLeod insisted.

"Sergeant, please, this is not Paris Island, and I am not a recruit. I have presented myself to you willingly. A gift bestowed, so please allow me to continue at my pace. Now, where was I? Although Rojo was in FBI custody, imprisoned, and eventually deported at a Cuban intel debriefing, his information was already known. Therefore, after the Rojo debriefing, no one considered you a serious threat after all these years."

Stopping the discussion for a moment, Doss pointed out, "The wind has picked up; let's go inside." He stood, grabbed his cane, and walked into the mall. Fortunately, there was only one bench directly inside near the decorative waterfall. Billy, as a precaution, made sure it was available. With a gesture, Doss sat on the bench and offered a seat to McLeod.

"I despise Max as much as I loved Anh Li and utterly hate myself. So, the unreasonable within me has decided that by giving you the information on that Russian, I can strike a blow for those dead Marines. Convoluted reasoning, I know."

McLeod strenuously interjected, "Why did you participate in my team's ambush? They were young Marines; they had no beef with you."

"As a child, I believed in what I was told, the moral teachings of Marx, Engels, and Lenin, the theory of collectivism, and the sinfulness of capitalism. I evolved step by step into believing I could, and most importantly, act rightly in serving the end without considering the means. So, dedicating my life to the result never prompted me to consider the symbioses of communism and the required totalitarianism. On the contrary, my intellectual curiosity led me to think of myself as a soldier on a perilous mission. Therefore, the killing of Team 33 was not only a necessary act of war but, on my part, a courageous act.

If that is an answer, you surely deserve an answer. Looking back on the truth of what prompted me to act in such a treacherous, malicious manner, I assume I had an answer at the time. I am currently unable to answer your question. It is pathetic of me. Besides, in the present, the question is moot."

"Are you done? Or is there more gut-wrenching nonsense?"

"I loved Anh Li very much, and I miss her. Interestingly, there were two faces of Anh Li, an absolute contradiction, don't you think, Sergeant?"

"How much longer?" McLeod was in no mood to discuss the irrelevant.

"Sergeant, I promise, the end is near. However, I have some news that will wilt your arrogance and self-righteousness. When you killed Anh Li, you murdered the mother of your child."

McLeod's mouth went dry, and he was shocked into silence; he could not respond. His first reaction was that Doss had fabricated this incredible lie solely to extract pathos, regret, and bitter contempt. He again lamented the killing, as it had not allowed Anh Li the time to explain. Lit, McLeod knew that Doss could be telling the truth. He saw a picture of a baby girl in Anh Li's arms.

"Yes, Sergeant, your revenge destroyed the life of an innocent, and that innocent is your daughter." Doss noticed the effect and continued.

"Well," Doss noticed the discomfort, "Sergeant McLeod has stumbled. It is hard for one to believe the ever-vengeful Paladin is speechless. I know you will want to doubt my claim. However, I also know you will accept the killing of your daughter's mother as a base, immoral, and unnecessary event."

Doss reached into his pocket and tossed a key to McLeod." Here, it is for a locker at the downtown bus terminal. In this locker are all the files Anh kept on Max the Russian. Then, sensing McLeod's impatience, Doss pleaded, "Give me five more minutes, Sergeant McLeod."

With that statement, Doss walked over to the nearby payphones, pulled a phone card from his jacket pocket, and dialed.

McLeod overheard him saying, "Please make the most of your life. I love you as I love your mother. Goodly."

Then, Doss hung up, faced McLeod, reached into his other pocket, and pulled out a snub-nose Smith & Wesson 38 caliber pistol. Then, obligingly, he put the barrel into his mouth and pulled the trigger.

The sound was electrifying. His body slumped onto the floor. McLeod stood up and walked out the way he came in.

LAS VEGAS, Miami, PANAMA

The thought of fathering a child was not only emotionally troubling but also too fantastic to accept. There must be more to the story, so McLeod shelved that thought in favor of a beeline to the bus station.

Prudence would dictate that he wait. He checked his impulsiveness, but McLeod was hell-bent on satisfaction, setting caution and prudence aside in favor of immediate relief. He thought of the timeline between his sexual liaison with Anh Li and the child's age. She must be twenty-something today.

He arrived at the bus station, parked, and moved directly inside the vacant locker area. He reached into his pocket for a second or two, thought of a bogy trap, and at once discounted the idea that he could not wait any longer. Then, with the key in hand, he raced to locker number 272, inserted the key, and turned.

He found two large, stuffed, manila-colored packets, one stacked on top of the other. He reached in, snatched them, and returned to his car. He fought off his desire to tear into the material then and there, but instead drove home.

McLeod went into his office and opened the two packets. One packet held photos; the other included documents, business licenses, addresses, phone numbers, contact persons, schedules, and critical personnel patterns. The organizational chart of holding companies, subsidiaries, and wholly owned corporations was interesting but dated.

McLeod pulled out the contents of one packet, a letter rubber-banded on top of the pictures:

Sergeant McLeod,

I am dead. Before I ended my life, I assured you that your murderous act destroyed the life of an innocent. This innocence is of your blood. You took from her a loving mother and the only person I ever loved.

I committed a cowardly, treacherous, and unforgivable betrayal; conversely, Anh Li was a dedicated soldier, fighting a war for the side she believed was righteous. The two of us are now dead. If my death serves some purpose of redemption for those Marines long ago, I am pleased, but killing Anh was nothing less than murder.

I have enclosed all the pictures of Anh and her daughter; regretfully, the daughter's photos are of her as a child. I included these photos in the hope that you will suffer. I want you to feel as much pain as possible for your crime. But, of course, you are a cold-hearted killer, a psychopath, and you may have no conscience. I can only hope that I am wrong.

I have included a copy of his Cuban passport; as you will note, it is ten years old. The picture on the passport is not the treated GRU agent; it is a fake. I have not seen him in more than ten Years. He lives in Cuba but often leaves the island on his 210-foot, specially designed, equipped yacht.

I have sent Anh's daughter all the information I have gathered about you. She never knew her father; now, she knows her father killed her mother. I wish you a lifetime of pain and suffering.

Billy, using his door code, entered the apartment and approached. McLeod handed the letter to Billy. Satisfied that his boss was safe in his apartment, Billy did not read the letter; he folded it back into the envelope and placed it on a nearby desk.

"You need some alone time. I'll be here tomorrow, 7:30 A.M." Billy knew his boss well. He left and shut the door behind him.

The day's actions, the Doss letter, and Doss's daughter's claim had an effect. He chose not to read it twice. Instead, he walked to his bathroom; his sleeping pills were on a small table. He took a double dose.

McLeod woke up early. Expecting Billy at 7:30 a.m., he dove enthusiastically into the Doss documents. By the time Billy knocked at his door begging for coffee, McLeod had drafted a rough plan.

"Damn, this coffee is good," Billy exclaimed. "How in the hell do you make such good coffee?"

"It's all about the water and the correct portion of Illy's."

"Billy, I have read these documents and devised a rough idea of my next few moves. You will be the only person who will know my intentions and destination. I may be gone for a while. My days in the gaming trade are nearing their end. I will leave after the hotel is sold to new ownership. After that, Delores will take over my position with the Confederation. In the meantime, I'll give Sepúlveda a call and enlist him in my new direction."

A stunned Billy asked, "You're leaving Vegas?" Billy felt anxious. "What about..."

"There is no what about," interjected McLeod, stopping Billy short of finishing his question. "Confidentially, I am leaving Vegas. If you haven't had enough of me, you can visit."

Billy smiled with relief and embraced the offer, knowing his friend's purpose was revenge. Satisfying his friend's lust for revenge was dangerous. He was familiar with danger; for years, his sort of danger was tethered to acting stupid and ridiculous. He rejected McLeod's danger because it served a morally induced purpose.

Time passed, and the Aladdin Hotel was sold; Delores was then installed as Director of the Confederation. McLeod told all interested parties that he had decided to take a leave of absence to rest and recover.

For months, McLeod, with Raymond Sepúlveda's counsel, spent hours developing a plan to lure the Russian. This scheme required the resurrection of a confidential business transaction that Anh Li and Raymond had worked on before her death —a stand-alone righteous transaction to rekindle a Spanish insurance company's interest in acquiring Old Dutch Indemnity.

With renewed vigor, McLeod reread Anh Li and the Doss inventory of information, paying particular attention to Raymond Sepúlveda's interface on the Spanish company's influence on Old Dutch.

To complete his research, McLeod hired a firm to investigate the operating status of Old Dutch Indemnity, Ltd. This St. Kitts, West Indies, company appeared on Anh Li's documents as one of the Old Dutch legal representatives. The firm reconstituted an audit and confirmed Old Dutch's operations and domicile were in good standing, noting that its premium income had grown over the last ten Years. Moreover, since its start, the company has had the same London legal representatives: Longfeather, Lithgow, Boylston, & Rivington.

McLeod sent a communiqué to Sepúlveda requesting a meeting in Panama City. Sepúlveda responded and suggested McLeod fly to Panama on Tuesday and check in at the Marriott Hotel under the Sepúlveda reservation. He wished McLeod a safe flight and confirmed that he would knock at his door on Tuesday at 11:00 a.m.

Finally, the day before Tuesday arrived, McLeod checked into his room and awaited the morning. As promised, at 11:00 a.m., there was a knock at the door.

"Señor Sepúlveda," McLeod said, "Good morning, my friend; please step in. As always, it is good to see you exactly on time."

"Sí, mi amigo, you look great. Welcome to Panama, the land of milk, honey, double-dealing, and private banking. It has been exciting working with you over the last couple of years. I had no idea that meeting you would create a new business opportunity. With your guidance, marketing gamblers and collecting casino debt, as you predicted, have their upside."

Raymond Sepúlveda embraced McLeod; the two friends wrapped their arms around each other, gently patting one another on the back.

"So, life is good for my friend?" McLeod declared.

"I have no complaints, although I miss the days when lean and mean ruled my life. Now, fat and comfort dictate. I have less hair, and with my chest dropping onto my stomach, there is more of me in all the wrong places. If that was not enough punishment for the audacity of living a long life, I must drink and eat less. Sin embargo, I am still alive to enjoy the sunrise and sunset. But enough chit-chat; let us get down to business."

McLeod had grown fond of Sepúlveda and, although on the payroll, considered him a worthy associate. Knowing that "let's get down to business" was many minutes away, he poured a cup of coffee and grabbed a bran muffin. "Do your men waiting outside the door and hallway want coffee?"

"No coffee for them, and my mi amigo Americano, I still have my traveling entourage. Admittedly, I have become obsessed with tradition and my particularities. Despite my once-held belief in youthful immortality, the passage of time has finally worn down all resistance; aging has taken its toll. I have become a replica of my father's quirks, but, factually, I am comfortable and satisfied with my present. I have many regrets, and my uncompromising Conscience will not allow me to delete them. So, my best shot at the divine everlasting is a first stop in purgatory."

McLeod passed a hot cup of the hotel's Panamanian java while discussing the reason for the meeting. Sepúlveda took the cup, put it on the nearby table, and sat on an oversized brown leather chair. McLeod sat on a sofa. The two were across from each other, with a coffee table between them.

McLeod began. "You're familiar with my quest. I have decided to approach this Russian by offering a business incentive, as suggested. I have drafted a plan that requires your engagement to be effective. Money is not a concern, but this could be dangerous, or, should I say, this will be dangerous."

"Danger is a matter of tolerance; my tolerance level is low." I do not engage in dangerous endeavors," Sepúlveda admits. "From my perspective, you are in danger, not me. He paused to sip on his coffee and then continued. "My tolerance of and for danger, I warn you, ranges from zero to none at all."

McLeod reached into a medium-sized canvas bag and pulled out a manila folder; he handed the folder to Sepúlveda. "Here is the plan," McLeod declares.

"It's an overview," McLeod informs Sepúlveda with a comical smirk as he hands the folder over. I'll call this version my conceptual, requiring your editing. Then, after your consideration, we'll call it our plan."

Before opening the single-page folder, Sepúlveda comments, "For a Yankee, you know how to entice us, Spaniards. Unfortunately, we, blood descendants of Ferdinand of Aragon and Isabella of Castile, suffer from conquistador syndrome."

"The conquistador syndrome, never heard of such an affliction," McLeod notes with a smile.

"It is the pretense of converting the heathens to Jesus while stealing their gold, exploiting their innocence, all at the risk of losing one's life and all its blessings. This old Spaniard who sits before you, even when young, has never considered such adventurous schemes. However, I would not be here if I did not trust your judgment. I want you to know that your skill at maneuvering me to serve your interests has not gone unnoticed."

"Maneuvering you? Impossible," McLeod joked. "The only person who manages you is you."

Sepúlveda smiled and then got down to business. He opened the folder; enclosed was an 8X10 white sheet of paper with one word in large black letters: insurance.

"We must shake the right tree. I think," McLeod suggests, "if we create an enticing business incentive, the lure may catch the attention we seek. This Russian Max never leaves Cuba. He is guarded 24/7, except when he's on his boat, surrounded by water and an eight-man crew.

"Be it boat or island, both sound very tentative," Sepúlveda added. "But frankly, getting a firsthand accounting of this elusive one will require several masterstrokes intertwined with incredible suerte. In other words, an enveloping maneuver has a better chance."

McLeod questions, "What is this enveloping?"

"Let us incentivize Mike Marin Garzia, the president by default of Old Dutch, to introduce us into the operational mix to meet this Russian fellow. Of course, I have a cause for such an introduction. That is the enveloping action."

"Yes," McLeod concedes, "Your history in the insurance business is just one of the essential factors of importance. The other is your historical insight into Old Dutch. You worked for Dr. Li's Old Dutch off and on for Years. For example, the company's attorneys wrote a disclosure document signed by Dr. Anh Li stating that Old Dutch had hired Raymond Sepúlveda to approve a non-binding letter of intent and initiate confidential acquisition discussions with the company's name redacted. One phone call from you to Marin should get that program into implementation mode. Don't you agree?"

"I do agree. But how did you find out about Old Dutch hiring me?"

"A man close to Anh Li, who is now dead, passed confidential documents onto me," McLeod responds. McLeod continues, "I wonder why you did not offer this entrée into Old Dutch a month ago."

"Maybe," as Sepúlveda hesitates while searching for an answer, "the older I get, the more irrelevant the words why and because. So, I will pass on answering the question and confirm that the idea is solid. Yes, I see the opportunity," Sepúlveda affirms.

"However, as I understand the process, once the shareholders' meeting takes place, per the company's Operating Agreement, Anh Li's daughter will be in firm control. And before you ask, I am sure that is a fact."

Sepúlveda continues, "There is an outstanding question about convertible debentures. The rumor, if it can be believed, is that Doctor Li somehow seized physical control of these debentures or nullified their effect. Verification will need to wait until the shareholders' meeting."

"Well," McLeod submits, "The Russian's alias: José Martinez González, his Cuban name, my source also included the schematics on Ivan's custom-made yacht."

"I assume," Sepulveda confidently declares, "is Anh Li's dependent, a man named Doss."

"Of course, you had to have met the man," McLeod concedes.

"I understand Doss, or whatever his birth name was, took his own life. Now, back to business. The Russian took no active part in Old Dutch operations, nor was he an appointed corporate officer. He was solely a passive investor; our Russian has no business relevance.

"Mike Marin Garcia, however, is, in our scheme, the critical player. He took over as provisional president because he was duly licensed to manage the organization's affairs. There is no evidence that Marin and your Russian worked together. I can verify that Marin functioned under the supervision of Dr. Li. The Doctor knew that Marin was a prolific gambler, a profiled client of Casino Nacionales and the casinos of San Juan.

As referenced in my notes, Marin is our best lead to a Russian introduction."

McLeod concurs. "So far, he is our only lead." With a nod, Sepúlveda agrees.

"You've known this Marin guy for Years; fill me in on his background," McLeod requests.

"Señor Mike Marin Garcia is Cuban, born in Havana but raised in Miami; his family left Cuba in 1955. His father's wise and deliberate move ahead of Castro's success framed his future. Having professionally solid fraternal ties to Miami, the family joined the ever-growing North of La Habana society. In other words, Mike was well-parented by a great family. He attended the University of Miami, graduated in the top ten in his class, and passed his CPA board on the first try. A mathematical genius: one would think another Cuban American headed for greatness. A top Miami money-management firm with robust European funding recruited him; he then joined their Latin American division. One of his first clients was Old Dutch Indemnity. After that, his career was moving along at jet speed. He even married into one of the wealthiest families in Venezuela."

"Our Mike Marin has had a story-book life," McLeod interjected.

"Not without self-induced tragedy," Sepúlveda continued. "At 35, Mike found Atlantic City, the Bahamas, Vegas, and sports betting. Things turned negative; he lost his wife, job, and a significant part of his mind to cocaine. For some time, Mike Marion was untraceable, had no utility billing address, had his driver's license suspended, and had no phone registered in his name."

"Then," McLeod notes aloud, "he turns up working for Old Dutch and advances to running the place."

Yes," Sepúlveda says, "a little miracle. He appeared on Old Dutch Indemnity's board of directors seven years ago. Today, he is the president of the company. How is that for a success story, Mr. McLeod?"

"One cannot predict the comings and goings of dumb luck. So, you think Marin had some help from our Russian?" McLeod questions.

"Old Dutch was his first legitimate insurance company client. Sepúlveda points out. "It is reasonable that someone of authority associated with the company noticed his ability. So, someone recruited the guy, reorganized his life, and trained him. Such is the modus operandi of Anh Li's recruiting style. Some have said this recruiting story is a rumor, and I know what you told me about information founded on assumptions and presumptions."

"Yes," both men recanted in unanimity. They will get you killed in combat," they chuckled.

"This alignment of insurance and Marin is time-consuming and boring," McLeod decries.

"I understand," Sepúlveda responded. "Please be mindful that even if the plot and plan align perfectly with the situational reality, killing this Russian is still impossible. However, let us not let the negatives get ahead of us. Marin is our target. I will research Old Dutch's operational particulars and develop a professional introduction to Marin to verify Ivan the Russian's whereabouts and viability. In my mind, the dice are rolling. I will get back to you in a week." Sepúlveda asks, "Where will you be?"

"Jockey Club, North Miami; you have my number?" McLeod affirms, "Yes, I do. We will meet in Miami, 10 to 14 days (about 2 weeks) from today. Oh, there is one other item. I am currently working for someone who may have conflicting consequences. It's a speculative possibility for now. However, when actionable," Sepúlveda infers, "I will pleasingly divulge."

"Be sure," McLeod emphasizes, that whatever the conflicting possibility, it has nothing to do with my plot or any of the characters therein."

Sepúlveda nods his head in agreement. Satisfied that the meeting had gone well, McLeod retreated to his bedroom, took the all-too-regular sleeping pills, and went horizontal. Dreaming, he started to push away the present in favor of the past. Until he arrived at Dong Ha, Vietnam, chatting with Gunner Hagerty while loading his M-14 magazines and putting tracer rounds in last. Archer approaches him with an open letter in hand and begins to speak.

"Hey, Sergeant McLeod, my girl has made up with me. She sent a picture with lipstick impressions and red hearts stamped all over it. Isn't that something? After all this time, she has come around to loving me. She says she will meet me when the plane lands. Only two more weeks, and I will be in her arms."

The hotel room phone rings, startling McLeod out of Vietnam, "Señor McLeod, Buenos Días, this is your wake-up call."

McLeod hung up the phone and hit the shower. The flight to Miami was at 8:00 A.M., so it was time to rise and shine.

Charlie

Ten days had passed since McLeod's meeting in Panama City. Sepúlveda called from Miami airport and was expected at the Jockey Club within the hour. McLeod's in-house phone rang. It was George, head of Jockey Club security. "Mr. McLeod, you have a visitor, Mr. Sepúlveda; he says you expect him. Shall I escort him to the elevator?"

"Yes, George, by all means; please escort my friend to the elevator." Within moments, Sepúlveda had entered the condominium and was seated comfortably.

"I came directly from the airport to drop off these documents." Sepúlveda reached into his worn leather traveling bag, pulled out a thin file, and handed it off to McLeod. "After a week of what I will simplify as research, there is only one sensible discovery. As explained in the paperwork, I consulted with the Spanish insurance company interested in acquiring Old Dutch. Because of my familiarity with Old Dutch and with permission from the acting president, Marin, I am to advise the Spanish insurance company in the Old Dutch acquisition."

"I see," McLeod pleasingly says, "the sky parted and converted a speculative possibility into an actual one. The gods of fortune have smiled upon us. I assume Marin would love to meet up."

"Yes, Sepúlveda agrees. As you often say, dumb luck has rained on us. I am exhausted and heading to my hotel to rest. I will return at 10:00 a.m. tomorrow. We can dig into the details then."

Satisfyingly, McLeod, pleased with the pace, escorted Raymond down the elevator and into his awaiting car.

Eager to read the documents, McLeod returned directly to the condominium. He moved over to his reading area, and then the phone rang. He answered with an irritated, "Hello."

A female voice responded, "Mr. McLeod, I have timely and specific information on a person of interest to you."

"Who is this?"

"Presently, who I am is unimportant. I have had a long-term relationship with the man you call 'the Russian. I can arrange a meeting for reasons that will remain confidential. Is that of value to you?"

"Yes, a meeting would be of value," McLeod answered, relaxing his tone.

"Then I will be in touch," the female voice acknowledged and abruptly hung up.

McLeod was intrigued. He fought off an impulse to call Sepúlveda to inquire. Who was this woman, and how had she gotten his private number? She spoke with confidence, knowing he was the intended recipient.

McLeod pondered. Typically, one would ask for confirmation before discussing a sensitive or exclusive topic. It could not be a prank; no one knew the Russian. He pushed the phone's trace function, added his code, and waited for the response.

The recorded voice answered in seconds: "International call, no number available." Frustrated, McLeod hung up the receiver.

"Well," McLeod muttered under his breath as he reached for the Sepúlveda documents, "at least the surprise was only a phone call."

As promised, at 10:00 a.m. the next day, Sepúlveda announced himself to George at security. He arrived, and the meeting commenced.

"Before we get started," McLeod cautioned, "Yesterday, my private phone rang within an hour of you leaving. A woman's voice suggested she could help organize a meeting with the Russian."

Sepúlveda exclaimed, "Instead of guessing who, let us agree that the female will call back and identify herself. You did run a trace on the phone?"

"I did," McLeod responds, "but the call was international. So, I assume it's a real person intending to communicate."

"Oddly, this could be the break we needed," Sepúlveda suggested. "No matter her motivation, it can only help us. We will wait until the next call."

"Yes, but how did this person know to call me on my private phone and mention the Russian?"

"The answer," Sepúlveda to that question, will come when this woman calls again.

Sepúlveda gets back to the business at hand. "As you can see, I have designed this presentation under Critical Business Preference. Emphasizing real money is done in the appreciation of publicly traded shares. And that, as a standalone, is the cause to sell Old Dutch."

"Yes, okay," McLeod confirmed. I am listening, but I'm interested in whatever works to induce Marin into introducing me to the Russian."

"I understand," Sepúlveda affirms. "And, of course, we need to meet Marin, but we need a relationship, not just a meeting. His interest is to safeguard his position. He must find a compelling way to secure his wants while having him enable our objective." Distracted, McLeod was only half Listening, still thinking of the call.

"Do you think," McLeod ponders, "considering Doss and Anh Li knew of me and now Anh Li's daughter, that the Russian knows me by name?"

"Possibly, but remember," Sepúlveda emphases, "Vietnam was twenty-odd years ago. I doubt anyone involved would keep the names Sergeant McLeod and Team 33 at the forefront of one's thoughts. The only other connection to you would be Cornfield and Gomez; of course, we only know what we think we know. Our first reason is to sell this acquisition idea to Old Dutch and Marin. Let us worry about that dragon for now."

"Agreed," McLeod pronounced.

"I think by the time you get to Panama—within a month—I will have met Marin and be ready to contract with Old Dutch."

"So tomorrow, you're back in Panama?" McLeod said in an inquiring manner.

"Yes," Sepúlveda affirmed, "and you'll be here in Miami wondering when she will contact you again."

"It was on my mind," McLeod admitted.

"All in good time," Sepúlveda stood and walked to the door, "until we meet in Panama. Stay safe, my friend." He paused for a moment, then turned back and warned. "But keep this possibility in the back of your mind. What if Doss lied? What if the caller is the daughter of the Russian? If so, they may seek revenge, something for you to contemplate over a glass of Blue. Adios, mi amigo."

Three days passed without a word from Sepúlveda or the mysterious caller; then, there was a ring on the house phone rather than the private line. McLeod answered.

"Mr. McLeod, I have an envelope in my hand. Shall I bring it up?"

"No, George, I'm on my way down; I'll pick it up."

McLeod opened it to find only a phone and a local number on plain white paper. Though planning on a three-mile run, curiosity got the best of him, and he returned to make the call. He stumbled at first, but then slowed down and connected on the second try. The phone rang and rang, but there was no answer. He hung up and tried again; once again, it rang, but there was no answer. McLeod repeated and repeated, but there was still no answer. Frustrated, he tossed the note under the phone and headed for a run.

Returning an hour later, he headed for the shower, dressed, and redialed the number. It was six in the evening. Finally, it was the same voice.

"Mr. McLeod, please listen; my name is Charlie. I will meet you tomorrow at the Sheraton Hotel in Bal Harbor at or near 1:00 p.m. Wear your Marine Corps cap, sit at the bar in the lobby, and I will contact you."

The phone went dead. McLeod was pleased.

As asked, McLeod was sitting at the bar of the Sheraton Hotel, nursing a neat Johnny Walker Blue at 1:15 p.m. He was getting anxious when a beautiful young Eurasian woman tapped him on the shoulder.

"Mr. McLeod, meet me at the lobby entrance." She then abruptly walked away.

McLeod paid his tab and looked for the young lady, spotting her at the lobby entrance. She walked out of the hotel, past the valet parking cars, and over the walkway. He followed. She stopped, waited for McLeod to catch up, and introduced herself, "Mr. McLeod, my name is Charlie. Please," she handed over a medium-sized black leather bag, "carry my bag and follow me; we're going to the shopping mall across the street."

McLeod glanced around to see if they were alone and deduced they were. As they walked, McLeod noticed her body's firmness, deep curves, strong muscular legs, and long, thick black hair; he found her allure and performance captivating.

While he observed Charlie's apparent attributes, McLeod sensed a combination of sensuality and physical strength, creating a vibe of confidence. Though she could only catch a glimpse, her sizable ebony eyes reflected the intensity of her purpose. She was on a mission. Charlie steered him into an outside seating area of the mall's restaurant. They sat across from each other.

Once seated, Charlie unexpectedly said, "I know Anh Li's daughter very well. We grew up in the same environment created by the same genetic circumstances. We are both half Vietnamese Kinh and the other half Anglo. Mutually, our conception was due to the chaos of war. We attended the same private schools and shared the sadness of having an imaginary father. We look so much like each other that we could be sisters."

"Mr. McLeod, I realize you have questions. Nonetheless, aside from helping you meet with the Russian, I am not here to answer any questions, so please do not ask." McLeod motioned a desire to speak, but Charlie's outstretched index finger pressed against his lips, denying him the opportunity.

"There is a common purpose between Anh Li's daughter and me, and your interest in this Russian. Without getting into my friend's concern, she is extremely interested in helping you rid the world of this son-of-a-bitch, as she describes him. Ok, Mr. McLeod, you may now ask me anything that pleases you, noting my restrictions, so we do not waste any time having me repeat myself."

The waiter arrived and took their order for drinks. She ordered a large bottle of Perrier, asked for extra glass and limes, and cautioned no ice, graciously passing on the day's specials.

"How do I know you're not working for the GRU Russian agent?" a suspicious McLeod asks.

"And here I thought your first question would be, who is the father of Anh Li's daughter?

"Maybe your intimidating mannerisms cowed me otherwise."

McLeod continued without waiting for a response, "So, what's next?"

"You are taking me shopping," Charlie declares. My only clothes are in my bag, and since I will move into your place...."

"Move into my place?" McLeod interrupted. "You will not like the bed in the guest room."

"I do not plan to sleep in the guest room. I plan to sleep with you, Mr. McLeod."

"You are bold and brave, maybe even a little pupule, a Hawaiian word for crazy," McLeod commented, trying not to look shocked by her boldness.

"Oh yes, you were born in Hawaii. Pupule, you say, but I am not even a little crazy," Charlie assures. "I fear the dark and need the calming effect of inhaling your manliness. As with most men, you are a snorer; your snoring comforts me. You should know, Mr. McLeod, that my daughter and Dr. Li's daughter have been together since childhood. I am very sexual; it is a large part of who I am. And yes, I am looking forward to sleeping with a man old enough to be my father in an entertainingly perverse way. Are you shocked by my frankness? I am what I am, and I have no intention of creating a pretense about who I am. Nonetheless, I presume there will be no resistance to my desires."

McLeod said nothing; the waiter arrived with the drink order, closely followed by the meals, which allowed McLeod time to recover and respond.

"What makes you think...?"

"Please, Mr. McLeod, a woman knows when a man looks at her with lustful intent. Whatever your issues are, ejaculation will rid them from your mind. I want, you need, so let us not complicate a natural wanting.

"So, the advice is to sit back and enjoy." McLeod pauses and follows up with, "OK, I submit."

"So sweet of you; tell me about your plans to approach the Russian?"

"Simple as that: you offer sex, and I should give you our plans, and that is how we coordinate our joint efforts?"

"Mr. McLeod, I know what Doss passed on before he died. If Anh Li's daughter, my friend, will be on hand to help, she needs to know the plan—that is, if there is a plan."

He wondered how much he dared tell her.

"The plan is in development," McLeod proclaims. "I have a friend, and we have an operation in progress. It deals with Old Dutch."

"With Mike Marin?" She calmly asked.

"How did you know?" McLeod responded.

"I did venture out of Switzerland as a child. As a child, I spent time in the presence of the Marin and caught sight of the Russian a few times.

"You've met the Russian?"

"No, not really; I said I had seen him from afar when traveling with Doctor Li. I have been on his boat. Now, let us go shopping."

Intrigued, McLeod wanted to hear more about the Russians. She denied knowing very much. She had not seen the Russian since she was ten.

While she shopped, McLeod contemplated the forthcoming Charlie relationship. This young, beautiful, aggressive girl decided that not only was she moving in with him, a stranger, but she also insisted on sleeping with him. McLeod chuckled about Charlie's presumptive confidence.

"Well," he thought, "this was a different therapy." The last hard-on had cost the recipient her life. It was close to six in the evening when they arrived at the Jockey Club. McLeod signed her as Charlie-Charlie since she refused to give him his last name. He found that silly, considering she must have had identification on her, and all he had to do was wait to take it from her, but then, the entire day had been mysterious.

Charlie settled in the guest bedroom while McLeod sipped a diet tonic and lime. Finally, Charlie emerged from the bedroom and entered the living room, wearing only her newly purchased panties. Her body was perfect.

"How old are you?" McLeod asked.

"I am standing here with nothing but my panties, and you want to know my age? Age is not a relevant factor. Not your age or mine; what matters is whether we stimulate each other.

I have often fantasized about meeting my father. You are the same age and share the same military circumstances as my father. Frankly, that is intoxicating for me, but of course, aside from all that, the thought of it all is a perfect segue into realizing my "father" fantasies.

As Charlie was talking, she knelt between his legs. Then, gently, she started stroking his inner thighs. McLeod quickly and surprisingly became aroused.

"You see, Mr. McLeod, seduction is incisive."

As she spoke, Charlie seductively massaged McLeod's most sensitive spot, and he responded with lustful intent.

Then, as abruptly as she had entered, she returned to her room, all the while voicing to McLeod that she was looking forward to tonight. She returned in minutes, dressed in a bathrobe. She sat across from him on a chair she had pulled in from the corner of the living room.

"Now, dear Mr. McLeod, as I mentioned at lunch, you have a plan?"

McLeod stood dumbfounded. Nevertheless, in seconds, his brain was operational and his composure intact. "Indeed, I have a plan."

"I am all ears," Charlie eagerly remarked.

McLeod is not about to give a stranger, known for a couple of hours, even a general plan. He hesitates with the truth and says, "I have no idea who I am addressing."

"So," Charlie concurs, "presently, there is no plan other than thinking about the possibilities. Firstly, a blueprint depends on Mr. Sepúlveda's brilliance, and yes, I know of Raymond; when I turned teenager, he worked for my friend's mother."

"I think you have captured the essence of the plan, Charlie." McLeod paused for a moment and then changed the subject.

"Do you think you could or would recognize this Russian?"

"No, he wore dark glasses and often wore a black cowboy hat, and he always had so many people around him that it was distracting. I was a child when I was aware of his presence. As a teenager, I do remember the boat. It was large, had a terrible diesel smell, and made an excessive amount of noise. I also remember men with guns."

"You say you went there with Anh Li's mother?" "Yes, she was a sweet, loving person. "

"What about your mother?" McLeod inquired.

"I would rather not speak of her."

"Got it," McLeod confirmed.

"So, your plan now, Mr. McLeod, is to wait."

"Yes, I am waiting for a call from Sepúlveda.

"Waiting is boring. Good thing you have me," Charlie muses aloud.

"Well, Charlie, what will you do while I wait for the plan to mature?"

Confidently, Charlie declares, "I will be here waiting with you. Who knows, I may have some ideas."

"Our concerns are in common, but for varied reasons. That is all I am going to say about that subject. Now, Mr. McLeod, how about some dinner?"

"The menu is on the kitchen table. Pick a meal and call it in; order whatever you want."

"And what can I order for you?"

"A chicken Caesar salad, please," McLeod responds.

"I like this ordering and delivery program; there is no kitchen mess. However, one night, I am going to cook for you."

"Cook for me!" McLeod responds.

"Why not? I cook!"

As they spoke, McLeod's private phone rang.

"Hello."

"McLeod, it's me. I have some news. I met Marin this afternoon at the Marriott Hotel near the convention center. We shared a meal and discussed generalities. I requested a second meeting to present our acquisition plan. Everything went much smoother than I anticipated. So, please arrange your passage to Panama to arrive in ten days."

"Panama, yes, I will decide tomorrow. And I appreciate the good news."

"OK, see you, Anh." McLeod hangs up.

"Your plan is taking form?" Charlie queries.

"I am apprehensive, or, should I say, a bit anxious by your automated insertion into my life...McLeod confesses."

"You mean my demeanor or having sex with me; you're fearful of sex or sex with me?"

"Sex with you could make me an uncontrollable addict," McLeod playfully responded.

"I am going to make you an addict," Charlie responded. Hmm, that is on you. I look at sex as I look at enjoying a tasty meal, not knowing when I will eat again. Tonight, the sex will be as natural as cuddling with your pillow. We sleep naked, Mr. McLeod; I need you instantly vulnerable to my yearning."

"Where did you obtain such confidence? Does Anh Li's daughter have your forthright nature?"

"Mr. McLeod, now and forever, no questions about my friend. Remember, that was the understanding from our very beginning."

"You are insistently tough," McLeod comments.

"Tomorrow," Charlie explains, "I will inform my dear friend of the non-plan and your travels to Panama. I am not sure what her reaction will be. Hopefully, she will want me to accompany you to Panama. Now, dear host, how about a glass of Carpe Diem's Pinot Noir?"

"You have inventoried my wine cooler and invited yourself to Panama."

The evening progressed with enjoyable, witty conversation; each gave proportion to the taking. Before long, the entire bottle of wine was emptied. Charlie went to the guest room, and McLeod came to his. However, within minutes, Charlie was in his bed.

Just as Charlie had insisted, they slept together naked, exhausted. Sleeping with another was rare for McLeod. Then, in the wee hours of the morning, McLeod awoke. Skin against skin, he felt her breasts press his back as skilled hands found his hardening cock. On his back, he began to turn towards her.

"Stay," she whispered as her hand grasped his penis and into her mouth. Before McLeod could ejaculate, she mounted him, forcing him into her. Within minutes, McLeod orgasmed.

McLeod was up first. He fixed some coffee and sat on the balcony overlooking the inland waterway. It was a beautiful day. Within an hour, Charlie, covered in a bathrobe, joined him. He poured some coffee; she added sugar and cream. By lunchtime, they had wandered down to the pool. They finish a bottle of wine without paying too much attention to its effects. Then, both jumped into the hot and soapy shower. Bathing with each other was a delight.

Charlie gestured to McLeod for a kiss; he obliged. Their lust for each other forced them out of the shower; still wet, they moved toward the bed. Naked, she spread her legs, reached for, and inserted his penis into her vergina. She then asked McLeod to put his hands around her throat. McLeod agreed, putting both hands around her neck. She whispered harder, he squeezed harder, then hesitated, not wanting to go further. She begged him not to stop but to press harder. She repeatedly said, "Fuck me deep, again, harder, please, harder, this is how I like it. You've done this before, haven't you?" She finally screamed in orgasmic joy.

Over the following days, Charlie coached McLeod in her methods of lovemaking. Overwhelmed by her smell, touch, voice, and sexuality, McLeod had fallen in lust with a woman he hardly knew within a week. A woman who had an instinctual insight into his sexual needs, he now understands her earlier prognosis: I want, and you need."

Although seduced by her sensuality, anxiety ran concurrently. Charlie, coming into his life, could not intercede in his bloody quest. Instead, in a practical sense, a shared objective might tactically enhance the quest to kill his number one target. Even though she abducted his sensibility, eroded his rationality, and damaged his prudence, Charlie became the value he desired to protect.

His feelings for Charlie were convincingly apparent to an observer. Charlie never offered the slightest measure of equal response. Without the requirement for emotional display, Charlie seemed pleased with the earthly pleasures of food, drink, sun, and organisms. Her actions indicated a desire to live under her own rules, disregarding concerns for anyone or anything. Nothing moved her to the left or the right. She took life as it gave; she ceded no quarter and required none. McLeod assumed that she could casually take him or leave him. Nevertheless, instinctively, she knew how to be only his when making love, which was a unique means of enticement.

McLeod found Charlie packing her few things into a small bag one morning. "My dear Mr. McLeod, I am leaving and will be gone for a while. So please do not concern yourself about the time of my return."

"Are you going to satisfy some obligations?"

"Perhaps, Mr. McLeod, but for now, you know I am leaving. Rest assured that I will return. Besides, mystery in a relationship is essential. It is one of my many allurements."

"OK, mysterious one," McLeod responded, acting as if her departure was something he felt impassively unconcerned about. But, on the contrary, he was anxious and hurt.

"And by the way, my dear Mr. McLeod, there is a folder I think you will find very interesting on your bed." Within minutes, holding the same bag she had arrived in, she was out the door, not a kiss, a good, or a look back.

Cornfield

McLeod was astonished by Charlie's sudden, cold-hearted departure. McLeod's emotional reaction evolved from lingering disappointment to a state of frustrated bitterness. Allowing Charlie in his life, trusting her, and now she was gone, thoughts of betrayal aimlessly wandered across his mind. But a betrayal of what or who? The feeling of sorrowfulness had the effect of a twenty-four-hour cold, and as with most emotional viruses, the homeopathic medication was time.

After a restless night and a few cups of morning coffee, he picked up the fat, brown-colored legal file folder Charlie had left him and emptied the contents onto the bed. Inside were photos, names, addresses, contact information, photocopies of passports, and contracts. Unlike earlier information on Calvo, this intelligence source was current, detailed, and voluminous.

McLeod read that Colonel Calvo had done very well after the war. His encounters with the CIA, Banco Santander, and Banco Bilbao Vizcaya led to profitable consulting agreements. Cuba's government was the counterparty to each of the agreements. Most surprising was that the colonel used his real name. Also, all the photos showed him with the usual mustache. The only noticeable change was the appearance of white hair and other signs of aging.

There was even a business card: Eduardo Calvo, President, Argon S.A., with phone numbers in Madrid, Gibraltar, and Miami. McLeod was amazed by his brazen disregard for anonymity. The Colonel must have cured his issues with Ivan the Russian and Castro.

McLeod contemplated the merits of the information, noting that the man had outfoxed his once dire circumstances by some extraordinary means. The man who commanded the Cubans who killed the Marines of Team 33 thought he was safe. Calvo's misplaced confidence would serve McLeod well.

McLeod called Calvo's Miami phone number. "Good morning," the operator answered. "Argon Consulting Corporation, how may I direct your call?"

"May I speak to Mr. Calvo, please?" McLeod asked.

"Yes, of course. Hold for Mr. Calvo's assistant; one moment."

While waiting for Calvo's assistant to connect, McLeod thought finding him was effortless and straightforward. "Hello, this is Patsy Maze; may I help you?"

"Yes, my name is McLeod, and I would like to speak with Mr. Calvo regarding service retention."

"Mr. Calvo is extremely busy satisfying his current obligations. As a policy, Mr. Calvo does not take on new business without a recommendation from an existing client."

"An existing client recommended me."

"Well, how lovely," Ms. Maze countered. Please fax the client's name, contact information, and a brief explanation of why you need to retain Mr. Calvo. I will fax you to schedule an appointment or decline the opportunity within a week. Thank you very much for calling; goodbye."

"Hmm...access to Mr. Calvo is not so effortless," McLeod said after hanging up on Ms. Maze. Moments later, his private line rang.

"As scheduled. Are you all set for tomorrow's flight?" Sepúlveda asked.

"As it turns out, no, I have some unfinished business. An opportunity that I need to take advantage of just popped up."

"Is this a new opportunity, something that needs my services?"

"Nothing you need to be involved with," McLeod answers. Sepúlveda, a veteran of life's entanglements, suggested, "Just remember, mi amigo, the prize, and whatever you do, take care not to jeopardize the prize."

"I will keep that in mind," McLeod assured; all the while, he knew that killing Calvo was what was in front of him, and the 'prize' would wait.

"I have lots of work to do here in Panama. Let me know when you are ready to head south."

"Of course, this should not take long," McLeod assured Sepúlveda and hung up.

It was late afternoon. Now, with the day's priorities behind him, longing for Charlie crept into the space between his ears. Loneliness set in and aggravated his lustful longings. He walked into the guest room. Since her entrance weeks earlier, she had been with him constantly, day and night. He began to wonder. He searched her room for the second time; all the purchased clothing was neatly in place, and she had taken nothing.

She took the clothes she had arrived in and her oversized gym bag. Feeling she would not return, McLeod reached for the Blue Label in the liquor cabinet and contemplated a pour. Rejecting a drink, he returned the bottle, read the incoming decline to meet Calvo's fax, and tore it up as trash.

Bored, McLeod decided it would be wise to stake out Calvo's office. He thought he needed a Charlie distraction, grabbed his binoculars, and headed out.

McLeod parked his rented Town Car directly across the street from Calvo's freestanding office building. He sat and stared at the front door of the building, waiting. But before mentally adjusting to the dull monotony of bird-dogging, the handled bar-mustached Calvo was out, escorting Commander Cornfield to an awaiting black sedan. McLeod's jaw dropped.

Not trusting his naked vision, he pulled out his mini binoculars and confirmed. Not waiting for the driver, Cornfield opened the back door and got in. The limo pulled forward, its left-turn blinkers flashing, and motored back onto the road in the opposite direction of McLeod's car. McLeod started his car, made a U-turn, and followed.

While following the sedan, his mind was seeking an explanation. The one thing that did resound was Cornfield's earlier statement that Calvo was innocent and knew nothing of Team 33 or their ambush. He now appreciated Charlie's accusation that Calvo was right in the middle of designating who would make the actual killing.

The sedan pulled onto the airport highway. Cornfield was getting on an airplane; sure enough, the sedan dropped Cornfield off at the departure area. He noticed Cornfield's carry-on luggage; the trip lasted only one night. Speculating that Cornfield and Calvo had a history, he surmised this was not the first Cornfield trip to visit Calvo. McLeod headed home and called Billy in Vegas.

"Billy!" McLeod exclaimed.

"Well," Billy responded, "I'll be. It's the man. Terrific to hear from you. What's happening?"

"You remember Commander Cornfield?"

"Hell, yes."

"Well, I want you to stake out his house in Arlington for five days. You have his address on Military Road?"

"I do; you know, I data bank everything. What has the good Commander done now?"

"After you make travel arrangements, call me, and I will fill you in on the nasty details. I need you to document Cornfield's 24/7 pattern."

"Upon your command," Billy replied.

McLeod briefed him on the Calvo–Cornfield connection. Billy agreed to meet McLeod in a week at Bar Panache, a well-known hangout in Arlington. In the meantime, McLeod had staked out Calvo's office building. So far, Calvo's operation has proved mundane and uneventful. McLeod headed for the airport to catch his 1:15 p.m. flight to Washington, D.C. Billy was in baggage claim to meet McLeod. It had been seven days since they last spoke, and for five days, Billy had been surveilling Cornfield; the two friends then embraced. McLeod grabbed his suitcase and headed to the airport car park.

Billy conveyed a detailed report of Cornfield's comings and goings.

"His only friend is the liquor store proprietor who sells him his indiscriminate choice of liquor. His entertainment is a timeworn television, an old radio, and a trash can full of varied chocolate candy bar wrappers. He eats a burger or a tuna sandwich at this coffee shop, just three blocks from his house, once a day. A car is in a two-car garage, but I have never seen it being driven. The house is on a large lot down the road, protected on all sides by tall trees and bushes. He leaves the house at 1:00 p.m. every day for the coffee shop and eats alone. He sometimes stops at the neighborhood bookstore on the walk back to his house, browses magazines, fingers through a book or two, and proceeds to walk home. At 4:00 p.m. sharp, a black sedan pulls up in front of his house every day, including Sunday. He travels to an office building at 105 S. Market Street in Washington, toting a worn black briefcase. At 10:00 p.m., he's taken home. The entire home-to-office trip takes 20 minutes."

His work schedule is eight hours a day. It sounds like a West Coast schedule or even a trip to Hawaii. It could be anywhere from western Mexico to Canada. At any rate, I'm guessing he works telephonically, complemented by computer-driven enhancements. Floppy disks and fax pages are scattered throughout his office, covering the desk and floor.

Billy continued to explain, "There are no family photos or pictures of girlfriends; there's a formal naval uniform with medals hanging in his bedroom. The highest personal medal is the Bronze Star, but without the "V" for valor. His clothes squared away as if he were ready for a commanding officer's inspection. Frankly, the guy exists as if he will die tomorrow."

"Well, maybe not tomorrow," McLeod interjected.

"I found his extra house keys and made a copy for you." Billy handed over the keys to the back and front doors, noting them accordingly. Billy continued the debriefing. "The basement had ten black metal cabinets, two with locks. The unlocked ones had nothing but junk. I don't think this guy threw anything away. I obtained the model number from the locked ones and returned it the next night to be opened. I found a few files in each of the locked cabinets. One was personal: his family's pictures bore a resemblance to those of his mother, father, wife, and son. Also included was a newspaper article and an obituary noting the death of his wife and son from injuries suffered when the mother with her young child in hand fell down the stairs; both were found by Cornfield when he returned from a neighborhood chore."

"Hmm..." McLeod contemplated, "That's interesting, convenient for him, both falling from the top to the bottom of the stairs."

"Digging in, I found over three Years a series of complaints of physical abuse noted by his wife to the police, both civilian and military. Following several reprimands and an equal number of appointments with the chaplain and five commanding officers, ordered visits were made with the unit's psychologist. I assume that Cornfield killed his wife and child and faked their death to look like an accident."

"What a bastard," McLeod muttered.

McLeod stared at the medical report and smiled. "Great work, Billy."

"Thanks, mon Capitaine. This guy, Cornfield, has gotten away with murder for a long time." Billy paused. "OK, now for the psycho-weird part."

"Psycho-weird," Billy distinguished. "Killing one's wife and child is a murderous act. Lucifer would be proud."

"That's a fact," McLeod agrees.

"Well," Billy continues. "Try this on for size—a two-story house with an attic and a basement; however, he shut off the upstairs by placing a crudely constructed four-foot-by-eight-foot wall. The wall is made of two-and-a-half-inch unpainted plywood; the basement door has a two-by-four nailed across it, denying access to the downstairs area. The dining room used to be in the bedroom, and the living room features a large, old, and expensive desk, along with two phones, a typewriter, a computer, and a fax machine. The kitchen has enough food for a few days: canned tuna, chicken, and individually wrapped transparent plastic bags of preserved fruit. He has a microwave and a can opener. His plates are paper, and his eating utensils are plastic."

"As you said," McLeod repeated, "the man has his issues."

"Exactly," Billy confirms.

Billy pulled out a home map and marked three places with an X where pistols were hidden. One was taped under the frontal shelving on his desk. He told McLeod that he had left the pistols loaded and untouched but had removed the firing pins.

"That's it on the information side of things. How are we going to approach this guy?"

"You have been, as usual, invaluable... but there is no 'we.' What I am about to do is not something I want you involved with," McLeod informed Billy. "I will deal with Mr. Cornfield myself. I want you on that plane tomorrow, heading for Vegas."

"I understand. It's personal."

"Yes," it's personal, but it's also feloniously illegal, immoral, and, when I'm done, a mortal sin."

It was Tuesday afternoon, nearing 4:00 p.m., and McLeod had posted himself outside the driveway of Cornfield's house. At 3:58 p.m., a black sedan pulled into the Cornfield driveway. Cornfield stepped out of his house and into the waiting car within a minute. McLeod waited 15 minutes, drove his vehicle a block away, parked, and walked back toward the residence.

As he passed Cornfield's home, he scanned for movement in or near the house. As confirmed by Billy, it is evident that Cornfield lived alone with no stay-behind personnel, such as a housekeeper or security guard.

With a mini flashlight, a high-voltage stun gun, black leather gloves, a 3⁄4-inch nylon line, a waterproof poncho, riggers tape, and a tape recorder enclosed within a green-colored canvas bag, McLeod entered the house from the back door. The porch and kitchen lights were on, and a kitchen chair was placed in the dark corner facing the door. He sat and waited.

At precisely 10:20 p.m., McLeod heard a car door closing. Cornfield stepped onto his porch; within seconds, the key was in the front door lock, and the door opened. Cornfield walked in. He put his briefcase beside his desk, just a few feet from McLeod. He threw his keys on the desk and started to disrobe while he headed for the bathroom, just out of McLeod's sight.

The shower and the radio competed for the most noise. The music was classical. The announcer declared the following selection a modern rendition of a Wagner tradition.

The shower lasted about seven minutes. Cornfield stepped out wearing green military-issued boxer shorts and a white t-shirt. He stepped back into the bathroom and turned off the radio. He walked back out and headed directly to his desk. Cornfield sat in his chair and turned on the desk lamp. McLeod sat quietly. Then, sensing he was not alone, Cornfield looked up and saw McLeod. Visibly shocked, he stepped back and bellowed, "Ha! It's you!"

"Yes, it's me," McLeod answered calmly.

The shock froze Cornfield; initially discombobulated, he started to stand.

"Please sit, Commander; let's take a few minutes for a situational adjustment." While reaching for the pistol in its holster, taped upside down, in a readily accessible location under the middle shelf, Cornfield sat willingly. McLeod allows Cornfield's movement. Commander Cornfield slides the 9mm (about 0.35 in) pistol out of its holster in seconds and points it at McLeod. "I am amazed; you've come a long way, Gunnery Sergeant of Marines, but as evidenced by the pistol aimed at you, not far enough. Don't worry; I won't put a bullet in your heart. That's too immediate and pain-free."

"You are a genuine sociopath," McLeod declares.

Cornfield aims at McLeod's legs and pulls the trigger. There is no discharge; he pulls again, the same result. With a surprised facial, McLeod touches the Commander across the shoulder with his hand-held stun gun; the surprise turns to shock. The pistol falls out of the Commander's hand, and he collapses, twitching to the floor. He then went limp. A few minutes later, securely tied to an oversized metal chair, Cornfield awakens and tries unsuccessfully to overcome his traumatized state.

McLeod tells him, "I am here because you lied to me. You told me Calvo was not involved with the killing of Team 33. Then, I found out that Colonel Calvo had handpicked the men who murdered my team members. I am a bit troubled and dismayed by your choice to deceive."

"Troubled and dismayed? Tough shit," Cornfield mockingly remarked.

With a smile on his face, McLeod responded. "Tied up and brazen, I'm impressed."

"Well," Cornfield responded philosophically, "How did you figure me out?"

"Tied up and disadvantaged, and you want to know how because you already know why you're in this position. Amazing! A lucky break led me to Calvo's whereabouts. Then you, accompanied by Cavo, walked out of his office. What a kicker of good fortune. You lied when you stated that Calvo had nothing to do with my team's killing. By the grace of Mars and a stroke of dumb luck, I am here to listen to your restatement.

"Well said, Sergeant; my hubris fooled me into thinking I had outfoxed you."

"Let's not demean your traitorous intent. A Commander of the U.S. Navy in business with a heroin dealing, narcissistic psycho; what am I to make of that, Commander Cornfield?"

Cornfield confronted the inevitable. "So, let's get to the point. You want access to Calvo so that you can kill him. Surely, you intend to kill us both. What if I do one better and make a bargain?"

"That would be quite the bargain," McLeod conceded.

"You will take my offer," Cornfield smirked.

"Then please, Commander, let's hear it."

"First, you need to understand the background, Cornfield pleaded."

McLeod rolled his eyes. "You're offering to deliver the Russian," McLeod suggested.

"I thought that would get your attention," Cornfield continued. "However, having you understand my relationship with Calvo is vital. This business with Calvo is a classic case of the handler or regulator going to work for the person or people he once managed. Calvo was a CIA source that I accessed while serving in Naval Intelligence. We spent hours together after he was discharged, and when I retired, he offered me a job.

The Navy made me a Commander, but then forced me into retirement. After a lifetime of service, I was handed my discharge papers and escorted out of the building. Calvo was the only offer that came my way. Of course, I understood the complications; I knew he was an amoral survivalist. Nevertheless, he treated me respectfully, and the job paid well."

"Commander, get to the point," McLeod impatiently demanded.

"There are only two people, aside from Castro, who have access to the Russian. As disclosed, Calvo hated and intensely feared the guy. A few years ago, the former GRU agent and Castro thought it best to eliminate the one person who knew of Cuba's link to Southeast Asia's heroin trade. Hence, Calvo was an agreed-upon target.

At the time, Calvo worked for the CIA; his value lay in providing names, dates, and places. Most importantly, so he purported, he knew the whereabouts of the Castro family's cash, tens of millions of dollars deposited in respected banks. But like all relevant things, time erodes viability; Calvo's information becomes dated and irrelevant.

The war that no one wanted to revisit was over. Before the CIA contract was over, Calvo had already sensed the forthcoming situation and prepared. He had invested his energy into an agreement with El Banco Bilbao de Vizcaya in Madrid: a proposal to fund the bank's capital in Cuba. The bank required a joint-venture agreement with the Cuban government. Calvo approached Raul directly, and with the help of the Cuban Embassy in Madrid, the embassy cleared the deal. Once again, Calvo recreated himself and assumed significant responsibility for the mutual benefit of Cuba and Spain by representing Spain's investment interests. In other words, Castro, the communist, and Calvo, the practical entrepreneur, canceled one approach to remedying past issues and concerns in favor of a newly created phoenix of understanding and commercial engagement."

"I assume this deal that Calvo put together included the Russian's cooperation," McLeod suggested.

"The Russian had no say with the deal; before you ask, no, this was all the Castro family's decision. So, Sergeant McLeod, Colonel Calvo is no ordinary exploiter of cards dealt. This man is extraordinary; I have learned much from this individual."

"I assume you told me about this Calvo exploit for a reason. So far, I have learned that Calvo has access to the Russian, has deferred death once more, and that you respect him; he is one of two. Who is the other?"

"The other is the daughter of Dr. Anh Li. Thanks to you, or so it is rumored, her mother is no longer among the living. Her daughter lives in Paris. I have had telephone conversations, but I have never met her."

Although taken aback, McLeod stayed calm and searched for more information without seeming too eager. He challenged the integrity of Cornfield's explanations instead of zeroing in on Anh Li's daughter.

"Though interesting, this bargain of yours has not taken any form," McLeod pressed. "So far, you have told me you know persons close to the Russian. Exactly what does that mean to me? What was the mother's interest? Why was she a client?"

"In the beginning, she worked as a consultant, a casualty insurance company officer, and then, of course, she was the CEO of Old Dutch. She was extremely competent and solidly connected with the Castro family. Over the last six years of employment, Calvo and I have met with Dr. Li several times, but neither of us has ever physically met the Russian or Dr. Li's daughter."

"If," McLeod emphasized, "neither you nor Calvo has ever laid eyes on this Russian, how do you know he's alive? And spare me, you feel that he exists. Do you have first-hand evidence of his existence?"

"Nothing firsthand," Marin responds. However, I do not doubt his existence," Cornfield answered.

"Now," McLeod forcefully questioned, "are you going to tie all of this to me killing the Russian?"

"I said I could deliver the Russian. Whether you can kill him or not is on you."

"Well, Commander, you played every side there was to play. You are duplicitous—a despicable murderer of your flesh and blood. Your treasonous self also worked for the Russian, Calvo, and, during the Vietnam War, the communists."

Avoiding any response to murdering his family, "That's ridiculous; I served my country," Cornfield implored.

"You started as a counterintelligence officer, but you were not exponentially successful despite hundreds of hours of hard, diligent work. You could not separate yourself from the herd and turn the day-to-day into the extraordinary until you met Dr. Anh Li.

" My assumption," McLeod continued, "is that you met her at a Red Cross function in Da Nang." She convinced you to trade intelligence over time by offering informational enticements. You gave yourself the excuse that you could turn her to serve the American side, but never alerted the folks at the CIA or Naval counterintelligence. At first, it was minor stuff, a little of this for a little of that; your superiors, not knowing the whole story, noticed and congratulated you on your success. Appreciation from superiors was an enticement that became addictive. When the promotion finally blossomed. Your ambition overrode your integrity; you told yourself that I was not taking money or favors. Most importantly, the line Marines received incredible insights into the distribution of NVA Battalions in I-Corps. You took information from Anh Li and turned it into actionable intelligence. Hell, you got the Bronze Star for your competence. You were magic."

"How in the world did you put this together?" Cornfield asked with remorse in his voice; he admitted, "I traded a bit here for a lot there. I ensured we gained much more in this game than we lost."

"Even now, while admitting to your betrayal, you still cling to one misrepresentation after another. One lie, one misdirection, followed by another," McLeod aggressively responded. "A documented elitist who on the outside reflects a respected Annapolis graduate, a field grade officer reaping the reputation thereof, while on the inside, you are a lying, scheming traitor, a wife and child beater. You are, through and through, a rat."

"You're wrong! Even the GRU agent gave up valuable intelligence at the war's end because he and Calvo didn't care who won; they wanted the war to continue. All they cared about was the heroin business, which is why the trade of intelligence always ended in our favor. That's the truth."

McLeod stayed on track. "You want me to believe it was an innocent trade for information between two counterparties, each servicing the interests of the other. You, the representative of America's war effort, and the other heroin distribution partners found no inherent conflict. Interesting fable: surely this story helps you sleep better at night."

"It was an equitable trade of information." Cornfield declared, "And I have no issues with sleeping."

"That might have been true until the North Vietnamese used your past actions for extortion. Then you were stuck, and Dr. Li, the deeply placed NVA spy, knew that whatever she wanted, your only response would be, yes, Ma'am."

As an admission of truthfulness, Cornfield could not directly look at him; McLeod continued assessing. "Those were just by-chance photos my team took of the Russian and his key personnel. A couple of those in the photograph were high-ranking South Vietnamese officers. Staff enhanced the photos in Quantico and passed them on, unaware of the significance of the procedure they had followed. Once you saw the results, you knew your GRU agent was exposed. In the hands of U.S. counterintelligence, those photos will result in arrests. You stashed the photographs by sending them back into the system. That bought you much-needed time."

"I suppose you want me to confirm and confess?" Cornfield asked.

Ignoring Cornfield's remark for the moment, McLeod finalizes his supposition. "Utilizing Anh Li's connections with the bad-guy network, you initiated the orders to place Doss into his Executive Officer position at 1st Force Recon. You provided the information to create the means to kill the real Doss. The timing could not have been better, with Force Recon's commanding officer in Okinawa on a temporary duty assignment. Only you had the access and ability to orchestrate such a move. You were the go-to guy for that sector's intelligence. A year before retiring from the Navy, your TTY Duty for the CIA allowed you to bury your treasonous behavior."

"I did what I did. I survived," Confield reasoned.

"A voluntary confession, the Naval Academy graduate officer will confess. The traitor who consorted with the enemy for career status and promotional gain finds confessing necessary. Where exactly is Calvo?"

"He is in Spain."

"You know I have no more time. You say Calvo is in Spain, but I don't care now." McLeod removed a small bottle of oil from his pocket.

"OK," McLeod conceded, "I should, out of reluctant charity, give you one more chance. Let me be clear: If you do not respond convincingly, I will zap you again and dump peanut oil down your garbage hole. Yes, I know that your peanut allergy is death-inducing. Suffocating is not a fun way to die."

"Calvo is in Panama," Cornfield exclaimed. He met with Mike Marin regarding an acquisition proposed by Sepúlveda for Old Dutch Indemnity. Calvo and I are on the insurance company's board."

"Now, that was good," McLeod assured Cornfield. "Where is Calvo staying?"

"When in Panama, he stays at the Paitilla Holiday Inn. He is one of the owners."

"Excellent!" McLeod continued. "How long is he staying, and where does he go from there?"

"I assume he stays until the new opportunity is affirmed, and from there, he returns to Miami." McLeod reached into his canvas bag and pulled out an army-issued poncho; he placed the hood firmly over his head, put on a diver's facemask, and ran his hands and arms through the poncho slots. Cornfield stared, looking puzzled, a bit bewildered.

McLeod believed nothing else after Cornfield's admission and Calvo's information. He reached for and grabbed Cornfield's .45 pistol, placed it on the desk. He replaced the firing pin Billy had given him with no hesitation. Pistol in hand, McLeod rammed the barrel into his mouth, smashing his teeth and cutting his lips. Blood gushed down his chin. With the barrel inches into his mouth, McLeod paused for a few seconds, allowing the full impact of what was coming to settle in Cornfield's mind. McLeod squeezed the trigger. The explosion blew off the back of Cornfield's head. McLeod set the pistol on the floor and vacated the area.

Panama City

McLeod boarded American Airlines Flight 507 headed for Panama. Thoughts of Charlie were near to his mind as he ordered a scotch and reconciled that this woman was out of his control, beyond his reach. McLeod slid that arrow into his quiver of memories and moved on. Once past customs, McLeod headed to Sepúlveda's usual parking space. In moments, the two old friends were chatting it up.

"You look terrific; I see the young lady and the Miami sun have taken good care of you," Sepúlveda observes.

"I stayed out of the sun," McLeod then grinned. "But the young lady was much more than I ever expected. I was smitten and abandoned, all in a matter of days."

"All part of this Greek tragedy we call life."

"Yes, so it seems, dear friend, so it seems," McLeod confirms.

"Mindful," Sepúlveda adds, "if only to track you, she could be working for the Russian. But, of course, you're not that hard to kill, so why bother?"

"Thank you for that analysis," McLeod retorts.

"Yes, of course," with a chuckle, "just trying to earn my fee." Do you remember Marin's gambling debt?

"Yes indeed," McLeod quickly responds.

"Well, as part of the deal, Marin requests that I pay that debt as an upfront token of good faith," Sepúlveda stated.

"When you say pay off, you mean McLeod pays. As an added incentive for Marin's cooperation," McLeod presumes, Sepúlveda's turned into the marina parking spot where McLeod pointed to a 105-foot, 1944 converted minesweeper docked just offshore. "

"Yours," Sepúlveda assumes.

"Yes, mine and the fates of wind and sea, I'll have you aboard. You will enjoy the attributes of my crew, all two of them," McLeod smiled.

"I am sure of it."

"Until tomorrow at 11:00 a.m., my friend and I will not pay off Marin's gambling debt," McLeod confirms.

McLeod departed with bags to the end of the slip, where a Boston Whaler awaited him on his boat. Aboard the converted minesweeper, McLeod showered and enjoyed a night's sleep. In the morning, Sepúlveda's driver picked him up and delivered him to his office. The meeting with Marin was at 1:00 p.m. McLeod was not to be a physical member of the meeting; instead, he placed himself in a joining room equipped to hear the conversation. The large painted landscape was a one-way mirror that allowed McLeod to see everything.

Sepúlveda, utilizing the dead time before the meeting, discussed the agenda and parts of an overall plan to initiate the action with McLeod.

"McLeod, I want you to know I like this project. And do you know why?"

"You need to tell me," McLeod conceded.

"This purchase by the Spanish insurer will dramatically appreciate the stock of the public subsidiary, which is part of the acquisition currency. McLeod, this Old Dutch acquisition is my last hurrah."

McLeod asked, disinterested in the Old Dutch business, "Have you thought through a method of getting close to the Russian?"

"No," Sepúlveda implores. "As discussed, the means to kill the Russian is your expertise. I honestly believe killing this fellow is impossible. That is why I am not so concerned about my physical danger. Today's focus is the presentation with Marin."

"I do agree," McLeod responds. "Doing in the Russian does seem highly improbable, and near impossible; nonetheless, the near impossible gateways through Marin."

"Yes, that's your mission. My primary has developed in another direction. My function is to sell or, more accurately, align Old Dutch's interests with the merger with the Spanish insurance company. If my primary somehow aids and assists your mission, all the better."

"Then we have a new understanding," McLeod acknowledges.

"My interest is to kill the Russian. Yours is to make the most money out of the Old Dutch situation."

"Yes," Sepúlveda affirms, "Since I will segregate some of my shares for you, I don't see any downside."

"I will be an Old Dutch Shareholder. How considerate! Of course, Father Time will determine your no-downside assumption," McLeod declares.

"Well, at 54, Marin is the youngest senior management member; the company needs new blood and increased revenue to sustain a profitable future. They must sell, reorganize, or buy into a new business model matrix. They need dynamic thrust in one direction or another. In addition to all their stagnation issues, Dr. Li died. As the CEO of the holding company, she was a force of reckoning; more than likely, she endeavored to enact some significant realignment. She is gone, and the insurance company is the worst for it."

McLeod avoided commenting on Anh Li and the company's stagnation issue. Instead, he states, "Hope is such a poor reliance. However, I hope this acquisition transaction will lure Marin into an introduction to the Russian."

"Upgrade hope into faith," Sepúlveda suggests. "I would not fight a battle wherein the odds of winning are unfavorable; besides, the Spanish company is eager and ready. Is this tactic a good lead for Ivan, my target? Who knows? It is precarious. Therefore, we leave success up to fate and continue putting one foot before the other."

"How very Panamanian of you. However, money is your center focus."

"Business and killing the Russian until now have run in parallel lanes; however, separation was inevitable. That does not mean we cannot satisfy them both," Sepúlveda implores.

"All right, remembering the original reason you're on board," McLeod responds. And with that last statement, McLeod stepped into the adjoining room to observe the meeting while Sepúlveda stayed back in his office awaiting Marin.

At precisely 1:00 p.m., the outer door buzzer sounded, and the security guard escorted Marin and his associate into the reception area. The receptionist rang for Mr. Sepúlveda and then turned her attention to warmly greeting the guests, confirming that Mr. Sepúlveda was seconds away. Sepúlveda entered the reception area with a big smile and an extended hand. Marin responded kindly and introduced his associate as Lucy. Sepúlveda invited the guests to the boardroom to sit at the conference table. He offered them water, coffee, and soft drinks.

Marin's assistant puzzled McLeod. She looked to be in her mid-forties and wore her hair pinned back, with no lipstick or makeup except for heavy rouge on both cheeks. Lucy lacked the slightest hint of a bosom, dressed in a long, white-sleeved shirt buttoned at the wrist and neck. She wore thick-rimmed glasses and had no indications of latent beauty. However, what stood out for McLeod was that she did not look anyone in the eye, with her head slightly lowered. Her function was to take notes.

Marin was of medium build and about five feet nine inches tall. He had indistinguishably faded black tattoos on his forearm, which looked like the artistry of a jail cell tattooist striving to imprint something nautical. Wearing brown-framed, lightly tinted sunglasses, one could see through the lenses. The perfectly aligned pressure marks on his nose suggested that—sun or no sunshine- he must only remove his glasses when sleeping. Regarding appearance and image, Marin was a remarkable contradiction; he was respected in his field and a proven manager of a highly regulated, detail-specific business. Wearing a bright ALOHA shirt confirmed that Marin was not a fashionista, nor was he sensitive to the fashions of Haute culture. A Dodgers baseball cap completed his ensemble.

The report on Marin indicated he had no pretensions. He was ordinary in every way. He understood his business, and his reputation proved he was no fool. His predominant weaknesses were gambling, alcohol, and excessive smoking. He spoke softly with little enunciation or emphasis, a cigarette at the ready either in hand or pocket. Listening to Marin for fifteen minutes could quickly put one to sleep. Fortunately, he spoke when spoken to and rarely wasted words. He was an excellent listener.

Marin started the meeting with a hint of sarcasm, "I assume you're going to tell me that this opportunity is essential to the survival of Old Dutch."

"Essential to survival? That's an exaggeration," Sepúlveda replied. "But frankly, Old Dutch does require exponential revenue growth, and by affirming this acquisition, the possibility of such growth is highly probable. The acquisition is a compelling shot of adrenaline directly into the heart of Old Dutch. Before selling Old Dutch to the profitable Spanish insurance conglomerate, is the do-it-now prudent thing for your board to affirm?"

"I'm sold on the concept," Marin concedes, "but then there are those nasty details."

"Agreed, nasty details are a transactional component," Sepúlveda affirms. "As discussed, I have disseminated a non-binding letter of intent approved by the buyer detailing the merger's terms and conditions. Concurrent financial, legal, and administrative audits are required; however, the buyer will require you as president to sign a separate, not yet drafted, binding agreement to represent your intended interest in this opportunity in ten business days."

With a broad smile, Marin initially moved from at least the pretext of hesitation to full-throated enthusiasm. After the sale confirmation, I have only one question: will the buyer renew my five-year contract as President of Old Dutch?"

"That's a question for the buyer's board of directors," Sepúlveda answers.

"And we know the board's response. Don't we?" Marin suggests.

The receptionist called, ringing the phone twice before hanging up; as they spoke, it was a code to let Sepúlveda know there was someone or something important. Sepúlveda excused himself and went to investigate.

McLeod saw a man standing before the receptionist with the security guard behind him. He was tall, slim, and eloquently dressed, with a distinguished handlebar mustache. The stranger, burdened with a heavy Spanish accent, introduced himself:

"Please forgive me for my tardiness; my name is Colonel Eduardo Calvo. I am a director of Old Dutch and late for this meeting."

"So pleased to meet you. My name is Raymond Sepúlveda; please follow me."

Marin stood as they entered the meeting room, and Lucy moved her chair to the far corner of the eight-chair conference table. Delighted at the recent arrival, this was McLeod's first view of the former Cuban Colonel. He looked aged, but every bit accurately reflected the descriptions given to him.

Marin addressed Calvo, "Senior Calvo, I was not sure you would be here; I am so pleased you could make it."

"You may address me as Colonel Calvo; please fill me in on the highlights. If I have disrupted this meeting, my apologies; now, Marin, please fill me in on the possibilities." Colonel Calvo sits next to Marin, introduces Sepúlveda as the presenter, and asks him to retell the presentation.

"Colonel, do you have any questions?" Sepúlveda picked up on the rank. Calvo motioned negatively with his hands and the slight movement of his head. "However, I have a question."

"Please, I am very interested in your thoughts," Sepúlveda remarks.

The Colonel continues, "What is the cost to Old Dutch paid to your person for structuring and facilitating this endeavor?

Sepúlveda responds, "Firstly, I will require an exclusive on the proposed deal and a corporate resolution appointing me to the Old Dutch board of directors. My efforts will require a 5% stake in Old Dutch stock before the merger. Upon the merger's success, the other five percent of public company shares will be required," Sepúlveda clarifies.

"Thank you; I now understand your wants," Calvo replies. "However, the board must meet and formally schedule a shareholder's meeting; before or at the shareholder meeting, the disposition of the outstanding Bearer Shares must be revealed and evidenced."

Sepúlveda continued, "Thank you for mentioning, but of course, such details are the responsibility of Old Dutch management. Sepúlveda handed Marin a notebook containing the generalities suggested and assured Calvo that he would have a duplicate before leaving. In short order, Sepúlveda stated the venture's reasoning while fitting the project snuggly with Old Dutch's financial concerns. McLeod noticed that his positive body language signaled Marin's engaging manner. Calvo displayed no emotion but listened intently.

The meeting concluded on a positive note with a handshake. Lucy stood silently and left the conference room. Marin, before departure, stated that he was impressed with the possibilities and intended to review the nonbinding LOI and respond within a week on Sepúlveda's terms.

After the three guests departed, McLeod joined Sepúlveda in the conference room and said, "I thought that went well enough."

"I agree. It could not have gone better," Sepúlveda affirms. "I bet that Marin will call in less than a week. I will make it in three days: that's my wager. Of course, Calvo showing up was a bonus."

"And that pretentious ass, Calvo, requiring 'Colonel' to precede his name is particularly touching." McLeod sarcastically shook his head. "However, his interest in the disposition of the Bearer Shares was apparent. Something's in the wind; bringing up Bearer Shares in a Sepúlveda acquisition presentation seems odd. He was addressing Marin as to the whereabouts of these shares.

McLeod changes the subject and asks, "Are you coming over for dinner aboard the minesweeper tonight?"

"Yes, I'll be there at seven," Sepúlveda replies.

Calvo, Up Close, and Personal

A little over ten years earlier, McLeod, instead of collecting a $25,000 gambling debt, traded the debt for the collateral of a 105 minesweeper. McLeod, aside from understanding starboard, leeward, astern, and bow, knew nothing about diesel engines or boats. So, in time, he understood the former owner's glee at exchanging a gaming marker for the boat title. As it turned out, the blessing was not the boat but Maurice and Philomena's retention and continued employment. This couple assumed the positions of captain, engineer, cook, server, and the day-to-day duties of a crew. If not for Maurice and Philomena, McLeod would have remained bound by the anchor of good sense and stayed landlocked to a permanent tether.

McLeod sat comfortably on the deck in an oversized, bamboo-framed, cushioned chair with armrests large and flat enough to hold a drink. Maurice approached McLeod. "Mr. McLeod, the water taxi with Mr. Sepúlveda is approaching."

"Good. What's on the menu for dinner?"

"I will ask Philomena."

"There's no need, Maurice, but when you find the time, fetch me another bottle of Blue Label."

"Oui; tout de suite, Monsieur McLeod," Maurice shouted as he moved at an exaggerated pace to help and greet Mr. Sepúlveda on board.

"Well, the Sergeant in his lair," Sepúlveda chuckled as he approached the boat's fantail. "Please don't get up. I'll take the same position on your chair's twin; these chairs comfort an old body."

Maurice poured Sepúlveda his light Puerto Rican rum with lime and ice while McLeod had his Blue Label served neat. Simultaneously, they raised their respective glasses in a toast to each other.

"Dear friend," Sepúlveda started, "my sources have confirmed some bad news."

Viewing Sepúlveda's sudden change from cheer to solemnity, McLeod braced for the worst: The Russian was dead.

"I can confirm our Russian lives in Cuba. In the past, he traveled on business occasionally, but now he never does. He is a Cuban citizen with Mexican and Belizean passports; remarkably, he traveled with a Canadian residence visa. As reported, he powers his yacht offshore occasionally but never leaves Cuban waters. His business contacts or associates must meet him in the open sea, or not meet him at all. He is a cautious man."

"Damn," McLeod relaxed. "I thought you were going to tell me he was dead."

"Dead, no, but it is reasonable to believe that Marin, in his present position in Old Dutch, has the means to make the introduction. However, maneuvering Marin to act, I'd say, is improbable."

Maurice poured another drink for both.

"Patience, in this case, is the right measure," Sepúlveda cautioned. "The situation regarding this Russian is not positive. Capturing or outright killing him has moved from difficult to near impossible."

"Well, we have both been in this position before," McLeod said, as a veteran of challenging situations.

Sepúlveda acknowledged by a lift of his glass and toasted, "We need a bit of luck; here's to suerte."

They enjoyed Philomena's tasty dinner, agreeable conversation, and the starry Panamanian night. Both men philosophized about accepting the terms of their own lives.

Two days passed, and McLeod and Sepúlveda found themselves at a local restaurant near the Marriott Hotel. McLeod had ordered the chicken-and-rice special, but Sepúlveda declined to order food and stayed with his coffee.

"So," McLeod initiates, "a meeting with Marin at 2:00 this afternoon."

"Yes, as forecasted, Marin is eager. He told me the proposed venture was a resourceful remedy to address the issues of Old Dutch," Sepúlveda stated in between sips of coffee.

"A kind of collateral benefit to the mission; besides, you are a veteran of making money. What else could have happened?" McLeod winked. "I will be waiting here for you to return."

"Why don't we make it easy for you? I'll meet you on the boat around 6:30," Sepúlveda added. "Maybe I can enjoy a drink or two."

"All right," McLeod concedes, "until later."

McLeod left the café and took a taxi back to the dock. He had just missed the shuttle and had to wait at least 30 minutes for it to return.

The waiting area was empty, except for a group of children chasing one another. He sat on the bench alone. The children's ruckus brought back memories of his childhood, his life with Sister Maria and Mother Clara, the Black Hawks gang, and that sacred tree. The tallest and most challenging to climb, the one every Black Hawk captain had climbed as a rite of passage. Mother Clara declared the same tree off-limits for practical safety reasons under the penalty of severe spanking. He remembered when Sister Maria caught him up high in the tree; he envisioned the spanking and pain as worth the satisfaction of reaching the top. Before disobeying Mother Clara's standing orders and Sister Maria's screams to climb down, he scratched his initials on the tree bark, alongside those of other previous Black Hawk gang captains, using a large nail.

"Mr. McLeod? Hello, Mr. McLeod!" The boat launch skipper yelled out. "Are you ready to board?" Shaken out of his daydream, McLeod stood and waved positively to the skipper. In a matter of minutes, he was boarding his boat. While he walked towards the fantail, Maurice greeted him with an apology, "I am so sorry, but I went ashore for groceries, and Philomena was down in the galley... somehow, this young lady got on board. The shuttle skipper is under strict orders, so she must have used a private boat."

"A woman, you say?" McLeod asked.

He turned, and his jaw dropped as he saw Charlie sitting comfortably on a deck chair. She looked fantastic. As he walked closer, she stood, reached out without saying a word, and hugged him. McLeod stepped back, overwhelmed. Completely surprised, he stood there staring silently at her.

"I'll have that drink, Maurice." McLeod finally converted his thoughts into words.

"Water with ice and a lemon wedge for me would be wonderful," Charlie added.

He reached for his wide-rimmed woven fedora and fixed it on his head. Then, the two sat while McLeod tried to collect his dismembered emotional self. Charlie said nothing, just looked at him as she waited for his next move.

Finally, she broke the silence, "Well, I did say I would be back."

"Indeed, you did. I had lost all hope."

"Not all hope," Charlie contested. "I know you had some tiny bit of hope left in you; after all, Miami was an experience that neither of us will ever forget."

She wore a loosely revealing halter top and bent down purposefully to fiddle with the ties on her shoes. Her superbly designed breasts burst out as if summoned by the sun. Charlie continued, "So... please, tell me you retained some hope."

At that moment, Maurice delivered the drinks; sensing the lingering discomfort, he withdrew without requesting any further service.

McLeod felt a driving sexual desire; knowingly, weak and vulnerable, he knew his want was apparent. He wanted to inhale her whole, rip her clothes off, and thrust himself between her legs. Sitting on the oversized cushioned chair, she pulled up her dress and spread her legs; she knew his wants. McLeod's heart pounded. He stared at her.

"McLeod..." Like a siren calling one onshore, Charlie whispered his name, saying, "Let's go to your cabin; this waiting is torturous." As if unleashed, McLeod took her hand and guided her below deck. The lustful longing of reunited lovers was not so easily satisfied. The lovemaking was hard and soft, kissing, licking, and sucking; enough was an imperfect sensation; desire ruled the moment, gratification once realized was not lasting. Finally, the lustful carnal gave in to exhaustion.

Hair brushed to her acceptance, a newly attired Charlie joined McLeod on deck. The sun was no longer as bright. Maurice had brought a pitcher of icy water with lemons and a chilled bottle of Pouilly-Fuissé with two glasses.

Charlie sat across from him, smiled, and asked him to pour her a glass of wine. He obliged.

"Well," McLeod said as if in relief of an itch scratched, "I do admit that I am curious."

Charlie stopped him. "Wondering and speculating about where I have been and what I am doing here is more than curious." She stopped to sip her wine and continued, "You probably also want to know how I found your boat and person."

"Indeed, if you wish to answer."

"Yes, Mr. McLeod, I will answer, but first, I want to discuss my original reasoning for contacting you. I must revisit my motivation if our lovemaking has clouded your memory."

"Clouded my memory," McLeod repeated. "That's a bit arrogant of you."

Ignoring McLeod's response, Charlie continued, I am here as an intermediary, assisting in fulfilling our mutual disdain for the Russian."

In a frustrating mood change, McLeod asks. "Will you clarify your motivation? Why do you want to help me kill this Russian?"

"Is that so important?" Charlie asks.

"Yes!" McLeod responds. "Do you have a plan?" McLeod asks.

"A plan? No, I'll leave that up to you and your partner Sepúlveda; I'm here to assist you dribbling the ball for the layup, an advisor, but I am not the planner or the executor," Charlie affirms. "I have stirred up some contention," Charlie playfully stated. "Yes, Mr. McLeod, I have a connection to Cuba from Panama. You look surprised. Yes, I know the man you seek is in Cuba; he has been there for years, but only within the last ten has his paranoia made Castro's Island his permanency.

"I assume you know Marin?" asked McLeod.

"Yes, as I mentioned at our initial encounter, I know of Mike Marin. McLeod, you are putting great faith in Mr. Raymond Sepúlveda."

"Yes, and he has proven very resourceful."

"Mr. Sepúlveda is a brilliant veteran of the grand game," Charlie compliments, "however, he does have his vulnerabilities."

"Vulnerabilities; what do you mean by that?"

"I mean that trust has nothing to do with much of anything. The plan is to meet, greet, and kill...." Charlie hesitated, "This, Max or Eduardo, this plan to kill the Russian is flawed when you assert trust as a reliable contingent."

"And you're suggesting my trust in Sepúlveda is a detriment?"

"I think," Charlie said, "contrariness is helpful in this game. The game takes no prisoners and gives no quarters. For his entire business life, Sepúlveda made a living by not favoring one side. He was always faithful to his benefactor's interest; he never sold out his employer or ratted to the authorities. Sepúlveda of old was ambivalent to ideology or popular sentiment; now, he is helping you assassinate this Russian to satisfy your revenge? I say, importancia de ser muy cuidadoso, Cuidado!

"I enlisted Sepúlveda in this endeavor in a very transparent manner," McLeod sternly responded. "Other than the moneymaking possibilities as a motivation, I never asked him specifically why he joined with me to erase the Russian from amongst the living. I had explicitly told him the cause of my revenge; however, other than his initial engagement with certain information, he was bound to silence. We have become friends; unlike a female, I do not engage in personal questions or have an innate need to know everything. Aside from instilling in me a sense of doubt. Your fluency in pointing out that Sepúlveda may have a counter to my agenda. What exactly are you getting at?"

"Mr. McLeod, such an alpha male response." Charlie sternly proclaims, "You're engaged in a dangerous game. This conceptual in-development scheme to kill this dangerous individual is as predictable as next week's weather. Is it impossible to anticipate an outcome with so many variables?" Though a bit aggravated by Charlie's very poignant concerns, McLeod had never considered Raymond anything but trustworthy until that moment. Nonetheless, her considerations were rational, and that doubled down on his aggravation. Was he recklessly innocent in his assessment? Contrary thoughts create doubt, uncertainty, and questions of trust, and the continuance of such erodes confidence. Unable to put these thoughts aside, he asks Charlie a more straightforward question: "How did you find me here in Panama? How did you get here?"

Charlie noticed his tone change and softly responded, "Finding you was simple; the anchor berth is in the name of the boat: Triple Threat, and you told me about Sepúlveda and your upcoming trip to Panama. I got here directly from Miami and indirectly from Paris. I want to help you with the Russian because my friend owns most of Old Dutch."

McLeod finally admits, "Doss insisted that I have a daughter. I assume your friend in Paris is that person. And that's why you are familiar with the Russian, Marin, and Sepúlveda."

"You've captured about half of the obvious. My friend's mother is Anh Li. She was remarkably close to the Castro family and familiar with the GRU agent; however, my friend might be your daughter; of course, only a DNA test can verify that."

"Hmm...interesting," McLeod responds. That's all good, but getting back to your original statement of help, how exactly can you help me?"

"The exactness of my help will depend on you. Have you further developed that plan of yours?"

The question goes unanswered at that moment; Maurice enters and announces the arrival of Mr. Sepúlveda, who walked onto the fantail and spotted Charlie.

"Well, McLeod," Sepúlveda exclaimed, "I didn't know you had a guest. Here I thought it would be another boring night of male jousting over drinks and cigars." Without waiting for an introduction, Sepúlveda reached out with his right hand, "My name is Raymond."

"Just call me Charlie."

Raymond replied, "I have heard about you, and I believe we spoke on the phone once."

Charlie made no reply. The three took their seats. Drinks and cigars were delivered, and the gentlemen cut, fired, and puffed on their hand-rolled Cohibas.

"Don't tell me I was the subject of this evening's conversation?" Sepúlveda asked.

McLeod jumped in. "Charlie is the same 'Charlie' I have talked about in Miami. Before you boarded, Charlie mentioned she knew your name and may have met you as a child.

At that moment, Charlie stood up from her chair.

"Well, I can see you boys have things to discuss; I will take my leave." Charlie interrupted the sit-in by calling it a night. Charlie stood but continued talking, "Please do not get up, Raymond." She reached over, kissed McLeod on the forehead, and headed downstairs to the quarters below.

"Well, Mr. McLeod," Sepúlveda said, smirking, "I see your heart has won over your normally prudent Anglo heart. So, I have met the infamous Charlie; she seems delightful."

"I am totally and completely in lust for her." McLeod leaned in.

"Just remember, my encumbered one," Sepúlveda cautioned, "she is a serious woman with an agenda of her own." He pointed his index finger at McLeod's chest and said, "You should never forget that."

"Agreed, that is a reality. But it's also a Chandler mystery thriller —a page-by-page, unpredictable, episodic whodunit that stimulates and intrigues. It's the danger of unreliability that makes Charlie so carnally exciting."

Sepúlveda, I see you have leaped into the abyss of susceptibility. She has seduced your body and spirit. There are no words I could use to sober your delirium. Permit me to change topics."

"Of course, please change the topic."

"This afternoon's meeting with Marin was everything I could ask. Old Dutch is interested in the venture's probabilities. However, I could not take one step closer to meeting this Russian. Killing this fellow will take a great deal of luck."

"As a fatalist, I want to believe Charlie is here for a reason," McLeod said. "She is not here, though I wish otherwise, because she misses me. She did say that she is awaiting some information."

"You can't get off this, Charlie girl. Well, whatever motivates her is her business at this point. You need help, and she could be the help you need."

"How about meeting with Colonel Calvo? Do you think his showing up is meaningful?" McLeod inquires.

"I assume the Colonel's attendance at the meeting was more curiosity than due diligence. The infamous Colonel may engage if the venture progresses."

"Maybe you should call a meeting," McLeod suggests.

"No, that's a Marin obligation."

"You are correct," McLeod concedes. "Besides, considering they both need to die, our primary objective, the Russian, is in serious competition with our secondary, Colonel Calvo."

"Yes, however, I need to stay focused on business, not your revenge," Sepúlveda points out. Marin is the focus and interest of our offering. Until we can guarantee what's in it for him, they, them, and those will inevitably require some concessions to sweeten the deal. For the deal to close favorably, Marin is our linchpin."

An hour flew by, and Sepúlveda exited only after noting that he was running late for a scheduled breakfast meeting with Marin at the Holiday Inn. As he left, he let McLeod know he would return directly to the boat after the meeting; McLeod headed down to his stateroom.

Charlie lay naked under a single sheet on McLeod's bed with her head propped on two feathered pillows. As McLeod appeared, she pulled one pillow behind her head and placed it beside her. McLeod approached, unbuckling his pants. He removed his shirt while Charlie lifted the sheet, exposing her naked self and inviting McLeod to partake.

Lovemaking and deep sleep consumed the night. At 6:30, the smell of coffee floated across the room, enticing McLeod to shower and dress. Charlie had no such inclinations.

By 9:00, Charlie had risen and joined McLeod on deck. "Good morning, Sergeant McLeod. What a lovely Panamanian day! " Anticipating the filling of an empty stomach, they devoured their breakfast on the fantail in silence. After the second cup of green tea, Charlie spoke. "My dearest Mr. McLeod, I must leave you for a few days."

"Hmm... in and out just like a Marine on shore leave."

"I am leaving. But I will be back before you can say, 'Charlie, I love, hmm, lust for you very much.'"

"Well, if that's the time frame, you've already returned."

Charlie finished her tea and moved directly over to McLeod, still sitting. She pushed the table away from his chair far enough to wriggle in, spread her legs, and straddle him. She looked into his eyes and kissed him on the lips.

"Mr. McLeod, your sweet words will beckon me back." Then she was gone again, motored to shore, occasionally pausing to turn and wave. McLeod begrudgingly returned the goodbyes. The day trickled on, drip by drip; the night would have been even slower if not for Johnnie Walker Blue. In the morning, Maurice shook him awake. The abruptness of light and the smell of coffee moved him on deck. He found a sealed white envelope next to his cup of coffee. McLeod opened the letter and found a note written in pencil: Tonight, 9:00 p.m., lobby, Panama Hilton Hotel. No signature was required. McLeod understood and recognized the author's identity. His connection between Vegas and Panama City had come through.

To secure the 9:00 p.m. meeting and reserve time to recon, McLeod needed to be at the Hilton Hotel by 8:00 p.m. He adjusted his schedule accordingly. Either the endeavor is a clever, opportunistic event that yields a fortuitous result, or a deadly trap. He had decided to go unarmed; he's dead anyway if it's a trap. If Calvo or the Russian use the Panamanian police to do their dirty work, carrying an unlicensed concealed weapon is an instant arrest.

A current employee of Aladdin named José Luis has a brother in Panama. Alfredo was his name. He arranged this nighttime rendezvous. Because of the prize, despite its danger, McLeod is determined to follow through on the opportunity. The Hilton's open-air lobby had two main walkways: one led to the valet and the street, and the other to the rear of the hotel and the pool. The hotel's restaurant and bar were near the pool.

McLeod arrived around 8:00 p.m., took a quick walk around the grounds, settled at the bar, and ordered a drink. He had less than an hour to wait. However, within minutes, a young girl, familiar to the bartender and a liaison, tapped McLeod on the shoulder, leaned in, and whispered, "Alfredo asked me to get you."

McLeod slapped a twenty under his beer glass and followed the young lady to a taxi, waiting without saying a word. The cab drove them to the Marriott Hotel and dropped them off. The young lady led McLeod through the front entrance, the lobby, and the back exit into a waiting car. After opening the rear door, the girl disappeared. Once inside, the driver spoke, "My name is Alfredo. My brother spoke of you often; my older brother always looks out for me."

José Luis, Alfredo's brother, had worked for McLeod for over ten years and never mentioned that he had a brother in Panama. After a casual chat with Billy Lamb, Luis informed McLeod of his connections in Panama. McLeod stored that potential, and when Calvo showed up in Panama, he asked Luis to introduce Alfredo.

"We share the same mother but not the father," Alfredo explained. "His father was an American Latino, so, unlike me, the son of a Colombian, he had direct access to the States. Anyway, it is my pleasure to bird-dog this Cuban. Your person of interest is a member of a private club located in a secluded area of Panama. The club is one of Columbia's most secretive and notorious. The principal owner is a favorite of Raúl Castro. Not sure what a Raul favorite is, but that's the club's rep."

"When you say secret, what do you mean? Is it a whore house, strip joint, or a straight-up private club?" McLeod asked.

"The club satisfies every kind of sex one can imagine. You think of it; the club will arrange everything, which is costly but free of scrutiny. No one can walk in. Only when accompanied by a member is a nonmember granted entrance. Or one must be famous, a person of note with the required connections. My sources inform me that Calvo, your Hombre of interest, is an equity charter member and an erratic individual with varied and peculiar preferences.

Initially, he befriends his victims with smiles and courtesy. Encourages a friendly chat, starting with kisses and ending with the victim sucking on his penis. Then, before ejaculation, he grabs them with the hair and pulls them away. He slaps them across the face, and with a whip in hand, his assistant forces one to have sex with another. He also enjoys, while masturbating, the performance of violent sex in his presence. He and others are cruel, sadistic bastards; as members, there are no limitations. If death or severe injury occurs, the parents or guardians are paid 5,000 USD."

"How long has this place existed?"

"Not sure; I know that this Calvo person knows all the Panamanian big shots; the privilege of membership is expensive. Pulling to a stop. We are here," Alfredo announces."

The car stopped in a clearing off the road directly across what looked like an upscale residential house.

Alfredo continued, "We should stay on this side of the street. There is only one entry and exit. You can see the entrance; it is directly across from us."

"Nice house, double doors." McLeod points out.

"Sí, but that is a false front; the real entrance is behind those double doors. Cameras are everywhere, but uniformed security personnel typically restrict themselves to the building and the immediate area in front of it. A 24/7 staffed gate controls private car access inside the compound. Member-owned private cars can drop off and pick up; however, parking is not available. Calvo is inside; he has been there for the last hour. My sources indicate that his visits typically last from three to four hours. He leaves no lingering at the bar or restaurant. A Holiday Inn staff driver picks him up and stops at his preferred local tapas café. The man is unescorted by the driver, who never leaves the car. Tonight, he is wearing dark-tinted glasses and a navy blue floppy hat half a size too big. Another significant consideration: I took the extra precaution of having a friend remove the bulb from the right taillight at the hotel. So, you will follow a white, four-door Cadillac with the Holiday Inn logo on the driver's and passenger's sides and one taillight logo. I know he is leaving Panama tomorrow on the 1:00 p.m. flight to Miami."

Alfredo stopped to point McLeod in the direction of a waiting vehicle.

"The keys are in the unlocked car. Don't worry; this is unknown to the employee's well-insured car. The employee will report it stolen at the end of his shift, which ends at 9:00 AM tomorrow. Leave the car wherever it suits you, and don't forget the gloves."

"You are a resourceful man." McLeod complimented Alfredo, extending an envelope thick with $100 bills, "My appreciation is enclosed."

"Good luck," Alfredo exclaimed.

McLeod exited the car and walked over to the vehicle provided. As requested, he found the keys to the driver's side wheel, binoculars, and a pair of black gloves on the passenger seat, along with a worn, faded baseball cap and a short, black, sharpened tire iron.

McLeod was counting on speed and surprise as his deadliest of weapons. McLeod rested his binoculars on his nose; his line of sight was the double-door entrance. He'd been watching for over an hour.

Waiting prompted contemplation; the waiting before initiating the ambush was particularly susceptible to remembrances of Vietnam. McLeod recalled the stillness before an ambush, the boredom of waiting, the body ache that came with disciplined stillness, and the unease that accompanied it. The mental stress of remaining focused and calm before squeezing the trigger and throwing grenades, the adrenaline kicking in, the anticipated sounds and smells of gunfire, and the screaming and moaning of the injured.

McLeod knew this killing was precarious. At best, the chance of predictable success was 60-40 against gratification. But killing a man like Calvo required the blessings of por fortuna, the tactic of spontaneity, and the acceptance of substantial risk. McLeod wanted this killing to be nose-to-nose, personal, with no martial dignity. I want to be killed by a standard workman's tool. I want him to know a split second before I bludgeon and stab that the moment of his death has arrived.

At that moment, a Cadillac with the missing right rear light pulled up to the double-door entrance; a man stepped out, opened his rear door, and climbed in. The Cadillac pulled away. McLeod followed. After a 20-minute drive, the Cadillac was parked across the street from the destination. Calvo exited and walked across the street. His unwaxed mustache flopped loosely on both sides of his face. He confidently entered the café.

McLeod parked his car, put on his thin leather gloves, adjusted his cap, and dropped the keys on the floor.

Wanting to look like a man seeking help for a flat tire with a tire iron in hand, McLeod headed directly to investigate the whereabouts of Calvo's person. His hasty ambush required finding an unsuspecting Calvo sitting by himself inside the café. As he walked in, the espresso bar was dark and dim, crowded, and people were milling about disorderly. He scanned the room; patrons were on their way to drunkenness, comfortably satisfying their taste for liquor and socializing at long tables with barstools on both sides; a drinking customer occupied every stool. As is common in Panama, the music was deafening.

In the corner, alone, to the extreme left, was Calvo sipping his espresso and nibbling on a small sandwich. His head was down as he stared into his cup while he chewed.

McLeod made a split-second decision to attack, and he was within reach with an abrupt half-left turn. Just like boarding the insertion helicopters in the early morning at Dong Ha, the last few steps were as if each foot weighed fifty pounds. He held the sharpened end of the tire iron by the middle portion with his right hand.

McLeod walked up to Calvo. Calvo looked up and stared for a second into McLeod's eyes. At first, from McLeod's perspective, Calvo had a look of bewilderment, but within seconds. Panic ensued. Calvo instinctively started to stand. McLeod's left hand grabbed the top back of his head and pulled down, forcing Calvo to sit on the chair. Calvo looked naturally up at McLeod; with his left hand, McLeod firmly grabbed the back of his head. He rammed the tire iron into Calvo's right eye. The tire iron hesitated on the bone, but with a firm grip, a quick, crunching adjustment with added pressure forced the iron into the brain with a distinctive crunching sound.

Leaving the tire iron in place, Calvo slumped forward onto the table and then onto the floor. Calvo was dead. Without looking around or making eye contact, he walked calmly out of the café. Once outside, McLeod's hands shook as adrenaline rushed through his veins. McLeod headed to the darker side of the street; he took off his short-sleeve shirt, revealing a black T-shirt, and pulled off the long, oversized pants, revealing a pair of dark Bermuda shorts. He cut into an enclave, rolled his cap, gloves, and clothing into a bundle, and walked with the bundle in hand for about six blocks. He then found a garbage can and deposited the clothes.

With Calvo dead, McLeod's thoughts turned to the getaway. He crossed the street and headed back in the direction he had just come from earlier. In hours, he was at the marina waiting for the shuttle.

A Friendship Ends

In the early morning before sunrise, after boarding his boat, McLeod went below and knocked on the captain's hatch. He woke Maurice and Philomena. Without declaring a cause, he ordered Maurice to weigh anchor and head north to Cabo San Lucas. Responding instantly, Maurice started the engines and disconnected the anchor line, freeing the boat from its berth. Lashing and securing loose items, Philomena prepared the ship for sea. McLeod withdrew to a hot shower and a double pour of Blue. Without causing a swell, the minesweeper slowly meandered between other boats at anchor, out of the harbor, and onto the open sea.

The night was replaced by the slowly rising morning sun. Below deck, daylight forced its way through every open crack and crevasse. Awakened, McLeod was out of Panama aboard his minesweeper, stimulated and comforted by the aroma of Philomena's freshly brewed coffee. He hurriedly dressed. He raced on deck to be cleansed by a brisk northerly wind; satisfaction eased its way across his mind. The humming noise of engines, a slight smell of diesel, and the unmistakable aroma of brine evidenced a clean getaway. The minesweeper was cruising against the wind at 18 knots. In five days, he would be in Mexican waters. Confidently knowing that this voyage was his last, he stood at the fantail, inhaled the smell of the ocean, and envied Maurice and Philomena, who considered the sea their home. The five-day voyage lingered, rendering cause for melancholy contemplation; McLeod realized an episode in his life had run its course. Once again, he must leave a friendship that has stood firm against the headwinds of an ever-evolving, unpredictable, multi-situational life, suffering cinema, titled The Revenge of Team 33.

On approaching the Marina La Bonita, Chetumal, Mexico, Maurice slowed and gently maneuvered the ship into the protected harbor. Lowered the anchor and set security for the night. Philomena prepared dinner. McLeod had requested an early dinner. He wanted "all aboard," were his exact words, to dine together on the fantail. The harbormaster had pledged to arrive at 7:00 to clear customs and immigration and check into an airport hotel before darkness chased away the starlight. His morning flight by private plane was early, and he arrived in Miami in the late afternoon. Tomorrow will be a long day.

McLeod initiated the after-dinner conversation, "It has been many moons since I acquired this minesweeper. I have benefited from your friendship and professional excellence for all that time." Maurice started to respond. With one finger across his lips, McLeod beckoned him to hold his thoughts.

"I will leave this ship and the two of you in a few minutes. We will never see each other again." At this point, McLeod reached for a large manila envelope resting on his lap. McLeod continued, "Dear friends, it gives me such sweet pleasure to legally render what you have always possessed. Upon reaching Miami, Philomena and Maurice will order a wire transfer of $250,000.00 into your bank account. This wire is for the last year of your contract, plus one additional year. Enclosed (McLeod handed the envelope to Maurice) are the notarized executed title of this boat, the insurance policies, and other relevant documents. Notice that I transferred the boat in your name six months ago."

Philomena pushed her chair away from the table; standing, she stepped over to McLeod, bent over, and kissed him on both cheeks.

Maurice held the envelope and said, "Monsieur, you have touched my heart. I am indebted." McLeod stopped him with a hand wave and a smile, saying, "The two of you know me well. I do what I do because it pleases me to do it."

Maurice insisted on completing his thought, "But I can never return such generosity." Neither Maurice nor Philomena asked questions or continued conversing. After years of Serving McLeod, the relationship unceremoniously ended.

"Philomena and Maurice have a long, comfortable, wonderful life." McLeod pushed the chair away from the table, stood, faced outboard, and said, "I see the harbormaster's launch is making its way toward the minesweeper. Goodbye!" McLeod turned away from the minesweeper and, without looking back, left for the launch.

Two Down, One to Go

In a day, McLeod was back in Miami. His first telephone call was to Sepúlveda. "Hello,

Raymond. I did not inform you of my decision to leave Panama; nevertheless, I'm here in...."

"Yes, you're in Miami," Sepúlveda interjected. "If your boat was gone after pre-paying for two months of anchoring and you left after less than five weeks, something must have prompted you. I also figured you would go to Miami."

"You're a regular Sherlock," McLeod joked.

"I'll be in Miami tomorrow," Sepúlveda informed McLeod. "I have some information we need to discuss."

"Great," McLeod responded, "see you in the afternoon."

McLeod sensed that Sepúlveda had a peculiar attitude; he sounded irritated. From downstairs, George called, "Mr. McLeod, Charlie is on the way up." Stunned by the announcement, there was a knock at the door before he could adjust to the surprise. He opened the door, and Charlie rushed into his arms.

"My dear Mr. McLeod, those delicious lips are like low-hanging fruit." She kissed him, sinking her succulent lips into his and tightening her arms around his upper shoulders and neck. He returned the embrace by lifting her into his chest. When she came up for air, Charlie dropped her bag, reached for his right hand with her left, and led him into the bedroom while offering a suggestion.

"No talking. Let's take off our clothes, jump into the shower, soap each other, and then dip ourselves into the huge bathtub with Jasmine. I want us to be clean and smell delicious when we climb into bed."

McLeod complied. Lovemaking ensued. The night evolved to morning; Charlie was up early. She made coffee. McLeod awoke. He put on his bathrobe and wandered into the kitchen nook.

"I wanted to thank you, Mr. McLeod," Charlie greeted him with a kiss. "It is always my pleasure to please," McLeod responded. "You should know that Sepúlveda is coming over this afternoon."

"That's fine, Mr. McLeod; I can hang out at the pool while you have your man talk."

"What is this, Mr. McLeod stuff?"

"You know, I have no idea. I start stuff for no reason. Please think of it as an endearment."

"Oh, by the way," Charlie continued, "Colonel Calvo was murdered in Panama about ten days ago. The police suggested the murderer was the parent of an abused child. Not surprisingly, the chief of police said that there were no suspects. Therefore, there is no case to follow up on. You wouldn't know anything about that, would you?" Charlie stated, her face twisted into a smirk.

"Colonel Calvo, you say. Well, as I understand it, he had it coming," McLeod remarked.

"The plane from Panama City arrives at 1:00, so I assume Mr. Sepúlveda will arrive around 3:00 this afternoon. Let's head down to the beach and go on a 30-minute run. We can run to the yacht basin and walk back. Doesn't that sound like great fun?" And asked, "What do you think?"

McLeod smiled, "Good ideas are all you've had since you got here."

By 3:00, McLeod was back in the Jockey Club. Sepúlveda was facing McLeod, sipping some iced tea; McLeod held a chilled glass of Pinot Noir. Sepúlveda opened the conversation, "Marin called me regarding some murders, one in Arlington, Virginia, and the other in Panama; he asked if I knew anything about them. Commander Cornfield and Colonel Calvo are dead; both are associated with Marin's insurance company. I think he's beginning to wonder if he's next." Cautioning McLeod, "I am not going to ask you anything that would prove compromising or embarrassing."

Sepúlveda continued, "On the same Marin phone call, he mentioned the killings and followed up by asking for a meeting with you. And he called you by name."

"The plot thickens," McLeod responded.

"He wants the meeting in Miami tonight in the Commanders Club at Miami International."

It sounds like a safe place to meet; I like it." McLeod comments. What time?"

"At 7:00 PM," Sepúlveda responds. "And one more thing: He only wants you at this meeting, not anyone else, including me."

"Now that's out of the park," McLeod exclaimed. "I wouldn't miss this for the world."

Sepúlveda says, "I don't know what to make of this development. He wanted me to know about the meeting; otherwise, he would have called you directly. He also wanted me to know about the disinvitation, which I found a bit rude. Aside from feeling better for seeing you in person, I wanted to inform you about the Marin meeting, hoping you might let Marin know that you wouldn't meet him without me. You should know that it's my ego that's disappointing. I am staying at the Miami Airport Hotel and leaving on the 8:00 AM flight back to Panama tomorrow. Please call me tonight and fill me in. Admittedly, my curiosity has gotten the best of me. I need to know what this guy is up to."

Sepúlveda stood and wished McLeod good luck as he walked toward the elevator.

Looking for Charlie, McLeod took the stairs to the pool. Charlie was sitting in the shade, reading Town & Country magazine, when she spotted McLeod approaching.

"Well, how was that man-to-man chat?" Charlie asked.

"Very intriguing; I've never seen Sepúlveda so out of sorts. He's anxious about something. He feels he is no longer the ringmaster. It is as if his ten-year-old self just found out his outrageously priced front-row seat for Saturday is worthless because the circus left town in the middle of the night."

"Now that is intriguing," Charlie admitted.

"Marin wants to meet me alone tonight at the Commander's Club at Miami International," McLeod shared.

"My dear Mr. McLeod, "this telling is the first time you have willingly brought me into the game. It could be that my seduction is a complete success, or developments have changed so drastically that you've decided there's a bona fide need for my input."

"Which of the two do you think it is?" McLeod sneeringly retorted, "So, you're asking which of the two?" Charlie repeats, "I prefer to think that it was both, knowing that without the seduction, the need for me may have never developed." Charlie confidently remarked while spreading her legs just enough to invite McLeod to seek further discovery.

"Legs are slightly spreading," observed McLeod, and with a smirk, whisperingly detects, "I see this seduction is ongoing."

"Well," Charlie explains, "you're a male and, as with most males, constantly on the hunt, compelled to chase after the never enough."

"Hmm, a woman's insight into the subtle distinctions of maledom predilections. But let's return to Marin's invitation," McLeod suggests. "You're thinking this out-of-nowhere summons is an invite into servicing an archaic problem or a recently matured development?"

"I have no idea, Mr. McLeod, but no charade is required for who you are or your interest. I assume there must be, at least in Marin's mind, an alignment and intersect of mutuality."

"Possibly," McLeod speculates, "this Marin meeting is the first stage of entrapping me. But then, looking at the practical, for reasons unknown, no assassin has shot me, beaten me senseless with an aluminum bat, nor has a Mexicana from Guadalajara run me over in a stolen car. Hell, I am as baffled, I assume, as Sepúlveda must be."

"I'll take you to the airport and wait. So, I will be the first to know. This airport meeting is an exciting adventure, Mr. McLeod."

"As I recall, you have no driver's license; well, at least in possession," McLeod commented.

"I see you've been snooping and scouring through my belongings again," Charlie rebutted.

"No, not again," McLeod responded, "from memory only."

Charlie took the passenger's seat, and McLeod drove. The airport was thirty-five minutes away, so they left themselves an hour just in case the unforeseen appeared. Charlie followed McLeod into the airport and agreed to wait at the bar across from the Commander Club. The club was upstairs before the departure gate security. McLeod pressed the button for entry. The door buzzed, and McLeod walked in.

As if forewarned, the attendant asked, "Mr. McLeod, I presume?"

"Yes."

"Lovely," the greeter commented, "follow me. Our member has reserved a conference room."

Upon entry, Marin stood and greeted McLeod with an outstretched hand. "We have never met, but of course, I have been aware of you for some time. Please sit. Coffee?"

"Yes, coffee would be perfect," McLeod answered.

Marin poured a cup and handed it to McLeod. "You take your coffee black, don't you?"

"You know my preference. You have me at a disadvantage," McLeod commented while grasping the coffee cup.

"Please, Mr. McLeod," Marin cajoled, "you're way too modest. I have experienced firsthand your ability to gather information. Coffee black was on an observation report I recently scanned in preparation for this encounter. As you can now observe, I am pouring a cup of coffee, adding a generous helping of cream and sugar, and I will likely drink several cups before our discussion is complete. But more importantly, permit me to move you to an advantage."

"You offer an advantage; well, we are off to a great start," McLeod chided as he sipped his hot coffee.

"And I would like to double down on that advantage," Marin continued. "Speaking frankly, I reached out to you to align your interests with mine. Such an alignment is possible. It certainly is sensible, but I also understand that such an alignment, at least in the first case, will be challenging for you to believe. You have every reason to distrust. Therefore, our first task is to establish a credible level of believability. I understand that all relationships have their built-in negatives. Nevertheless, the stakes are high enough for me to warrant a good college try, so I decided to ask for this meeting."

Marin reached for his cup of coffee and took a sip. "Mr. McLeod, Raymond, for reasons I can no longer remember, told me of his engagement with you. I never thought the Sepúlveda engagement would lead to endangerment. Of course, I was unaware of your history with Dr. Li. Richly connected in Cuba, she has made friends with the powerful and has used the services of Mr. Sepúlveda in the past."

Noting that tidbits of information regarding Sepúlveda as attractive, McLeod bluntly revealed, "I do not want to behave discourteously, but I think we do need to get to the reason you called this meeting."

"I see you are conversationally impatient. I welcome your bluntness. So, speaking pointedly, Mr. McLeod, Sepúlveda tells me that you, for reasons of revenge, want to kill, as you call him, the Russian. And I want the Russian killed, so we are in simpatico. And to that end, cheers," as Marin raises his cup."

"Well," a surprised McLeod responded with a reciprocal, "cheers." Regarding the Russian, although the director of human resources informed me at the time of my hiring that I would be working for Maximilian Ivanov, I have never had a one-on-one meeting with my boss. I had seen him at a distance. At least three other men always accompanied him when he rarely appeared. I understood I should never speak to him, not even a casual greeting. I was told never to look him in the eye assertively.

On the other hand, I have had many meetings with Dr. Li and have taken directives from her and her staff. But since her death, according to the corporate operating agreement, I should receive my guidelines and instructions from a scheduled board of directors meeting. I have not received any guidelines from the board. And there has been no corporate board meeting since the death of Dr. Li. Questions, Mr. McLeod?"

"Yes, sort of," McLeod injects. "Rumor has it that the Russian is not and has never been a person of decision-making authority; all the authority rests with Dr. Li."

"There's truth to that," Marin continues. "Dr. Li did assure me of the Russian's brutality, anticipatory genius, and innate predator innateness. Only God knows the truth. I can only relate my experience. All authority rests with Dr. Anh Li. She used that Russian as a bite noir, a bogeyman to keep me and everyone else in line."

"You want me to kill this bogeyman?" McLeod exclaims, "Why?"

"That's a good question," Marin responds," and one of the driving nails to build our bridge of mutual interest. Mr. McLeod, the business environment I have been dealing with is complicated."

"You can stop there," McLeod insists, "I am not interested in your reason. I am interested in the reasoning behind this, just the down-and-dirty details. Please, no more detours. I'm not interested in stepping onto the merry-go-round of your thoughts."

"Mr. McLeod, please, do not bully me with your insistence on brevity; I will try to edit; however, I am not reading from a prepared statement. Please allow me to continue at my meandering pace.

Marin continued, "Dr. Anh Li had discovered that two veteran board directors of the company, Calvo and Cornfield, were cheating the company out of hundreds of thousands of premium revenues. They perpetrated this scheme by redirecting policies that have historically paid commissions to house accounts and then directing these payments to one of their agent companies' benefits. I want to emphasize that no similar fraud has been detected in any audit. Nevertheless, Anh Li discovered the theft and waited for the right time to announce the missing capital. Because Calvo and Cornfield were very connected and regularly contacted the most valued clients, retribution for their fraud was a delicate maneuver. Stage left, enters Gunnery Sergeant McLeod. A person with a disconnected history and differing motivations hunted down Calvo and Cornfield. As if acting purposefully in the interest of the Old Dutch, our vengeful angel unknowingly made sure their embezzlement cost them their lives. And most blessedly, these acts of justice occurred before the sale."

"Wow! "You and yours are shrewd," McLeod assured Marin. "I'll be sure my accountants invoice you properly for services rendered."

You undoubtedly," McLeod affirms, did not invite me here to pound your chest and applaud your genius. Please tell me what it is you want."

A frustrated Marin says, "As stated, I want you to kill Maximillian!"

"I have been informed that Charlie is downstairs," Marin noted with a slight smile.

"You know of Charlie?" McLeod interjected, knowing the answer could have consequences.

"I met Charlie when she was a teenager; however, I do know for a fact that neither you nor Charlie works for the Russian," Marin, once again, out of context, confidently answers a question never asked.

He goes on with his aggravations. "The crux of my issues with Old Dutch started with Dr. Li's death. Since then, I have been managing Old Dutch. I have increased its B.E.S.T rating to a BB+ from a double C. However, with the sale, my efforts will be of little consequence to the new owners. I am often underappreciated, which fuels my pride, ambition, and strong need for recognition. I am the presiding officer of Old Dutch, and I am responsible for finalizing an acquisition that will result in my termination of employment. I have no employment agreement. Why would I willingly eliminate my position, per my affirmation of the forthcoming definitive agreement?"

The redness of his face slowly dissipates. Marin sipped his coffee while preparing to explain further, "I believe the time to act is now. I must belay the current deal until I gain absolute control over Old Dutch."

"The current deal is something Dr. Anh Li and Sepúlveda worked out?" McLeod inquired.

"Yes, which I endorsed, nonetheless. I am in a time-sensitive situation with little time left," Marin responded. "Dr. Anh Li expertly understood the company's nuances. She had the Castro family's blessings and had purchased their equity. Her daughter received and is presently in possession of all sorts of delightfully pertinent information. But most importantly, she has in-hand custody of the Russian's bearer shares, which, once affirmed in the shareholder meeting, will cede most of the Old Dutch to the holder.

"Just so I understand," McLeod interjected, "You are endeavoring to recruit Dr. Anh Li's daughter into your scheme, but you have not heretofore succeeded."

"Yes, that is accurate. I cannot attract the daughter's interest enough to even look at my offer." Marin replied.

McLeod asked, "Do you know if she has an interest?"

"She has conceded to the idea of meeting to discuss, but she is elusive about a date. Aside from the bearer shares, Anh Li's daughter has critically important legacy documents. I need to obtain this information before the acquisition audit is conducted. Now, I know I need to make it worthwhile."

"What exact information do you need?" McLeod asked.

"She inherited all her mother's acquisition deal rights," Marin declared. "But more importantly, her mother, and now I assume she has the minute book, all the corporate resolutions, unissued treasury shares, and other such items of importance. Without the documents, I am mindlessly blind; I have not read Dr. Li's revised company operating agreement. I must review those documents and amend the operating agreement before the acquisition audit. And you would desire in-hand possession of such documents," McLeod suggested.

"Yes, Mr. McLeod, you have grasped the obvious," Marin confirmed. And I would make her an excellent cash offer for her equity position with Old Dutch."

"As I understand the sequence of events, after affirming the binding letter of intent. Everyone waits for auditing, licensing, and vetting results by multiple governing domiciles; you're in a unique position within the company. The board has lost Dr. Anh Li's leadership. Today, you're the man," McLeod affirms.

"Hmm...well, yes, but what are you driving at?" quips Marin.

"Today," McLeod predicts, "you are the man; the president, post-merger, you're out with nothing but severance."

"You've captured the situation. My tenure as president is over as Anh as the deal is consummated."

"What is the reason you want this Russian dead?" McLeod asked pointedly. "You need to be very clear; why is killing the Russian so important to you?"

"Here I am aiding and abetting the killing of a dangerous man, the very apex of your revenge, and you need to know why. My reasoning is irrelevant. "

"Well, it may seem irrelevant to you, but unless you're willing to disclose the reason...," McLeod emphasized, "I think our pact may be mortally injured before we engage."

"You are as difficult a man as my briefings suggested. Plain and simple, I fear the Russian. Cornfield, Calvo, and the rest of the board relied on me as the licensed president throughout the purchase process. But post-merger, I know too much. I stayed too long. Therefore, they, possibly the Russian, will silence me. Frankly, Mr. McLeod, I need the Russian dead to ensure my survival. You have extracted the information there. Are we now in agreement to kill him?"

McLeod responded with an affirmation, "If you can accommodate the opportunity, yes, I will kill him."

"Reaching an accommodation with Anh Li's daughter is a matter of negotiation," Marin asserts. He then answers his assertion, "Well, yes is the short answer. But I think the daughter can do more than provide information. I need to review the documents to determine the exact scope of my corporate authority during the acquisition phase. She can vote for those shares in my favor before the acquisition takes place. In other words, she can guarantee an endorsement of my professional status." Marin continued, "My pre-approved employment agreement requires affirmation if it is not before the sale. I'm out."

Marin passes a thin white envelope to McLeod. Inside are two made-to-bearer Bank of Commerzbank, AG of Frankfurt cashier's checks for One Hundred Thousand U.S.D each. Marin advises, "If you agree right now, one is cashable today—the other upon my affirmation of the task completed."

"This is undoubtedly the strangest, most bizarre, outrageously convoluted meeting I have ever had, "McLeod surmised.

Marin explained, "These checks induce you to perform a task you profess as your intention. It is an additional incentive to rid the world of a notorious bully.

"That's motivating," McLeod concedes. "You will develop a plan founded on what?"

"Surprise coupled with access," Marin confidently touts two powerful tactics. Besides, I don't have an alternative. I can't simply walk away. He would kill me anyway. As stated, my only out is to act first."

"All right. Anything else?" McLeod inquired.

"I want you to end your involvement with Sepúlveda. I will be working closely with Raymond to finalize the sale of Old Dutch. I do not want any real or perceived conflict slightly influencing this for-sale endeavor."

"I can sympathize with your perceived predicament and will inform Sepúlveda. I'll take the first hundred; however, you understand I may not find it possible to earn the second. It all will depend on how you set up the opportunity. You have endorsed Max's super competence, labeling him a genius grandmaster. Now, at the risk of your life, you are betting he knows nothing of your plot and plan."

"You want this Russian dead because he played a part in the killing of Team 33. Since the incident, this has been your life's desire. You're executing this as your final act of contrition. However, for me, killing Max is a no-choice decision. For me to live, Max must die."

"Ok," McLeod acknowledged, "enough of this chit-chatting."

After you disengage, Sepúlveda contact me," Marin concluded.

McLeod responded, "I will not need to contact you. Sepúlveda will immediately call you."

Marin rose, extended his hand, and said he had a flight within the hour.

McLeod shook the extended hand and asked, "If you have not seen your boss in years and have not heard from him in months, how do you know he is alive?"

"Marin answered, "If he is alive, his death is yours to ensure. And if he is dead, you're $100,000 ahead."

"Good enough," McLeod replied and left the lounge.

Charlie was engaged in conversation with two male travelers at the bar. She had positioned herself to see McLeod when he returned to retrieve her—seeing McLeod, she abruptly withdrew from the conversation and started walking towards him.

"How do we get out of here?" Charlie asks. "I always seem disoriented in airports."

Still considering Marin's proposition, McLeod should have paid more attention to the exit signs.

After finding her way, Charlie cried out, "This way!" She reached down to grasp McLeod's hand.

They walked past the busy departure area toward the parking lot in silence. Once in the car, McLeod said, "That was not a boring meeting."

McLeod begins his recollection, "The only thing missing in that meeting was Bacall and Bogart. He wants me to kill the Russian. As a condition, Marin requires that I sever my Sepúlveda relationship and then stand by for further instructions.

" McLeod paused with a slight smile, then thanked me for assisting him with the disposal of Cornfield and Calvo and showed his appreciation by offering two checks totaling two hundred thousand dollars."

"Big bucks, considering you'd do it for free." Charlie asks, "What do you think of the guy?"

"Marin is a manipulative fabricator utilizing a whiff of truth to create a whole bunch of misdirection. For me, his nom de plume is "unimpressive schemer." He certainly is an opportunist. His time in power at Old Dutch is coming to an end. He is one shareholder meeting away from removal as president. Therefore, he is anxious, which has moved him into fits of desperate spontaneity. He is unpredictable and inclined to act upon what may not exist."

"I don't understand," Charlie said.

"He's betting that the three goddesses of fate will align with his perceived outcome," McLeod answered.

"Three goddesses of fate, are you changing the subject? You're still unclear, but setting that aside, did you learn anything new?

"Well," McLeod resolved. "He does not work for Ivan. Let me clarify this discussion with a definitive. I now doubt Ivan's dominating influence on anything material. This Russian is akin to the myths of King Arthur or Robin Hood. The difference is that Ivan did exist at least once and for some time, but I doubt his authoritative existence in the present."

"Myths akin to King Author, what does that mean? Are you saying the Russian, or Ivan as you called him, is more a legend than a threat?" Charlie quizzed.

"According to Marin, he has only seen the Russian from a distance, and that was long ago. At least until recently, his directives came from Dr. Anh Li."

"Therefore," Charlie declared, your assertion is?"

"That, more than likely, the holding company created by Dr. Anh Li is the linchpin that controls Old Dutch; the lingering variable is the Russian's bearer debentures. I don't believe Marin is much of a strategist. He's getting help from someone."

"Maybe, Sepúlveda? Ok, Mr. McLeod, enough of this subject; I'm hungry. Let's go to Joe's in South Beach. I have a yearning for some crab."

"Wow," McLeod exclaimed, "that's an excellent choice. Joe's place has an excellent bartender, and I could chew on a big fat steak."

At 10:00 AM the next day at the Jockey Club, McLeod drank his second cup of coffee. The phone rang. It was George, the valet.

"Mr. McLeod, Mr. Sepúlveda is on his way up." There was a knock at the door.

"Wow, what happened to your 8:00 AM flight?" McLeod inquired.

"I could be coy and offer some uninspiring excuse, but because you did not call. This morning, curiosity got the best of me. I just had to find out what that meeting was all about." Sepúlveda explained.

"Well, all right. How about some coffee? Let's sit out on the patio. It's still cool out," McLeod suggested.

"Coffee...perfecto! I can always use another cup of caffeine."

Once seated, Sepúlveda spoke first. "Well, fill me in."

"Marin started the meeting," McLeod explained, "with a thank you for serving his interest in riding the world of Cornfield and Calvo. Marin then offered me a hundred thousand to kill the Russian. However, he did insist that I terminate my business relationship with you."

"Terminate our relationship?" Sepúlveda questioned.

"He told me that your engagement with me was detrimental to his engagement with you. Of course, I had no idea you had an engagement, whatever that meant to Marin. We shook hands, and that's the meeting."

"Well, did the cash buy you off?"

"Yes, the cash has paid me off," McLeod answered bluntly and dismissively.

"Is our business relationship over?"

"Yes," McLeod confirmed.

"What! It took only one meeting, and that's it?"

McLeod answered, "The idea was to use Marin to introduce me to the Russian. Marin has offered cash and the means to satisfy my final quest. And for reasons unknown to me, you now have some agreement with Marin."

"Well, frankly, I am a bit shocked."

"Please stop there; if you have any monies owed, send me an invoice."

"Very generous of you, Mr. McLeod; nevertheless, I am disappointed and frankly still in shock," Sepúlveda declared.

"The grand game is over," McLeod announced. Sepúlveda stood and headed for the door. McLeod followed right behind him, moving a little faster and passing him on his left to open the door. A miffed Sepúlveda departed. Upon Sepúlveda's departure, McLeod realizes that Marin's request was a blessing regardless of his motive.

Sepúlveda was no longer a confidante. His viability was spent. But even beyond that realization. McLeod felt that Marin and Sepúlveda were in cahoots with each other for their private reasons. It was just a feeling, but McLeod sensed a setup was in the works. An unknowable negative floated across his mind. Regardless of all the nuances and entangled what-ifs, there was nothing left for McLeod to do but wait.

While waiting seemed to be the order of the day, Charlie nestled comfortably into McLeod's life. She engaged him at every conceivable level, but did so, at least outwardly, because it pleased her. Two weeks had passed since the meeting with Marin, and life was blissful.

"My dear Miss Charlie," McLeod beckoned after a delicious home-cooked dinner, "I have been waiting some more for Marin to act. He told me that time was running against him, yet I am here waiting."

"So," Charlie remarked, "you're tired of waiting? I do believe your waiting is ending."

"More insightfulness from Charlie, the clairvoyant. McLeod quipped. "Truth be known," McLeod continued, "I am not tired of waiting. Frankly, I have never been more content; I enjoyed this wait. There's only one thing pressing on my mind."

"Pray, tell," Charlie inquired. "What could that pressing thing be?"

"I think it is time I meet your friend, take a blood test, and see if she is my daughter."

"Wow, so forceful a demand," Charlie responded.

"Eventually," McLeod added, "Marin will contact me. He wants to partner with your friend, whom he believes is my daughter. Does it not seem reasonable to meet her before I act on whatever Marin prepares? I assume you are here with me because you have not received further instructions."

"It seems my cooking has prompted an after-dinner fit of feistiness," Charlie mused. "I'll need to check the ingredients in this recipe."

"My dear Charlie, I am much better with you. Nevertheless, if I have a daughter, even after all these Years...."

Her index finger crossed her lips, and Charlie stopped McLeod from talking. "Mr. McLeod," Charlie harshly stopped, explaining, "you have no rights even if she is your daughter. On the other hand, she has the right to reject or accept. She can manipulate, contrive, and distance herself from your presence."

"Damn, Charlie," McLeod forcefully injected, "I did not want to anger you."

"Well, then, select your words with caution."

"Ok," McLeod pleaded, "I believe my falling in lust with you has evolved into love. Withstanding its freakiness and disbelief, I do love the idea of it. I love the idea, even when it is obvious that your lovemaking is solely a carnal exercise. Although lovely, sex does not indicate anything meaningful. I accept that actuality as the price of participation. As you have said to me on more than one occasion, you are the intermediary, the messenger, and the loyal friend of a young lady who could be my daughter. Well, it is time to get this, whatever this is, settled."

"Fine," Charlie agreed, "I'll go to Paris to meet and chat with her. She may not be willing to meet with you."

"Wow," McLeod spurted out, "that's it? You're going to Paris? Is that simple?"

"What should I have said?" Charlie retorted. "You're demanding an audience; I'll book a flight for the next day."

"So, you're leaving me again," McLeod exclaimed. He muttered, 'But at least this time, I created the cause.' "Hopefully, you will stay in touch and return quickly," McLeod beseeched. Charlie did not respond.

"If you want to see her, you must fly to Europe. I know Li's daughter will not come to the United States."

"All good, Charlie," McLeod acknowledged. "I will willingly go to Paris."

"Then it is settled," Charlie declared as she left the dining room." True to form, Charlie refused a lift to the airport and left the Jockey Club by limo hours before her flight's boarding. Knowing her abrupt nature, McLeod had laid surveillance plans to access Charlie's whereabouts. The Jockey Club's limo driver, paid for by McLeod, was prearranged to report his passenger's destination address and call McLeod.

As she entered the car, Charlie asked the driver to stop at the Bank of America in Bal Harbor, just minutes away. When she got out of the limo, she told the driver 'Thank you,' gave him a tip, and said she didn't need him anymore. She gathered her bag and disappeared into the bank.

Although the drop-off was surprising, McLeod parked across the street from the bank's entrance and waited about 30 minutes. Finally, she emerged carrying a separate, medium-sized black leather bag. She walked onto the sidewalk in front of the bank; a black Lincoln Town Car sedan drove up with a driver and another man on the passenger side. The car stopped in front of Charlie. The passenger door opened, and a large man stepped out. He couldn't be sure, but the guy looked like one of the men she had been talking to at the airport while waiting for the Marin meeting to end. McLeod followed the sedan to the airport and witnessed Charlie's entrance.

All McLeod could surmise was that Charlie's purpose for this detour from the airport was to pick up documentation. He left the airport wondering.

After two weeks of Charlie's departure and Sepúlveda cast aside, McLeod was anxious, frustrated, and grievously lonely. Having not heard from Marin, he asks himself, Is it Marin who was playing a trick on him? He quickly answered, No, not after paying him a hundred thousand. Charlie was in Europe. Furthermore, she had not called either of them.

There was a knock at the door. It was George, "Mr. McLeod, a special delivery came for you." McLeod thanked George, closed the door, and opened the package.

The note reads: Mr. McLeod, enclosed, you will find an open return reservation for a first-class Delta ticket departing from Miami International to Charles de Gaulle, Paris, the following Monday. The return flight was not scheduled, and hotel reservations and an itinerary were enclosed at the Four Seasons George V Paris. The hotel will send a limo upon your arrival at Charles de Gaulle Airport. There was no signature or identification.

Finally, McLeod thought, she acted. Charlie was not stringing him along. He was delighted.

The flight to Paris was perfect. His luggage and the limo arrived as forecasted. It was a bit cool, with a slight mist in the air. The driver assured him that the fog was typical of Parisian weather at this time of year. Aside from the weather report, the driver asked no questions and offered no conversation. The limo pulled in front of the hotel.

Finally in Paris

The door attendant, accompanied by valets, bounced onto the luggage; the doorman's greeting was sincere. McLeod was impressed by the collaboration between the limo driver and the hotel staff. The staff knew his name and respectfully addressed him by it.

The hotel's resident manager came forward within a minute, accompanied by a hotel staffer, "Mr. McLeod, my name is David Fitzgerald; this is my assistant Jennifer. Would you please call me David? I am pleased to welcome you to the Four Seasons St. George V. Jennifer will escort and assist with check-in."

"Perfect," McLeod responded, "it has been a long flight."

"Yes, Mr. McLeod, you have my sympathy. And to relieve the discomfort, please, with the hotel's compliments, at your leisure, call our Spa, and they will send one of our skilled massage therapists to lessen the tension and aid with the time zone adjustment."

"Thank you, David," McLeod replied. "It is interesting to be greeted by an Irishman in Paris."

"Yes, Mr. McLeod, there is a commonality in labor trade; we Europeans are dispersed throughout Europe."

A young lady with a distinctive Scottish accent greeted and guided him. She, sporting a dimple-enhanced welcoming smile, welcomed him to Paris while passing an envelope with his name imprinted on the front. She escorted him to his room and told him about the hotel's restaurant, bar, and spa services on the journey. McLeod opened the envelope; it read, "Dear Mr. McLeod, Welcome to Paris." I'll give you two days to adjust to the time change, Charlie.

The note was satisfying, acknowledging his whereabouts and Charlie's interest. Still, it fell far short of her lying in his hotel bed awaiting his arrival or telling him to meet her downstairs at Harry's Bar.

As anticipated, two days passed without a word, and then the telephone rang on the morning of the third day.

"Mr. McLeod?" the caller queried.

"Yes," McLeod responded.

"My name is Varinia Michalun. The hotel contacted me, and the concierge called my office. I understand you are interested in viewing the daylight sights of Paris."

"Possibly," McLeod answered. She knew he had not asked for a tour of Paris, but thought this might be something Charlie had arranged.

"Shall we meet in the lobby, or what is your preference?"

"Please come up to the suite," McLeod suggested. "I will order a continental breakfast with tea and coffee?"

"Tea, please," Varinia replied. "I will have the hotel staff escort me to your room."

"Wonderful," McLeod exclaimed, "see you in the morning."

There was a knock at the door. McLeod opened it to find a young woman in her mid-to-late twenties. Varinia dressed conservatively, wearing a hat, gloves, and a thin, woolen, red-and-black checkered jacket to match the weather. A black purse strung over her right shoulder as she stood, arms at her side. She displayed a twinkle of innocence; her smile was wholesome and genuine. She was a disquiet young lady seeking confirmation that all was tranquil and sane with her new client as she endeavored to walk into his room.

"Good morning, Mr. McLeod; I'm Varinia Michalun."

"And a perfect morning to you; please come in and make yourself comfortable," McLeod countered. "The breakfast with tea service is on its way."

Varinia selected a seat, and the doorbell rang. It was the waiter with the tea service. In a few minutes, the tea was poured, and with coffee in hand, McLeod asserted, "I received a note informing me of your coming."

"Yes, that's normal company procedure," Varinia responded. I can assure you that you will not be disappointed with the magical beauty of Paris."

"So, you are a professional Parisian host. In other words, was the assignment just the luck of the queue, or was there a recommendation from my friend Charlie?" McLeod asked.

"I am not familiar with Charlie," Varinia verified. She then changed the subject. "I realize that the time change is a physical reality that has its effect, so please advise me when this adjustment induces you to sleep or just rest with your eyes closed," Varinia insisted.

"Time will not deter a lovely tour of the multi-cultural blessings of Paris."

"So," McLeod asked, "when does this Parisian adventure begin?"

"As you request, Mr. McLeod," Varinia answered. "I have scheduled some options depending on your preference."

"Firstly," McLeod suggested, "we could walk when you've finished your tea. Let's say for about thirty minutes. While walking, we can discuss these options while helping me with this cooped-up feeling."

"Of course," Varinia positively declared.

"By the way," McLeod inquires. "What does your firm charge for services rendered?"

"Because you are a premium guest, the hotel pays for my services." Satisfied with this response, McLeod prepares to depart.

The walk was brisk. Varinia took off on Rue Pierre Charron, reaching Av. The Champs-Élysées in a matter of minutes. Turning right, they continued with a series of right turns until they returned to the hotel. Varinia was disappointed when McLeod preferred waiting to see how he felt before confirming the next day's schedule. Nevertheless, she stoically passed on her business card and smiled her way through the goodbye, ending with a please don't hesitate to call and a firm handshake.

The next day, after his early rise and the first cup of coffee, McLeod went to the gym. Save for one, the gym was empty. McLeod endured a weight workout followed by a 30-minute run on the treadmill. Satisfied that he had done enough, he headed to his suite and that second cup. While making a pot of coffee, there was a knock at the door.

He opened the door to find Marin wearing a Dodgers baseball hat and sunglasses; at his side was Sepúlveda. The sight of Marin standing next to Sepúlveda stunned his senses.

Recovery from the shock was slow and visible. The accompanying uniformed hotel valet noted McLeod's disappointment at not being notified. Knowing he had broken protocol, the valet lowered his head and retreated. Marin and Sepúlveda walked in. Sepúlveda started to explain, nudged aside by Marin, who took off his sunglasses, folded them, set them in the right pocket of his light blue all-weather jacket, and began to speak. "I can imagine your utter shock to see us here together." "Yes, I'm slowly recovering," McLeod uttered. I am particularly impressed with the confirmation that even in this Five-Star hotel, a large tip to the right person will get you in a room without giving the guest a heads-up." Please sit. Coffee, tea, or liquor? Both men waved off the offerings.

"After our meeting in Miami," Sepúlveda emphasizes, "the acquisition deal advanced to a binding agreement. It is now critical to the deal that we settle with your daughter."

"And why are you convinced I am the father of Anh Li's daughter?"

"The assumption," Marin injects, "initially came from remarks Doss referenced; he said the father was a Marine Dr. Li knew in Vietnam. No one thought much of it. Now we know that Marine is you. Also, Charlie is all over you, and we know she is remarkably close to the daughter. I believe she's hanging with you for a reason."

Sepúlveda chimes in, "The Procedure is to call a shareholder meeting 30 days (about four and a half weeks) before signing the definitive agreement. Dr. Li's daughter must attend this compulsory meeting. Alternatively, proxy her vote or sell her shares. However, the lucrative sale to the Spanish company without finalizing a deal with Dr. Li's daughter is in jeopardy."

"And that's why you're in my hotel room?" McLeod inquires.

"Well, yes," Marin clarified. Charlie informed us of your meeting in Paris, so I took advantage of the opportunity to convince your daughter to accept my money and vote for my agenda in person."

Ignoring Marin's comment about his daughter, McLeod addressed Raymond. You were out of this madness. Hell, you made money, and you were out. Why do you want to come back?"

"My friend is upset with me; I thought my contribution to your quest was complete. I was never out; in Miami, per Marin's request, you dismissed me from further service."

"Raymond," McLeod responded, "I prefer to believe what you have said is truthful. However, our business dealings ended some time ago. Now you're here in Paris with Marin. Frankly, that's a bit disconcerting."

Marin interrupted, "As I understood the situation, the evil one is the Russian Max; he should be the target of your wrath, not Raymond. The Russian is the source of your revenge, the central perpetrator, the very one who ordered the killing of your Marines."

"Gentlemen, I understand the invite from Charlie was to see, per a blood test, if I am the father of Dr. Li's daughter. Killing this Russian is high on my list, but my interest is to see Charlie and settle the daughter issue. Not to discuss this Max guy's behavioral dysfunctions."

"Mr. McLeod," Marin inserts, "your daughter indirectly invited me here. She surely wants us to discuss my business offer and have you present. I took this as a positive occurrence."

"That sounds like you know something I do not," McLeod replied.

"Possibly," Marin asserts. "But I am not aware of any special insight."

"Charlie explicitly told me," McLeod affirms. If I wanted to meet Anh Li's daughter, I must do so in France."

"And how's the welcoming?" Marin inquires. "Any indication on when you'll meet?"

"I have received no communications from Charlie, McLeod insists. Then you show up with Sepúlveda after you told me you would develop a plan for me to kill this Russian. All this is happening while you're developing a business coup d'état that requires equity control of Old Dutch. To top it off, you're feeling is that Anh Li's daughter wants us to meet, but it's all conjecture."

"May I clarify?" Marin requested, and without waiting for an affirmation, he continued.

"So, I am extremely interested in seeing Anh Li's daughter and completing our agreement. The only other interest I have is our deal. The last I heard but never witnessed, Max is recovering from an injury and is recovering on his boat, which is impossible for you to penetrate."

McLeod switched topics without responding to Marin's explanation and asked, "Where is Charlie?"

"I have no idea," Marin replied. "I assume that she is here in the city."

"An assumption," McLeod sarcastically remarked. Gentlemen, this entire episode doesn't feel right. Unless I hear from Charlie, I plan to fly back to Miami. I am not feeling good about this, whatever this is."

"Mr. McLeod," Marin noted in an exceptionally soft, respectful tone, "it is time for me to leave. Raymond, why don't you stay and speak with your friend? We'll meet up later at our hotel for dinner." Marin walked out of the room, and the door shut behind him. Sepúlveda, in a meek conciliatory manner, as if trying to reconcile what he perceives as McLeod's disappointment, speaks, "I thought killing the Russian was the mission supreme."

"Raymond, you should say less than more right now; on second thought, it's better to say nothing. You know I distrust this Marin fellow. Your alignment with him is your business, but to be clear, I have no interest in either of you. Showing up in Paris with Marin and all these events together. Well, they verge on a negative that prompts many questions."

Sepúlveda, in a suggestive manner, Sepúlveda responded, "It was my work for you that induced me into this endeavor. Initially, I had no forethought other than to serve your interest. The deal unraveled, and bam, I'm in Paris with Marin."

"Sepúlveda, whether this explanation of yours spews the truth or not, I'll accept it. However, if I were you, I would make the most of the Old Dutch deal, take advantage of the risk-free opportunity, and get out of Dodge before Wyatt Earp shows up."

"Withdraw?" Sepúlveda quickly questioned. "That analysis sounds a bit extreme. Besides, without the physical evidence of the bearer shares, the situation," Sepúlveda explains, is all for naught."

Marin is a businessman striving to do his best for his interests. Because of his affiliations, you have read too much into Marin's position and intention. I am having dinner with him tonight. Will you join us?"

"Raymond," McLeod scowled, "I gave you my view of Marin. As a friend, I wish you had left it as we agreed in Miami. Many years ago, I was a lean, mean U.S. Marine. The simplicity of good and evil was evident, but that world is long gone. The replacement is an amoral, duplicitous, and often vacuous moving target of regret, wishing it were different. Pointedly, I am not that Marine of old."

"Remember," Sepúlveda enunciates, "your pursuit of revenge, the reason you contact me? You are one step away from satisfying your quest."

"Maybe! Chasing this Russian is like trying to capture a shadow. He is as much a myth as he is a reality. This image of him has been cast purposefully like a scarecrow guarding a farmer's crops. Everyone seems to play off him, but no one has seen him face-to-face in years."

Sepúlveda looked directly at McLeod, reaching up with two hands and cupping McLeod's shoulders. "Regardless of what you may presently think or what you may discover, I acknowledge that things have changed."

Sepúlveda's gesture and words did not sit well with McLeod; his former friend insinuated a foreboding already in place. He contemplates the terrain and situation, reminding himself that seeing Anh Li's daughter and Charlie matters.

"Remember," McLeod cautions Sepúlveda, "Marin is not the red Queen protecting her King but an untrustworthy mercenary Black Knight that can go backward as quickly as he can forward.

"We, you, always needed an insider, and of course, along with that insider is the inherent risk of being deceived," Sepúlveda stresses.

"All true, but as you said, things have changed. The mission no longer feels good. The truth is, regarding my analytical abilities, I have serious doubts. I am in Paris with no daughter, no Charlie, and no note or message. Marin is just showing up with you as his sidekick. If the Russian is as brilliant as his reputation, how did Marin travel to Paris without the Russian's knowledge? Most importantly, Charlie is not present, nor has she contacted me independently. Time to accept whatever this reality portends and head back home."

"I know my arrival in Paris standing next to Marin was a surprise, but maybe you're overthinking," Sepúlveda suggests, "creating dragons where none exist. You didn't even give him a real opportunity to talk and explain. Come to dinner; let's see what we can work out. Give an old friend a chance to redeem himself. We are staying at The Ritz Hotel. Dinner is in L'Espadon; the reservation is at 8:00; join us, and let's talk this through."

"You want to redeem yourself? Then, old friend, you should get on an airplane tonight and fly out of this mess. Forget about any obligation and walk away from everything," McLeod advised.

"Sorry, I'm not going to do that. I thought that our collaboration was about killing Max, the GRU agent. Whatever else I was involved in was irrelevant. I thought everything else between us would be fine. I was wrong."

They parted, each knowing the parting was their final act of friendship.

Diner at the Ritz

McLeod noticed the time was 11:27 AM, sensing something was going down, and decided to accept the Ritz dinner invitation.

There was another reason that going to the Ritz was inevitable. In the back of his mind lay a morsel of delusional thought, a thought that permeated his otherwise rational mindset. Melodiously delivered into his wanting-to-believe ears, a soft whispering tone seeped this illogical suggestion: "Charlie could be present at the dinner or even the daughter."

McLeod understood desperation, accepting that loneliness enables wishfulness, and the combination can create a mirage of what one wants to be true. Attending the dinner was a decision that had been made. Now, resting in his hotel room was the best way to cope with the boredom of waiting. Being close to a phone and sequestered is a usual situation. After a couple of hours, the hotel room phone rang. McLeod picked up the receiver. "Hello."

"It's me," the caller announced.

"Raymond," McLeod responded.

"Yes, you were right, Raymond acknowledged. "Since my engagement, I have not told you the whole truth. I worked with Dr. Li on the Spanish company's acquisition interest in Old Dutch, which involved several document reviews, as well as administrative and financial audits. One of the tasks was to investigate the workings of critical employees of Old Dutch and the personnel of the holding company Avoca. When I met you in Panama, I mentioned that I worked for a confidential source. I could not envision a conflict; however, if a dispute arose, I said I would drop my endeavor in favor of the other.

After Dr. Li's passing, I was able to leverage my position with Old Dutch and the Spanish insurance company. I knew the Russian was not an officer or director; the Spanish company never mentioned the Russian, and no one from Old Dutch, except Dr. Li, had communicated with him. Aside from that understanding, for my perceived benefit, I never advanced the possibility of aligning you in a position to satisfy your revenge. Per deception, I kept your revenge on the verge of a possibility that never existed.

I lied to myself and deceived you with a half-truth. This uncorrectable act has ruined our relationship; however, just between us, I request my confession and do not seek forgiveness or understanding."

"Well, Charlie did warn me.' McLeod notes, "I half-heartily decided not to believe her."

"Because of your Marine Corps Semper Fi mentality, it's understandable. I'm sincerely sorry about that. I have worked with Dr. Li, and the daughter knows me. Marin recognized the possibilities and offered a very lucrative alignment. The objective was to purchase the Bearer Shares and the essential documents; Marin felt that our relationships with Charlie and you were an advantage. Even though I passed on all information on your whereabouts and intentions to Marin, I convinced myself that my Marin partnership did you no harm."

"So, Marin did not care if I killed the Russian?"

Raymond interrupted, "The meeting at the airport was a sly cash-infused gesture."

"100,000, that's a lot of gestures," McLeod responded.

"Well, it wasn't his money; let's return to the primary. Marin recently informed me that plan B would be in place if the daughter failed to cooperate. He'd capture Charlie, kidnap the daughter, and force her into compliance.

The revelation of Plan B slapped me back into reality. I foolishly announced the immediate termination of my employment. My naivety became apparent within minutes, and I was too deep to extract. Marin pledged there would be no Plan B and pragmatically nudged me into traveling with him to Paris in a final attempt to deal with the daughter. The daughter messaged him that she was in Paris and was amenable to discussing selling her position in Old Dutch in person. Marin believed that the message proved her interest, and if approached correctly, the daughter would sell her position."

"You're traveling way too fast," McLeod cautions. "What did he offer you?"

"McLeod, you are always on point. His offer tantalized my ego, fed my greed, and incited my most base desires, and now I recognize that it created childlike aspirations, which prompted me to betray myself and you."

"Well, Raymond," McLeod started to respond.

"There is little time; please, I must speak uninterrupted. I have a son, grandchildren, and their precious mother. Years before there was a Margarita, I lustfully impregnated a young girl from my family's village near the Costa Rican border. She died shortly after giving birth, and I secretly took on funding to raise the child from afar. I wrongly thought my son, the child, was safe from my turbulence. It never occurred to me that any business affairs would jeopardize the safety of my son and grandchildren.

My son called, furious and scared. I have four grandchildren, three boys, and the youngest, Linda, is a kindergartener.

She is enrolled in a highly respected Catholic school near the family home. After school lunch, the nun scheduled a nap during the afternoon. The nun went to use the bathroom; she was gone for just a few minutes. When she returned, my little granddaughter was gone. Three hours later, she was walking home. She had a note in an envelope pinned to her dress. The note in English addressed to me read: Call this number 1-800-555-8888 within 36 hours (about 3 days) or the lives of your granddaughter and her entire family."

"My assumption," McLeod inquired, "is that you have moved your son's family to a haven."

"Yes, but a haven until when? My son's family is at risk. I cannot have the slightest possibility of anything happening to them."

"I am sorry," McLeod lamented. "Who is your primary suspect?"

Ignoring the question, Sepúlveda continued, "There is only one way for me to safeguard my son's family."

"How's that?" McLeod asked inquisitively.

Sepúlveda ignored that question as well and continued his explanation. "I excused myself from tonight's dinner. I have documents of immense interest to you; I will deliver what I have to your Miami address tonight."

Sepúlveda's voice was starting to tremble. His delivery was weak and hesitant. "I do fear that my situation is dire. In a quivering voice, "I strayed from my business ethics and moral convictions."

"All right, Raymond, calm down," McLeod coached.

"My dear friend, you cannot trust anyone. Castro has arrested Marcus Ochoa; do you remember the General? For my business interest and the specific harvesting of information, the General was, for Years, a primary source. I have a solution to protect my son and his family. Forgive me for my duplicitous behavior. I feel like a stupid old man who has lost the love and respect of his son. I just..."

McLeod interrupted, "Raymond, you leave tonight! Leave your bags; forget about the report. Just take what you can carry on your person and leave."

"I can't do that," he responded. The phone went dead.

McLeod immediately tried calling Raymond's room a couple more times. There was no answer. A shower and shave later, a rested McLeod headed to The Ritz Hotel. He called Raymond's room from the hotel's lobby phone. No answer.

Although the dinner was at 8:00, McLeod entered the Ritz at 7:30. He positioned himself to see the guests as they walked into the L'Espadon.

At 7:45, he was surprised to see Lucy. Marin's secretary from the Panama meeting walked briskly across the hotel lobby, wearing a loosely fitted formal business suit. With the guidance of the Maître d'hôtel, she walked directly to the awaiting table. Afterward, Marin alone showed up and sat across from Lucy.

Within minutes, the Chef de Rang appeared and joined the table in pleasant conversation. When conversing in Spanish, Lucy's mannerisms seemed more male than female. McLeod found her peculiar but pondered no more and ordered another lime and club soda.

Marin abruptly stood up from his table and walked directly toward McLeod upon noticing him.

"Hopefully," Marin suggested within earshot, "this means you have reconsidered and plan on joining me for dinner?"

"I certainly can join you," McLeod responded, "but if you don't mind, I'll drink my dinner. The time change still has me somewhere over the Atlantic. I have not adapted, plus, frankly, I am just not hungry."

"That's just fine," Marin responded. Raymond called. He said he was not feeling well, so we would have dinner."

The waiter greeted Marin by name, welcomed him back, and informed him that the chef had prepared his duck just as he liked it. Marin nodded with a pleasing smile.

"Are you a wine drinker?" Marin asks.

"Yes, I enjoy a fine bottle of red occasionally," McLeod confessed.

"Excellent!" Marin announced, "I will order you a bottle of the finest French grape. Of course, if you would like to include a glass or two of Walker Blue, please do not hesitate."

"Tell me," Marin requested, "Mr. McLeod, did Raymond call you this afternoon?"

"Yes, he did," McLeod confirmed. He told me he would lie down but looked forward to seeing me at dinner. I suppose he was persuading me to attend. Then, early in the evening, he called to tell me he was not feeling up to par and would not participate in the dinner."

"Hmm," Marin suggested, "earlier, when I left with you, he seemed perfectly fine. I'm a little perplexed by his absence, but you're my guest. And I am pleased. I will check on Raymond later, although Lucy called his room earlier, and there was no answer. Of course, he had the hotel hold all his calls."

"You seem worried," McLeod comments. "Is there something I should know?"

"Not that I'm aware," Marin responded. "Let's set Raymond aside for the moment. I have ordered a lovely French burgundy. I do love this wine. It is from one of my favorite vineyards; I know you will enjoy its flavor."

Marin was right; McLeod confirmed that the wine was delightfully full of discriminating flavors with no singular, pronounced taste. The blend made even an unsophisticated palate ask for more.

Upon opening the second bottle of wine, the first bottle had dispelled customary apprehensions. Marin was ready to discuss his essential topic. But just then, Lucy, who had returned from Raymond's room, rushed over to whisper in Marin's ear. One could see his concern. Marin stood up with a look of concern. "I'm so sorry, Mr. McLeod." Marin apologized. Raymond is not in his room; I need to inquire. Please finish the wine, and I will contact you very soon, certainly sometime tonight."

In a matter of minutes, McLeod left the restaurant. Satisfied that Sepúlveda had made a getaway, he crossed the lobby and headed for the hotel entrance.

"Mr. McLeod," Marin called out, spotting him. With two uniform hotel security personnel hurrying in his direction and accompanying Marin and Lucy, he could sense the urgency.

"It's Sepúlveda," Marin exclaimed. "When Lucy initially asked security to check on his room, they just checked his bed and lounge room. But on the second search, security on the second search found him in the bathtub full of bloody water. There was no note or evidence of any struggle; this unexpected event is very puzzling. I never figured him as a troubled man."

Marin asked McLeod before the police arrived if he wanted to see the body. McLeod replied, "Positively."

Raymond's tub was filled with bloody water, and he lay there. His eyes were closed, still fully clothed, less his shoes; the hotel phone was near the tub, and his tie was loosely knotted; his wrists revealed their mortal wounds. McLeod could not mindfully assimilate what his eyes revealed. He could not comprehend the meaningfulness of the apparent suicide. If a suicide, Sepúlveda had honestly acted out an unanticipated event. Without commenting, McLeod turned and walked out of Sepúlveda's room. He headed directly to the doorman and then took a taxi to his hotel.

The Abduction

Like an unpleasant aftertaste, thoughts of Sepúlveda's death lingered. All McLeod could think about was Sepúlveda's last conversation. Was this a sacrificial act? How did Max or Marin tie into this suicide? Or was he murdered? McLeod identified himself to hotel management as Raymond Sepúlveda's business partner. He noted that Raymond had no family and that if the hotel made all the arrangements, once the body was released, he would assume all the financial costs.

The phone rang. "Mr. McLeod?" the hotel employee asked. Mr. Marin is in the lobby. He would like to visit you in your room. Shall I escort him?"

"Is he alone?" McLeod inquired. "Yes, sir."

"Then yes, please escort Mr. Marin to my room."

Within moments, there was a knock; Marin responded to McLeod's unenthusiastic command, "Come on in; door's open."

"I assume the shock of Sepúlveda's death has not subsided," Marin quired in a conciliatory tone. Not expecting an answer, Marin immediately went on. "I certainly do not want to disrespect or seem insensitive to this tragedy; however, I have not heard from Dr. Li's daughter. Raymond's death unsettles me. I am at the Sheraton Airport Hotel at Charles De Gaulle this evening because I have an early morning flight tomorrow. This face-to-face is my only opportunity to speak with you."

Seeking a response, Marin paused; McLeod remained silent. Disregarding the awkwardness of the setting, Marin pressed on, "I sense that you are not ready to discuss the details of what I have created for the Russian's death. Nevertheless, I want you to know that my interest is the same as expressed at our first meeting. Let's give each other some time, say a couple of weeks. I'll contact you. I do believe in the kinship of our objectives. However, if your interest has waned, Mr. McLeod, I would be severely disappointed; I cannot overstress my need for your services." Without commenting on the substance of Marin's message, McLeod mustered a few insincere words, "Well then, in two weeks." McLeod walked over and opened the door; without another word, Marin walked out.

The tension created by Marin's appearance was real; McLeod could smell the stench of disingenuousness and the not-so-subtle twinge of a physical threat. Moreover, a spark ignited the infancy of a fresh revelation. Was it possible that Marin, insuring the house loss, was playing a shills' craps strategy of simultaneously betting on the come and didn't come? Wherein he'd hire me to kill the Russian while telling the Russian he's leveraging my relationship with Dr. Anh's daughter to locate and deliver the debentures? Or, quite possibly, Max the Russian is out of the playing field altogether.

If Marin does not favorably secure the debentures with Raymond's death, the sale of Old Dutch Indemnity is likely to be on hold or negated altogether; as a result, Anh's daughter will likely have supermajority control of Old Dutch by default.

As president of Old Dutch, Marin has no board members to limit his actions; he has unlimited power in an extralegal sense. However, if he fails to satisfy Dr. Anh Le's daughter, he must contemplate eliminating her physical presence. When sensing an unidentifiable danger in Vietnam, the hair on his arms and the back of his neck stood on end; goosebumps ran along his extremities. For McLeod, this once-familiar sensation usually signaled looming violence, a forewarning of mayhem and pending danger. Although unclear about his next move, McLeod knew that Marin had not successfully enlisted the daughter's cooperation in his offerings. As proof, he is leaving Paris.

McLeod knew he was unfamiliar with Paris; effectively, confined to his hotel and nearby surroundings, Charlie and Dr. Li's daughter's situation was not developing. He once again sensed an indescribable, lingering scent of lurking danger. He pondered the possible meaning of Marin's remark, "Let's say a couple of weeks." Marin's timeline was inexplicable. When coupled with the death of Sepúlveda and no sight of Charlie, everything seemed disjointed and beyond the reach of rational continuity. Instinctually, McLeod wanted to run, hightail it to high ground, or hide under the blanket of anonymity, but he could not act on any of those options. McLeod had a longing desire to see Charlie. A burning affirmation ignited deep between his ears; he knew he was resolute on one absolute. He's not leaving Paris unresolved. His next move came to mind; McLeod went directly to an idea that included Varinia. Now there, he thought, is someone familiar with Paris. She had even called to solicit more business. She was the person who could assist, but to help, she would need to learn his purpose.

Within minutes, McLeod had found her business card. It was 4:30 in the afternoon on the day after Sepúlveda's death. He called, and the receptionist answered. McLeod asked for Varinia. Although I was initially told that Varinia would pick up in a few minutes, she did not. McLeod waited. After what seemed like a drop call, Varinia came on the line.

"Finally," McLeod sarcastically commented.

"I'm sorry, but sometimes calls are jammed up, too many people. I apologize. How can I make up for my tardiness?"

"You can accept five hundred euros. Have dinner with me tonight at your favorite Paris restaurant, where we can plan a few days of private tours."

"A financially independent woman might decline, but fortunately for you, I need the money. Please leave the money at the front desk with my name on it. See you at your hotel at 7:00 tonight."

"I appreciate your acceptance; I'll do as you ask."

McLeod intends to persuade Varinia, using her Parisian expertise, to find Charlie's address. Far-fetched, but how many Anh Li's or Jadots' family members live in Paris?"

At 6:30, he passed the lobby, heading to Harry's Bar to wait for Varinia. As he stepped out of the elevator, a young man, uniformed in a black suit with a hotel nametag affixed to the left side of his jacket breast pocket, extended a greeting. "Mr. McLeod?" said the hotel employee.

"Yes, " McLeod responded." I'm surprised that the employee knew his name.

"You have a note," a miniature-sized white envelope was handed to me. McLeod read the note. *Mr. McLeod, I'm outside in a black Range Rover,* signed, an employee of Charlie. Once outside, despite the winter's early evening darkness, McLeod spotted the Black Range Rover. Only thinking that Charlie had finally contacted him after leaving an envelope with five hundred dollars at the desk, the obligation to Varinia fell from his mind. He eagerly sought out the Range Rover.

The double-wide lane for passenger pick-up at the hotel was not accessible. The uniformed employee escorted McLeod over the cement obstruction between the hotel and the avenue. As McLeod approached, he saw two boxes stacked on top of each other, occupying the vehicle's front passenger seat. He handed over a tip and stepped into the car. The car doors automatically locked. As the Range Rover slowly made its way onto the street, McLeod noticed that a window separated the passenger from the driver, like a New York City taxi or a stretch limousine. McLeod knocked on the window. He signaled his interest in lowering the window; the driver ignored the request. He knocked harder. Still, there was no response; a thin spray aimed at the passenger seats started McLeod. He cupped his hands over his nose, but it was too late.

Captured

Marin checked his hotel at the airport and readied himself for his early morning flight. At the same time, Lucy drives approximately five kilometers out of Paris toward Charles de Gaulle Airport. She turned right onto a two-lane highway and finally onto the backside of a refurbished former farmhouse, stopping long enough to press the electronic device that opened the two-car garage. The door opened, and she drove in. Lucy stepped out of the car, flicked on the garage light, and automated the closing. She entered and startled her employees with an unconscious McLeod in the backseat.

"Don't just sit there looking at me," Lucy ordered. Take him down to the basement."

Lucy handed off the car key and continued preparing, taking off her coat and gloves. Moving quickly, the two men unlocked Lucy's car.

They carried the now spread-eagled, fastened by wrist and ankle, McLeod to the basement as commanded. A naked, still not clearheaded McLeod found himself firmly buckled, standing upright, slightly tilted on an 8x4 ft. 3⁄4-inch clear fiberglass frame fastened upright for draining onto a bathtub. When Lucy removed the pillowcase from his head and the rigger's tape that sealed his lips, she revived McLeod with smelling salts. McLeod regained lucidity with a shake of his head and several coughs. Lucy was now setting up her cutting tools to sever flesh from bone. She barked orders to her two accomplices in the other room, ordering them to bring in twenty thick plastic bags and to get the furnace heated up to maximum centigrade so they could fire the dismembered parts into ashes.

McLeod was terrified. Thinking that the pain about to befall him would be excruciating. He struggled to free himself, but it was to no avail. He thought, finally, after many years of wondering, he knew how he would die.

Lucy stared directly at McLeod. "No worries, Mr. McLeod. I am about to inject you with a very potent dose of opioids. Although conscious, you'll be inducted into a sort of pre-death. You will not feel a thing. You see, I am not a torturer. After cleaving off pieces and parts, I must drain the blood; the drugs will induce a limp and nonresistant body. More than likely, the shock will kill you before blood loss."

At that moment, Lucy inoculated McLeod's right thigh. After a few minutes, Lucy checked the drug's effectiveness by stabbing a needle into his chest several times. McLeod did not flinch.

Hours later, as if in a stupor, sobriety did not come easy. McLeod fought to regain mindfulness. He remembered standing and being pinned against a hard surface. It was dark. Clothed in a white bathrobe, he was lying on a canvas cot. Free to move, he sat up. His bare feet touched the cold cement floor. Standing with hands extended as if blind, he walked to measure the square footage of his space. After several steps in four directions, he estimated the room to be about two hundred square feet. There was the sound of a turning doorknob, and then a sudden burst of bright light. The light blinded a recovering McLeod. Muscled from the room by two men along a long corridor. A man on each side forcibly guides him. They stopped; he could hear the metal-to-metal friction and the door opening. Seated on a soft, oversized leather chair, he could hear the men walk away and the door closing. Within minutes, his vision adjusted, and he squinted. He saw Charlie standing before him with a cute smirk on her face. She handed him a water bottle and told him to guzzle it all.

"Mr. McLeod, Mr. McLeod," Charlie shouted as she sought to test his awareness, "that was a close one."

Still suffering from the effects of Lucy's injection and the abruptness of seeing Charlie, McLeod was slow to respond from his dreamlike state and into sobriety.

Charlie continued, "Of course, I have been watching you, Marin, and his bodyguard, Lucy."

McLeod finally responded. "How in the world did you pull this off? How did you rescue me?"

With a grin, Charlie friskily suggested, "I do my best to watch over you." Charlie's face evolved from frisky to sober. "So, I think you had better prepare yourself for some revelations. I will make a fresh pot while you shower. A fresh towel and a Terry cloth bathrobe are hung on the shower door. Soap and hot water followed by a cup or two of java will revitalize you."

McLeod sat across from Charlie. A shower clean, McLeod was sipping coffee within half an hour.

Boldly, Charlie stated, "I am the daughter you've been striving to meet."

Without waiting for another moment, McLeod reacted. He stood up. "You are my daughter?" A bewildered, flabbergasted McLeod shrieked.

"Please sit down," Charlie commanded. "I said I am the daughter you seek; I did not say I was your daughter."

"Please explain."

"It's simple," Charlie declared. "Anh Li is my mother. But you are not my father. Now, that is the plain fact of the matter."

"Please continue," McLeod pleaded. "Who then is your father?"

"When my mother and Captain Doss left Dong Ha, they scampered to a safe house across the DMZ. Doss came down with malaria and was interned for treatment in a nearby NVA army facility. As scheduled, Ivan — I think that's his American-given name — came with his entourage to escort my mother to Hanoi. Doss was at the medical facility. Fortunately for Doss, within earshot of my mother, Ivan ordered three mercenaries to seek Doss out and kill him. Though not surprised by that directive, it was then that my mother suggested that, instead of killing him, an American might prove valuable. Besides, she implored that killing would serve no real purpose. The Americans would want him in some future trade. Ivan followed my mother's recommendation, knowing that killing Doss was an open-ended option."

"Your mother saved his life," McLeod noted. "So, he is...

"Wait," Charlie cautioned, "please don't jump to conclusions. Doss is not my father."

"I see; the mystery continues," McLeod assumed.

"Then let me get to the truth; my father," Charlie asserted, "is your most meaningful target. Yes, the Russian Maximilian Ivanov is my father."

McLeod had always considered this possible, but the confirmation was still mildly stunning. Did that union initiate any repercussions regarding his current situation? Potentials raced ineffectually across his mind, but all such activity abruptly stopped when Charlie went on with her revelations.

"Maximilian, my father, this Russian repeatedly, over the next five days, raped my mother. It took a week to arrange the extraction to Hanoi. During this entire time, my mother was a subordinate to his will. The repeated rape of my mother was the making of my conception. She never told me the truth that the rapist was my father. Thinking that you were forever out of her life, my mother told Doss that Sergeant McLeod was the father to satisfy the anticipated queries with her blossoming belly. There now, aren't you relieved?"

"Relieved that you are not my daughter? Well, considering our relationship, hell, yes, I'm more than just relieved," McLeod exclaimed. "I'm confused. Your mother went on to work for her rapist?"

"No, she never worked for him. Years later, she assumed a senior manager position after the war and functioned as that manager for many years."

"How did this come about, and what is that senior manager position?"

"My mother, with Doss in tow, arrived in Hanoi. But instead of working as originally assumed, she used her Paris political connections to be reassigned to the North Vietnamese consulate in Havana. The Cubans started to use her Vietnamese connections, and of course, she had many connections in the U.S. military and Viet Cong support organizations. It wasn't long before she transitioned from her position at the consulate to Raúl Castro's diplomatic staff. My mother was a brilliant leader and a gregarious person. She befriended the influencers and the elite connected to Castro. In time, aided by her innate good sense and prudent behavior, her acceptance into the Castro family evolved into the family's dependence."

"Quite amazing," McLeod stated. "I agree your mother was exceptional.

With no hesitation, Charlie continued, "My mother was a person of conscience who, as a young Parisian student, was exposed to the pseudo virtues of communism; she learned of communism in school as a theoretical idea. However, in Castro's Cuba, she witnessed the tenets of communist implementation.

The theoretical ideal, the academic model of economic uplifting of ordinary citizens, failed. Still, the price of subjugation to the will of the totalitarian state remained, creating an unelected class of omnipotent bureaucrats touting state power over the individual. My dear mother witnessed injustice to every Cuban, a false promise realized. In Cuba, she observed the apparent disparity of wealth and power between the ruling elite and the community of individuals, in practical terms, who were nonexistent. Her findings were immensely disappointing. She felt betrayed, even stupid, with a sense of guilt for her service to the communist cause. Nonetheless, in one fortunate and ultra-determined swoop, my mother stepped out of Cuba's Marxism and into Castro-style crony entrepreneurialism. She took to making money like Rich Uncle Pennybags was to the game of Monopoly.

"Did she ever run into Ivan again?" McLeod asks.

"Yes, a couple of years after the war was over, she was invited to the Russian embassy in Havana for coffee and cake on a regular Saturday afternoon. The Russian ambassador had a guest. The guest was the bastard who raped her, Maximillian Orlov Ivanov, the former GRU agent."

"What a shock this must have been," McLeod commented.

"Mother told me that although startled when she saw him across the room, she did not tell anyone she knew him. And upon being formally introduced, she did not greet him as someone she had known. On the other hand, disconcertingly for my mother, he greeted her as an old acquaintance. As the evening wore on, she could tell his host fronted him as a newly recruited resource. She told me that she felt a definite tension in the room, which even the personal guests of the Cuban government regarded as a hammer on the downswing. His reputation and physical sway instilled gut-wrenching fear. He held an intimidating presence."

Later, she learned that Max, short for Maximillian, was compelled to invest millions of his heroin gains in a Cuban insurance start-up controlled by Raúl Castro. My mother assumed that such an investment was made willfully in payment for Cuban sanctuary and protection. She remembered the independent GRU agent of yesterday and the Castro lackey of today. Today's GRU agent is dependent on Cuban goodwill. After a year, my mother, personally sponsored by Raul, was given the authority over the insurance company; within a year, my mother was the acknowledged lady of means and authority, and everybody, including the Russian, acknowledged that reality."

Charlie reached over to pour McLeod another cup of coffee. She then poured herself a cup of hot water over green tea leaves, commenting that tea suited her.

She said calmly, "I know you have questions, you know, personal questions, but that will need to wait."

"If you say so," McLeod agreed."

"I have defined myself as your daughter's close friend of a similar background. Although untrue, I have repeated that scenario over many Years. This portrayal of the daughter's friend has been gainfully productive, particularly over the last couple of years, with Marin and, most recently, Sepúlveda. My mother's idea was to create another identity, one where the daughter was more than just her appearance. My loyal childhood friend Charlie would manage all the other engagements. My mother's cover story would imply that her daughter was physically healthy but had certain deficiencies that restricted her social interface. Everyone accepted that answer. The truth is that no one cared to know about those specific deficiencies or disabilities, nor did they show the slightest interest in inquiring about them. As a little girl, I remember this story about me was like being anonymous while fully engaged. I thought it was a wonderful ruse; I learned that anonymity is the only true security."

"In an open society with the constancy of prying eyes and ears that cover story as you call it, is as close to anonymity as possible," McLeod endorsed.

"So, it was after my mother's death when Marin approached Dr. Li's daughter, that is, Charlie, via an arranged teleconference with one of my attorneys. Initially, he wanted to meet with me because the subject matter could only be discussed in person. I told him that person-to-person was impossible and steered him back to my attorney's office. He flatly refused that offer and insisted on seeing me. I told him I would see what I could do if he gave me a phone number. Finally, he agreed and gave me a number. After that, the idea of seeing me face to face, and I, Charlie, became the conduit to the daughter of Dr. Anh Li."

"He is a persistent fellow," McLeod stated. "What exactly does he want from you?"

"My mother, CEO of the holding company and President of Old Dutch, had affirmed a confidential non-binding agreement with a prominent Spanish insurance company. Years before, Sepúlveda had worked as a consultant for that very Spanish company. He was familiar with the company and its board of directors. Under my mother's employ, utilizing his contacts within that company, he helped put the deal together for Old Dutch.

"This is such a large transaction; I assume this is in keeping with the wishes of exactly who?" McLeod inquired.

"This idea of selling everything was a plan originated by my mother and wholeheartedly endorsed by Sepúlveda and the Old Dutch board of directors."

"Ok, but why," McLeod asks, "is Marin running around with his hair on fire?"

"Because Sepúlveda revived a dated LOI, made an edit, reaffirmed it with the Spanish company, and presented it to the board as Marin's own," Charlie responded. "So many questions; I see you are finally moving into the core of this intrigue," Charlie complimented McLeod.

"I am? Frankly, it's still unclear."

"The reaffirmed LOI has a six-month termination date, and three months have passed," Charlie clarifies.

"What does Marin want from you that you can deliver and benefit from?"

"Here's what I know: Mother had firm control over the company's operations when alive. Most importantly, she had a firm grip on Marin. My mother regularly briefed me on company operations, and I have a solid understanding of Old Dutch's accounting, legal aspects, and general insurance business practices. Since her death, Marin, the only duly licensed individual, was appointed president and given the insurance company's operational authority by default. The revenue from the insurance business is substantial. However, over the years, neither gross premium volume nor net profits has increased. The insurance business outside of Cuba is highly regulated. Marin has all the licenses and operational resources to conduct the day-to-day operations. However, he realizes he is having a shareholder meeting away from discharge.

"You're a substantial owner. Why don't you get engaged?" McLeod suggested.

"I love your straightforward innocence—very U. S. Marine of you, Sergeant McLeod. If only the world were so simple," Charlie despondently pondered. "To be fair, I did leave out one potent detail."

"Hmm..." McLeod murmured, signaling readiness for God knows what.

Charlie explains, "My mother bequeathed her Old Dutch shares held in Avoca Holdings LTD, a Bermuda Corporation, to me. I am the sole shareholder and president of the company.

"So, Marin mistakenly and desperately thought that the father, me, another mistake, his real interest in me is to get to you," McLeod declared.

"Exactly, Mr. McLeod, I think you're getting the message. Before the company's sale, I must attend the board meeting, as it is a legal requirement. Now, that's where our interests intersect. This is what you have always wanted, isn't it, Mr. McLeod?"

McLeod hesitated, then asked, "What have I always wanted? "

"Me, is it not true you want me?"

"I certainly will not quarrel with that," McLeod injected. "So, we are engaged in a mutual satisfaction of interest. I do for you, and you do for me."

"Exactly, Mr. McLeod," Charlie confirms.

"And Charlie goes on, 'I have a bonus."

"You know the whereabouts of Maximilian?"

"My mother told me that Max sustained a stroke while both were attending a Castro gathering; he fell forward and landed on his head, blood gushed, and they rushed him to the hospital. My mother took charge of the situation at once. He was unconscious for 48 hours (about 2 days); he could mumble but not speak with fluency. Touting the need for clinical recovery and security, she moved him onto his boat and ended his outside access.

While in the doctor's care, tests revealed advanced arthritis in his body's joints. The disease hampered his physical return to normal. The stroke caused by diminished blood to the brain permanently eliminated his ability to communicate fluently. He was limited to a monotone moan or groan. Within a month, the intimidating junkyard dog turned into a pussycat."

"So now the dreaded Maximilian Orlov Ivanov is a pathetic, disabled, dependent person. Justice is served," McLeod moralized.

"Ivan, 'the Russian,' as you once called him, though unable to walk unattended, gained portions of his voice and certain motor skills, and he was cognitive able enough to understand his disability. "Remember," Charlie pointed out, "this guy has spent his life intimidating people, and now he has no means to coerce anyone."

"So, your mother took advantage and captured Max right in his domain. Now that's an overt operation with a covert twist."

"Yes," Charlie concurred, "The rapist was under her direct supervision; she had absolute control. Max was, by practice, a secretive man. So, no one ever knew much about his habits. He is not a social being. For him, a daily pattern was dangerous. He's not a guy with friends. When missed, no one was interested in finding."

"Nevertheless, he trusted your mother," McLeod pointed out.

"Trusted my mother, hmm...let us say he learned to respect her work ethic, audaciousness, and her more right than wrong decisions. But most importantly, in his debilitating state, he depended on my mother not to enact vengeance on him for his past horrific deeds. Trust was a taste neither my mother nor the GRU agent ever acquired," Charlie corrected, annoyed by the silliness of the 'trust' comment.

Noticing the unease, McLeod changed the subject, "I wonder what Marin is thinking right now," McLeod wondered aloud.

"Probably quite content with the idea that Lucy completed the task." Charlie glanced at her watch. "He has just landed. "In minutes, he'd know how wrong he was. But that is just one of my problems. Marin is operating as the company's president; however, Marin knows that his power is tenuous. He must eliminate me to reign supreme, since I will never sell or convey my equity to Marin. Factually and quite sensibly, Old Dutch Indemnity is the only entity that should buy my shares.

If I, as the majority shareholder, must take control of Old Dutch sooner rather than later, and undoubtedly before the sale to the Spanish insurance company,

"Then, of course," McLeod proposes, "Marin is aware of that opportunistic feasibility.

"I'm sure Marin is aware," Charlie assumes. I am just as sure he has a plot and a plan to circumvent that action. Marin is not a shareholder; nonetheless, he is authorized to call a shareholder meeting to replace the vacated former directors. The nomination, taking place on Saint Martin, the Dutch island, will be Marin's proxies voting in his favor. Before the meeting is adjourned, he will propose that the current operating agreement be voided. Since he has the votes, the proposal will pass. This shareholder meeting requires a notice period of twenty-one business days. As a shareholder, I am naturally required to attend. My attendance will hinder Marin's proposal; therefore, it would be hazardous for me to attend.

"Interestingly, according to Raymond, Old Dutch's operating agreement cannot be changed without a shareholders' meeting. McLeod notes, "It's an amazing twist of probabilities that Marin seems to have in his quiver. How did this guy get into such a dynamically strong position?"

"Marin was recruited by chance, a quirk of fate. He had no connections with the Castro family. However, he was duly licensed and well-positioned within the broader Caribbean insurance sector. He desperately needed a job and a second chance. After being recommended by an insurance recruiter, Dr. Li decided that, after one interview, Marin had the requirements to fulfill her needs. My mother worked effortlessly with Marin; she taught him the value of adhering to her wishes. Over time, my mother gave him the opportunity, but to be clear, Marin earned his position," Charlie emphasizes.

"However, you were the one, Mr. McLeod, who did the most to elevate Marin to the presidency of Old Dutch."

"I put Marin into the presidency of Old Dutch," a puzzled McLeod astonishingly responded. "How in the hell did I do that?"

"You killed all of his rivals and the former president."

That truth silenced McLeod. Acknowledging that his actions and bloodlust created Charlie's threatening situation, he said, "Yes, I now understand. By the way," McLeod interjected to move on to a different subject, "whatever happened to Lucy?"

"I released Lucy unharmed."

"You spared her life," McLeod pointed out.

"Lucy is Luke, a soldier doing his duty. The female thing was just a disguise. Luke Patina is a Filipino American. A member of a Caribbean gangster family, Marin was their accountant. Marin recently hired him after securing the presidency of Old Dutch. Luke was employed as an administrative assistant; in reality, Luke was his bodyguard aide-de-camp. I suppose it allowed the two of them to be together, and no one imagined that Lucy in a skirt was his henchwoman.

"Lucy is a Luke. I got that when he prepared to chop me up into disposable pieces. You mentioned that you had some revelations. Is there more to this melodrama: As the World of Charlie Turns?"

"No more revelations, at least for now," Charlie confirmed. You have questions."

"I suppose Marin ordered Lucy to terminate my existence, and you, following me, paid Lucy to spare my life for cash."

"Well, that and the confirmation to Lucy that I would never sell my shares to Marin. And since Lucy's bonus was tied to Marin obtaining my shares, he took my cash and moved on."

"OK, I owe you. How do I pay off this debt? Killing Max, as you call him, is no longer a high priority for me. However, if required."

"My sexual self has squelched the flame of revenge for Mr. McLeod. I am powerful, or the tough guy is not so tough." Charlie asserted with a smirk.

"Are you mocking me- again? Incidentally, why did you seduce me?"

"Seduce you, sounding like a high school boyfriend wronged by a teenage vamp. Mr. McLeod, I have sex for pleasure. Admittedly, my sexual interest in you goes back to my mother's orally delivered novelettes about her sexual encounters with you and how she lusted for you. I was seventeen when she told me about that night in Dung Ha. As it turned out, that was the last night you were together. While masturbating, I imagined and embellished the encounter; it aroused me. The details endured as an unsatisfying fantasy. At an incredibly early age, lustful thoughts turned me on and on and on. I never thought I would ever experience my fantasy. And yes, having sex with you was an attempt at recreation. I wanted to; I did. The sex was good, but fell short of my imagined expectations. Does it matter why I had sex with you?" Charlie implored.

"I know I sound like some high school romance gone bad. I should never have asked, so let's drop it." Changing the subject, "I assume this Marin threat is a priority," McLeod suggested.

Charlie cautioned. "I can confirm his whereabouts. He can no longer hide his true intentions nor use Sepúlveda as an intermediary, purposed for misdirection. However, Lucy's failure serves as a warning. My opportunity to eliminate the Marin menace is now. I told him I'd meet him at the insurance compliance conference in Nevis to formalize the sale of my Old Dutch position, including the Bearer Shares. That satisfied his mindset and alleviated his concerns about the Old Dutch control.

"So," McLeod asks, "why did he want to eliminate me?"

"Because and why are no longer in my contemplative vocabulary; however, I'll satisfy your curiosity. Convinced, you are my protector and the killer of Calvo. He dreads your interference. Notifying him of my agreeing to a settlement, I believe, calmed him down and gave him cause for self-congratulations."

"You plan on residing here in Paris?" McLeod asked.

"Whoa, that came out of nowhere. For now, Paris is best," Charlie responded.

"And you're on your way to Panama," Charlie noted.

"Yes, how did you know?" McLeod questioned while acknowledging that the assumption was valid.

"I assume you ordered Raymond's body to Panama for burial, and I know you will be there for the internment," Charlie responded.

"Well," McLeod concluded, "your assumption has earned you a gold star."

"I have people who pick up a few coins passing information; this is not a CIA operation. All these people are looking to make a little money on the side. You are spending the night here. Your luggage was retrieved from the hotel and should arrive in a few hours; we have time," Charlie explained.

"Time," McLeod queries with a slight smile.

"Don't look so coy. You know perfectly well what we want," Charlie responded, taking off her clothes while heading for the bedroom.

As if she had read the script in advance, knowing the end before she initiates the beginning, she decisively acts with steadfast confidence. McLeod steps into the bedroom, her nakedness, hips, inner thighs, and nipples on her breasts. Her legs were muscular and shaped. Her eyes beckoned, her lips promising, and the clit between her legs was tastefully tempting. He wanted her. He could not trust her, but that was part of her allure.

Once he accepted his want for Charlie as an addiction, critical thinking surrendered to the reward of yielding. She was an undeniable compulsion.

Charlie's Murderous Plot and Plan

An hour later, McLeod awoke from a deep sleep; Charlie was gone. A note had been delivered; she had reserved his 11:00 AM flight to Madrid with a connecting flight to Panama. A limo was scheduled to take him to the airport at 8:00 AM. She wrote down her telephone number and told him to call after the burial.

McLeod caught a flight to Madrid and then to Panama. He called the funeral home and confirmed that the body was ready for burial. The service was at 10:00 am the following day. Since his wife's death, Sepúlveda had stopped all socializing, and after the kidnapping warning, no further family interface was expected. McLeod arrived early. The casket rolled out, followed by the priest and two altar boys. After a few words, dirt was shoveled onto the casket, and within minutes, it was over. Sepúlveda's final resting place is now assured.

McLeod did not linger. He had a 3:45 flight to Miami; the rapid change of time zones affected his circadian rhythm and assimilation into the new time zone. The for-hire sedan was waiting in the designated area at the airport. The driver saw McLeod approaching, stepped out to open the passenger door, and put McLeod's luggage in the trunk. McLeod stepped in.

"Senior McLeod" was the greeting of the man occupying the leeward side of the rear seat. "It's been so many years; you may not remember me. You knew me as Rojo, my alias at the time. What do you think of my ear before you question my intrusion into your life? Cosmetic surgery, please relax, Mr. McLeod. I am here to talk and nothing else."

"All right," McLeod replied, "what do you want?"

Rojo begins to answer, "I work for an interested party."

McLeod interrupts, sarcastically noting, "So you gave up the secret agent stuff and burnt off your conspicuous tattoo."

"I see time has not dulled your memory or sense of humor. Yes, working on the private side is a requirement that pays much more."

"Well, wonderful," McLeod commented. I assume this mysterious employer decided to have you greet me for some good reason."

"Let's just say," Rojo answered, "that we look out on all the players. One of your interfaces has been with the president of Old Dutch, so I thought you might tell me what those meetings were all about."

"What a silly opening," McLeod responded. "This Old Dutch information is not why you're here. Since I am still alive, you are not here to settle some score. Why the surprise? Your presence must have a definitive purpose since you have excellent informational access." McLeod suggests.

"I have monetized my communist ideology. I acted alone to meet you because I wanted you to know that I appreciate you setting my ear on fire instead of killing me; however, I do not owe you a debt. We will meet again; in the meantime, enjoy your flight to Miami."

Rojo left the car; McLeod ordered the driver to the airport. Before long, he was on the flight to Miami. Never able to sleep in flight, McLeod has hours to ponder. What could the insertion of Rojo as a messenger mean? There must be something to the occurrence; whoever they are, they, him. No, it must have been Charlie who sent Rojo; how else could he have accessed information, even if he acted independently? Well, one thing was sure: Marin, Charlie, Sepúlveda, and Rojo, even Lucy's interference, were scripted as if they were characters in a complex, mysterious novella.

Deducing the fact of the matter is as slippery as grasping a pole greased with lard.

Upon exiting Miami customs and immigration, an airport announcement operator bellowed his name, "Mr. McLeod," and asked him to pick up the white telephone. McLeod did precisely that: "Hello, McLeod here."

The caller was Charlie. "Mr. McLeod, please leave the airport and wait for a private car to pick you up. It will be a black Lincoln Town Car. It will take you to a private airport in Fort Lauderdale. I will be here waiting for you."

"I wanted to get home and relax," McLeod countered. There was a click, and the line went dead.

McLeod submitted Charlie's instructions. Upon arrival, the car was waiting for us. Without greeting, the driver opened the trunk and placed McLeod's luggage inside. He opened the passenger door, McLeod stepped in, and the forty-five-minute drive to Fort Lauderdale commenced. The driver stopped short of the private airport by turning onto a restaurant parking lot. Just as the driver parked, another car pulled in behind it. The driver of the other vehicle stepped out and opened the passenger door.

Charlie stepped out and beckoned, "Mr. McLeod, jump in; let's go."

"And what about my luggage?"

"The driver will deliver your belongings to The Jockey Club. They will be there upon your return."

McLeod opened the passenger door, stepped in, buckled up, and said, "You continue to surprise me. If it is not one thing, it is another."

"Well, things have developed, and we need to act," Charlie responded. Marin is in Nevis three days before the conference begins. I cannot allow him to attend this mandatory compliance conference."

"I assume that implies he has moved into a position of vulnerability, and you want me to act."

"Precisely," Charlie answered. The conference is an annual regulatory requirement that a company representative must attend for educational purposes and to stay informed about new and pending regulatory rules and regulations.

"He's a guest of the Four Seasons on the island. He has been there four times. His routine has become a predictable pattern. He checks into the hotel; the next morning, he plays an early round of golf. He'll rent clubs, buy golf shoes, 12 Titleist golf balls, a left-handed leather glove, and a hat. He plays from the white tees. He is terrible but loves the game. He never plays with anyone and has no witnesses, not even a caddy."

"I don't know why, but I never imagined him interested in the game," McLeod commented.

"I don't think it is the game per se," Charlie contributed. "It is his image of himself as the proper corporate honcho. His peers play golf; therefore, he must play golf; he's feeding an indulgence, something we've all contended with."

"I know you have a plan. This Nevis of Four Seasons event must be the opportunity you'd like to take advantage of."

"Yes," Charlie confirmed, "on hole twelve, the white golf tee is sunk deep, below sighting from above and hidden from view to the front. Golfers call it a blind shot. This hole has a sharp dogleg right, so one tries to get out from the tee in the middle of the fairway."

"You must be a golfer," McLeod inquired.

Charlie didn't respond but continued laying out the plan. "I will drop you off at the restaurant on the beach, about four hundred meters from the hotel and the golf course. The place is not open until noon, so the dock and beach area will be free of boats and people. The drop-off should not catch anyone's attention. Employees and tourists extensively use the drop-off spot."

"Sounds doable," McLeod comments.

"Charlie continues. "The boat will be decked out with fishing poles, so from a distance, it will resemble an angler getting an early start. You'll wear a golfer's ensemble with a hat and sunglasses. Track up the walkway to the golf course; you will have your map to help guide your way up to the seventh hole. A golfer will park his golf cart above the tee and walk down to hit his shot. Unable to see his cart from the elevated tee, he returns after hitting his shot. You'll be waiting, hidden near his cart with the 50,000-volt Taser at the ready. He will be startled and incapacitated. A few blows to the head with his driver should silence him."

"Additionally, I have put on a clear, colored, water-resistant plastic cape for you to wear when you approach him. There will be blood splatters. I also put on medium to large golf gloves on my right and left hands. Afterward, you will find a suitable place to dispose of the gloves and poncho. You packed the extra shirt and pants, your passport, cash, airline tickets, a hairbrush, paste, and a toothbrush in your blue Alpine backpack that you'll wear. Remember to take his possessions, you know, make it look like a local criminal, a drug addict needing quick cash. Advantaging an alone early morning golfer."

"You have thought this out," McLeod comments.

"Exactly," Mr. McLeod, Charlie affirmed.

"Damn, you're vicious."

"You do remember what Lucy, under Marin's order, had in store for you?" Charlie reminds McLeod. "Besides, unless Marin's terminated, I don't know how we could eventually have a moment's solace; he will be an everlasting threat."

McLeod fixated on one part of Charlie's response, which was the most meaningful.

"You spoke of us and solace."

"Mr. McLeod," Charlie offered a misdirected answer, "I have grown quite fond of you. In executing this act, you will have protected me from a dangerous man; there is nothing so stimulating for a woman than to be protected by her Paladin in shining armor."

"In shining armor, hmm...never thought of me as anything close to such a regal persona," McLeod comments.

"What am I asking you to do? Is this something you are going to have problems with?" Charlie asked.

"I have killed soldiers whom I did not even know. These individuals did nothing against me. So, killing Marin, who tried to have me sawed and sliced, no problem," McLeod assured Charlie.

"Excellent!" Charlie beamed. "You have your flight tickets to San Juan and Miami. We will reconnect in a few weeks; organizing will take me that long. Once I do, I will set up the opportunity to finalize your quest. After the Russian is dead, your duty to Team 33 is complete."

McLeod agreed and added, "Yes, that's all true, but because of you, the fire of revenge has simmered."

"Then possibly I have done you a disservice," Charlie suggested. "If you're not going to kill him, I'll find another."

"I'll kill him," McLeod conceded. "I don't want anything to happen to you."

Charlie steered the speedboat using navigational reckoning, following the sea path created by the ferry. McLeod viewed another exhibition of Charlie's previously unknown skill.

For conversational reasons rather than genuine interest, McLeod asked. "Where did you learn to operate and navigate this speedboat?"

McLeod noticed the shift in Charlie's expression. Where she had been quiet but relaxed, she was now rigid. Her jaw was visibly clenched, and her facial muscles were taut. She was staring straight ahead, lost in contemplation. She broke her concentration in a few seconds, saying, "From my mother, I learned everything of prime value from my dear mother."

Knowing that any comment on that subject line would be detrimental, McLeod stepped onto the pier, and the untethered boat sped off. Charlie waved goodbye. McLeod started tracking toward the twelve-hole with the map as a reference; it was easy to find. Following the golf cart lane, McLeod positioned himself behind a tensely green-leafed shrubbery close enough for easy access. In ambush mode, he sat and waited.

He considered Charlie's explanation of the Marin threat agitatedly exaggerated. Besides, her cold-blooded scheme did not fit his sense of righteousness. He thought it was best to talk with Marin. It was Lucy, not Marin, who kidnapped him. He felt it best to chat with Marin instead of killing him outright. He would explain that although he would lose control over Old Dutch, a lucrative cash and equity accommodation, it would assuage the effects of the loss; besides, there are profound negatives if you refuse. Within an hour, McLeod heard a golf cart descending the hill onto the tee area. Wearing a well-worn straw hat and appropriate golfing regalia, Marin arrived. He turned and faced the front of the cart downhill; McLeod observed him pull out an iron club and walk down toward the tee. In a minute, there was the sound of the clubface striking the ball. Then, with a loud curse, Marin returned to his cart, holding his iron in his left hand. Without the Taser in hand, McLeod moved toward Marin.

Marin turned and saw McLeod. Immediately, he dropped his club and reached into his right pocket with his right hand. There was panic in his eyes. Marin tilted his upper body to the left and lifted his leg as if trying to free the object stuck in his pocket.

McLeod noticed Marin's fright and said, "Hold on, I want to talk."

McLeod's words did not ease Marin's efforts to grasp what McLeod assumed was a pistol. McLeod continued his approach, repeating, "I just want to talk." A muffled but distinctive bang sounded within, and Marin fell to the ground, hand still in his right pocket. Blood flowed all over Marin's right thigh. McLeod was astonished; recovering after a minute or two, he reached for the object inside Marin's pocket with his left hand and pulled out a small, double-barreled, twenty-two caliber derringer. A panicked Marin shot himself. The bullets tore through his crouch and into his stomach. Within minutes, Marin heaved his last breath and died. McLeod put the pistol back in Main's pocket with a gloved hand. He surveyed the scene; Marin would be found in an hour or so. Authorities would trace his movements from his tee shot. The investigators would deduce that an assailant's robbery accidentally prompted the killing. There was likely a surprise and a struggle. The victim went for his pistol. And, for the police, the fact that Marin carried a gun onto the golf course proved he feared such a possibility.

From this point forward, time worked against McLeod. He had to push hard.

McLeod took his cash, left his body, jumped onto Marin's golf cart, and meandered across the course like a golfer skipping holes or returning to the clubhouse. Everyone was busy with the comings and goings of their vacation. No one noticed another golf cart meandering to the clubhouse.

Ignoring the rental cart return, McLeod parked the cart near the clubhouse, walked into the hotel as if to breakfast, and coolly walked out front to the hotel shuttle station to take him to the St. Kitts ferry. Before long, the clubhouse personnel would procedurally mark the cart and rental clubs as returned. Before the evening ended, an exhausted McLeod's flight landed in Miami. Within hours, he would be horizontal.

Miami Jockey Club

Two days later, Charlie received a call after the second cup of coffee in the early morning. Several rings, but no answer. He could not leave a message. The phone just rang; a week had passed since he left for Panama. There was a pile of mail, organized in layers, one letter on top of another. Reluctantly, he decided to deal with his mail. But instead of paying bills, he'd rather receive a call from Charlie.

McLeod reasoned that life and living waited for no one, which applied to significant household liabilities. So, despite his contrary inclination, he began going through his mail, writing checks, making notes, checking billing accuracy, and attending to all the other mundane tasks of being alive.

There was a ring on the internal phone line. McLeod answered. It was George, the bellman. "Mr. McLeod, I have your FedEx mail. Shall I bring it up?"

"Yes, please do," McLeod responded.

McLeod used scissors to open one end of the FedEx package. Inside was a handwritten message on a plain piece of paper torn from a small pad, like the kind used in hotels, placed next to the telephone.

Fly to San Juan, Puerto Rico, and check into the Ritz-Carlton Hotel in two days. I will contact you there. All's good, Charlie.

McLeod was relieved. Finally, the note gave McLeod the impression that Charlie was ready to start anew. Feeling excited and cheerful, McLeod returned to the mundane.

Set on the end of the table, partially hidden under some open envelopes, he reached for a flat, manila-colored package. When he brought the package closer, he noticed it originated in Paris, France, and was addressed to W. R. McLeod at the Jockey Club address. Other than the hotel's, there was no return address. McLeod opened the large manila envelope; the contents revealed the following:

Raymond wrote on a hotel notepad:

Why I Took My Life

I contracted and invoiced for services rendered to Old Dutch Indemnity for the month preceding my start date on your behalf. Initially, there was no conflict between your concerns and my other contractual obligations. I worked comfortably with Dr. Li to develop a strategically important acquisition agreement with a Spanish company and its publicly traded entity in the United States. Remember, I had no idea there was a personal history between Anh Li and you at the time.

Then things started to change after the Cornfield and Gomez interview in the Nevada desert. But it was after the killing of Anh Li that I earnestly began to deceive and betray.

Her death automatically terminated my lucrative consulting contract, which included 100,000 shares of Old Dutch as an added consideration. Anh Li's daughter would not return my calls, so prompted by greed and egocentric resentment, I accepted Marin's offer.

After a lifetime of making correct decisions, modest ambition, and never compromising my client's interest, I blundered big time. As an unwarranted excuse, the death of my dear wife impaired and destroyed what was once my sensible and prudent mindset. I assessed that the never-present Russian posed no discernible threat; all the big hitters were permanently absent. Marin was right; a management void existed. Opportunistically, Marin and I attempted to capture operational control of Old Dutch Indemnity and eventually an equity supermajority before the Spanish company merger. Regarding Max, the Russian, a man I had never seen, the Cubans effectively sold him or, more accurately, forced him to invest as the price for his Cuban residency. The Russian viewed the investment as the price of residency and anonymity, so he willingly purchased worthless (at the time) Old Dutch convertible debentures at par with an investment dollar-for-dollar value or fair market price, whichever was higher on the day of conversion.

Raúl Castro structured the debentures to the bearer's benefit, wherein the value is redeemable to the person or entity in physical possession of the bonds. I assume the Cubans thought swindling their former partner was clever, and the bonds could be retrieved if demanded. The means to transfer a few million dollars from his pocket to theirs, never thinking that the transaction would be of any value or that a start-up insurance company's worth could increase. However, due to Dr. Li's excellence, the conversion of these debentures to equity today means that the holder of those bearer shares controls Old Dutch.

Initially, the company facilitated the self-insurance requirements of government-owned Cuban businesses. Dr. Anh Li endorsed Marin's hiring and expanded the self-insured risk-taking to businesses other than those domiciled in Cuba. Anh Li's effort, though challenging, exponentially increased revenues, forcing the company's internal systems to become more sophisticated and comply with mandated financial transparency requirements. The persistently correct Dr. Li knew that when licensed in other than Cuban domiciles, the insurance regulator's scrutiny would require a Bermudian domicile, the vetting of corporate officers, directors, and, most egregiously, a list of all shareholders owning 5% or more of Old Dutch stock.

Consequently, about three years ago, Dr. Li started acquiring shares. The first to be bought out was the Castro family. She created and funded First Avoca Holdings Trust, domiciled in Bermuda, to purchase the Cuban-domiciled entity and hold these shares in its street name. The accounting conversion to U.S. standards, a requirement of the Spanish insurance company's acquisition, was problematic, but Dr. Li achieved the required compliance audit within nine months.

Marin is a clever opportunist. He knows that unless he finds a legitimate counter to what commonly occurs during an acquisition, his replacement is assured, encouraged by the absence of Dr. Li, Commander Cornfield, and Colonel Calvo, as well as the Russian's non-appearance. Marin thought, and I agreed that a vast vacuum within the upper management of Old Dutch was a call to action. He ended up as the last man standing. As he interprets it, his situation is a perspective of 'if not now, then never.' He is the only person with a company background and operational specificities. An excellent place to be, that is, until the consummation of the Spanish insurance deal. Marin brought me on board for apparent reasons, and frankly, the coup would have been successful, but only if I could have found a way to affiliate with Dr. Li's daughter instead of Marin.

Lucy is not Lucy. She is a man. As a freelance agent working for whoever pays him, I wouldn't be surprised if Lucy, while working for Marin, also worked for Charlie, unbeknownst to Marin.

A couple of hours ago, my hotel phone rang. A recorded message: Senior Sepúlveda, in your bathroom sink, is a razor blade; climb into the bathtub and use this blade to slit your wrists vertically. If you are not dead in the next two hours, your son and family will eventually be found and tortured till they painfully die. After the incident with my youngest granddaughter and the alarming anxiety from my son, how could I risk any other thought but to obey the recorded instructions?

As you must agree, my death was required. Although admitting to speculating, Charlie is the puppet master; Cuidado, mi amigo.

The revelation of Lucy's duplicitous allegiance meant that his near-death rescue was a sham. Charlie's use of sex and charm to achieve her determined result had been handed down from mother to daughter. Could my old friend be wrong?

The flight to Puerto Rico took less than two hours. McLeod was in a trance, brimming with remorse, questions, and regret throughout the trek to the hotel. He could not generate any deductive thinking, not even to explain why he had followed her most recent request. Just putting one foot in front of the other, McLeod was almost catatonic as he checked into the hotel.

Once inside his room, McLeod made a beeline for the refrigerator. Grabbing two mini bottles of his specialty-ordered Chopin vodka, he squeezed a lemon into a glass and poured the vodka over ice. He relaxed, knowing that the loss of sobriety would relieve him of objectivity. The phone rang jarringly. McLeod was almost lifted off his seat by its loudness. He reached over and answered, "Hello."

"Mr. McLeod, it is Rojo. May I come up?"

"Why not?" McLeod replied and hung up.

In a matter of minutes, there was a knock at the door. "Rojo, the door is open for old friends; my door is always open."

Rojo spotted the glass and the two empty mini bottles of vodka and surmised that McLeod was less than sober.

"I see that you've been...relaxing," Rojo commented.

"Yes," McLeod responded cavalierly. "Now, what exactly do you want?"

"Charlie asked me to come over to validate your arrival and explain tomorrow's agenda," Rojo replied.

"I see," McLeod snickered. "Your boss is busy, so she sends her employee."

Rojo suggested, "Maybe I should go and come back in the morning."

"There is an adage: no better time than the present; it sounds sensible. Anyway, what is it? Please spit it out."

"Charlie is on the Russian's yacht. Tomorrow, the ship will pull into Isla de Vieques Malecón in Esperanza; a small pier makes it easier to dock. I will pick you up tomorrow at 11:00 AM."

"Let's make it 9:00; we have a stop to make," McLeod demanded.

"You say a stop to make?" Rojo repeated.

"Yes," McLeod assured Rojo. "No worries, the stop is mutually beneficial, like facilitating cash reserves. I am attempting to buy you off with logic and cash."

"In that case, I misspoke. I'll pick you up at 9:00 am. A private helicopter will fly us to Vieques. Land, and I will point you in the right direction."

"I assume that Charlie is in command and control, possibly accompanied by the Russian." McLeod guessed.

"Yes, she is in command, but I know no Russian, Rojo responded.

"Am I getting on this helicopter at Charlie's invitation? But more importantly, you must ponder: Why are you the hombre to meet and greet? Think about it." McLeod's request.

"They pay me, I act, but surely, if you asked such a question, it is because you have a different answer," Rojo responded.

"Indeed, my answer is unlike yours. "You are here because Charlie wanted you over any other person," McLeod insisted. "She is aligning us for a reason."

So, you say," Rojo sarcastically queries. "Please explain because I have no idea."

"Soldier to soldier, the circumstances of our first meeting were unfortunate. Tomorrow, at our first stop, I intend to correct the misfortune of that first meeting," McLeod confidently remarked. I assume you will call Charlie sometime tonight to confirm my arrival and acquiescence to tomorrow's agenda. Please inform Miss Charlie that I will get on that helicopter tomorrow and emphasize my insistence on seeing her.

"Intriguing,"

Rojo declares. "Hmm, my boss was right, amazing! You must know her intentions."

"Yes, imagine that! I have killed your Miami compatriots, turned you over to

U.S. government lockup for two years, and finally, have the DOJ deport you back to Cuba."

"I am impatiently waiting for your explanation of Charlie's dual-purposed intent, and I assume this explanation has something to do with our first stop."

"Wow! Impetuously waiting, your federal lockup has vastly improved your English vocabulary. Yes, the first stop is at the bank, and the wire transfer of $500,000 has been sent to your bank account. After the wire transfer, I will satisfy your impetuousness."

"The lock-up did more than improve my English. After my release, I saw the world nakedly, void of ideology and unrequited zeal. Yes, the feds tried to turn me into a U.S. spy. Instead, I turned myself into a businessman. I put aside ideology in favor of cash. After depositing the five hundred thousand, I will pass on Charlie's intentions. Your presence in Puerto Rico and your insistence on tomorrow's agenda will please her immensely. Until tomorrow, Mr. McLeod."

Before McLeod could respond, Rojo turned and headed for the door. The meeting was over in a matter of minutes. Both men took away the discomfort of wondering about the sincerity of the other, Rojo's interest in cash, and McLeod's determination to walk into a trap.

Unconcerned with death or the pain leading up to his death, McLeod was ready for whatever. Mundane concerns would evaporate, and in short order, it would be as if Sergeant McLeod never existed. All he had to do was get through one more night. Resolved to accepting his probable demise, McLeod slept soundly, like a baby protected in his mother's womb, and he dreamt of an outing to Happy Times.

Amusement Park.

The dream comes to life. He is eleven. The proprietor, Mr. Morgenstern, invites all the Star of the Sea Orphanage children to the Smiling Charlie's Puppet Show twice a year. After the show, the children wander throughout the park; this is a cherished event. In his dream, everything and everyone is clear and natural. Standing in line behind Betty Sue is McLeod, obligingly waiting for a turn on the sissy ride, the merry-go-round. The line progresses, and following Betty Sue, he steps onto the go-round. Embarrassingly, he is the leader of the Black Hawks, trailing behind a girl. Betty Sue passed up a wild-eyed stallion and chose some pink bird thing ahead of the stallion. Sister Maria noted his gentile behavior.

The music starts, and the children speed up, cheering louder and louder. Mounted on his steed, McLeod leans forward. Long-tailed golden pigtails oscillated directly in front of his face on a secret Black Hawk mission. At each turn, the merry-go-round picks up speed. His buddies are on the ground waiting in line, and those who have completed their ride are looking on. McLeod reaches over the saddle horn like a lion towards his prey. Holding on to the brass pole with his left hand, he goes forward with his right. Defying the danger of a bucking horse running at a gallop, McLeod leans and stretches his free arm over the horse's ever-widening nostrils. He reaches for those oscillating pigtails. He lunged but could not grab the pigtails dancing on his face. Sister Maria sees what McLeod is up to and orders, " Billy McLeod, sit with both hands on the pole." His buddies egg him on. McLeod ignores Sister Maria and tries again. One good yank and a scream would be worth the spanking. Betty Sue is alerted. She turns, grabs her pigtails, and screams.

Memento Mori

The phone rang; McLeod answered, "Hello."

The automated voice says, "Good morning, Sir, your wake-up call."

In the morning, he had come early for W. R. McLeod. Around 5:30, his pre-ordered coffee, eggs over easy, and ham steak were cooked to perfection. Upon delivery, he savored his last meal, dressed, and readied himself. He left all his belongings in his carrying bag to drop off at the valet on his way out.

The phone rang. It was the valet. A car was waiting; McLeod left the key at the front desk and met with Rojo. A black sedan pulled up. Rojo and McLeod sat in the back. He offered salutations, and McLeod passed a note with directions to the bank's destination to the driver.

"Rojo," McLeod initiated the conversation, "I assumed you never contemplated why Charlie chose you over another to meet and now escort me."

"No! I never asked myself that question. However, I need to inform you that not only did I survive the lock-up, but I have also vastly improved my life. I'm unsure why informing you of my betterment is important. Nonetheless, upon assignment, I could not wait to see you. When Charlie told me of her intentions, insisting that you would come, knowing she wanted you dead."

"Well, Charlie has cast the characters in this melodrama. She wrote the script and assumed the role of producer. For clandestine reasons, she has decided that your attendance is vital. Does that not jar some curiosity?" McLeod asked.

"I have been working for the Li clan for some time. My relationship is excellent; they have been exceptionally good to me. Negative thoughts never crossed my mind. I have no lingering questions about why I was hired for this job or why I was selected for the position. Rojo continued, "What are you trying to tell me?"

"We are going to a sister branch of my U.S. bank to wire $500,000 to any bank account you designate," McLeod affirmed.

"And I assume your generosity has a price; you should know that since I gave up spy craft for business, bribery is within my operational scope. But what makes you think I have information worth such considerable cash?"

"Fortunately, I possess the worth in question," McLeod confidently responded. And I have some cautionary findings for you."

"Well, as you Americans say, I am all ears."

"Charlie will time my death with yours, maybe mine a little earlier; be sure to accept she has ordered your demise."

"And why," Rojo asks, "would Charlie want me dead?"

"Because she considers you as complicit in her mother's killing," McLeod insists. You did not inform the Cuban authorities about the information I shared with you regarding General Ochoa's family Christmas vacation. Her mother was not warned because of your less-than-truthful debriefing."

"How did Charlie find out?" "That tidbit of info came unintendedly from me to Sepúlveda when he found out where I had spent the Christmas Holidays and unwittingly passed on that information. I told him you informed me that it was the annual destination of the Ochoa family. I assume after discovering the death of Dr. Li, the relevance hit home."

After a few minutes of contemplation, Rojo asks, "What do you want to know?"

McLeod answered, "In our Miami encounter, I got the best of the situation. I assume Charlie believes you would vicariously enjoy instrumenting my demise as payback. Because of her hubris, as you said, she has disclosed more information to you than she should have. Besides, she knows your death is pending, and any information given would die with you."

"I'll tell you what she said to me after you have transferred the funds," Rojo responded.

The pair arrived at the bank. Information and details are exchanged, and the funds are wired.

Satisfied with the transfer, Rojo repeats what he was told: "After being repatriated to my homeland, it took me six months of desk-type work before I went back into the field. However, my fondness for intelligence analysis waned after a few months of desk work, which was incredibly dull. About nine months ago, a Panamanian law firm approached me through my chain of command in Cuba, suggesting I submit to an interview. They would not disclose the interviewer's name or the company's name. I attended an interview in Havana, and within five days, Dr. Anh Li called for a second in-person interview, which led to my hiring shortly after. I have worked for her daughter, Charlie, since Dr. Li's death."

McLeod asked. "Understood! Now tell me what the daughter of Anh Li has planned for me?"

Rojo explained that you would be hung, disemboweled, and dismembered. Rojo suggested that the safest route was not to go. McLeod agreed but insisted that an informed confrontation today is better than an ambush in the future.

On the drive to the heliport in a hotel limo, holding a zippered bank-issued canvas deposit bag, Rojo continued. "In the bag is a M1911 military-issued forty-five caliber pistol. I was ordered to hand you the unloaded pistol in a zippered bank canvas bag. I did question why he would comply. She berated me for questioning and then insisted that you consider her request a well-deserved and desired requiem, a final flagellation. She had no doubt you would follow her instructions."

Rojo handed McLeod a fully loaded seven-round magazine with one extra bullet in the chamber. He then inserted the pistol into the canvas bag. McLeod's right hand was to be inserted inside, gripping the trigger mechanism of an unloaded handgun. There was no other explanation or instruction.

Upon the helicopter landing, a Billy Lamb-driven truck was waiting to transport whomever to the marina. Rojo stepped out of the copter with McLeod; then, as a precaution, threatening pistol in hand, Rojo told the pilot, who undoubtedly worked for Charlie, to get out of the helicopter and move to the truck, where he was bound and taped silent.

There was a sense of finality as I walked onto the yacht, canvas bag in hand, after years of accepting dangerous assignments amid a lifetime of risk-taking. The unknown was how Charlie would deal with him once inside. There was no wind, the sun was blasting, and the humid heat was suffocating. The boat had a gangplank bridge from the pier to the midsection of the yacht. McLeod strode across the gangplank, looking at both the starboard and port sides, but one was blocked. After a few paces, he turned aft into an opening that led him down into a stateroom toward a bar. A young lady walked from behind the bar and said, "I will pat you down for weapons." Finding none, she walked away.

McLeod chose one of the two comfortable leather chairs and sat, resting the canvas bag on his lap. From that advantage, he noticed a flat, four-by-eight wooden table with four leather straps and metal buckles designed to hold down wrists and ankles. A 3⁄4-inch nylon rope configured with a hangman's noose dangled in the room's far corner.

He waited, eagerly anticipating the confrontation. Then footsteps! From outside the stateroom, he heard a salutation.

"Mr. McLeod." Although she wasn't in view, the voice was distinctly Charlie's. She continued, "So I see you have thrown caution to the wind. You conjured the worst, and you came anyway. But then I knew you could not deny this finality."

McLeod Charlie's footsteps were coming from below; she was moving upwards from the deck below.

"Well, how else could I see my beloved?" McLeod responds.

"Followed by two fearsome-looking men dressed in black leather, Charlie entered the room. Both wore black gloves, a black leather apron hung around their necks, a butcher's belt holstered a large cleaver, and two knives were bound around their waist. Hooded with large openings for their eyes, they noted that each was right-handed, toting a 9 mm pistol in their waistband. They stood at the ready next to Charlie.

"My dear Charlie, your air of confidence has vaporized; two armed bodyguards, you must think I have superpowers. McLeod joshed.

"But I like it. Pageantry interweaved with brutish intimidation is impressive."

Torturous Requisite Unfulfilled

"My, my, you're calm and collected. Is there something I do not know? Do you have the Marines on standby?" Overconfident and very satisfied with herself, Charlie smirks while gleefully taunting McLeod with her voluptuously exposed cleavage.

"No Marines," McLeod confesses.

"Hmm..." Charlie murmured, "All these years of working the quest, all the blood spilled in the name of revenge. What a letdown this must be for you; aren't you gravely disappointed?" Charlie paused to pour a glass of JW Blue. McLeod ignored the whiskey. Although the situation seemed dire, McLeod showed no fear.

"Mr. McLeod, do you know who I am?" Charlie asked.

"I thought I did," McLeod responded.

"Well, you know I am the daughter of Dr. Anh Li. She was my caring, always loving, sweet mother, and you, Mr. McLeod, are her murderer."

"Yes, I am that man," McLeod responded, "and once again, I dare to ask, am I your father?"

"I have answered that question, and now, on the verge of your demise, you ask it again. Your naiveté and convincing boyish innocence contrived a Peter Pan resilient to maturity. Conversely, my mother envied your guilelessness, your ability to remain mindful amid the killing and dying, to keep a steady rise above the chaos. Imagine if I were your daughter. How shocking would it have felt to have fallen into carnal lust with your daughter, Mr. McLeod? Perversely, foolish is my guess," Charlie suggested.

"Foolish? At a minimum, it is foolish, but that would be just the surface of my disappointment. I do wish that foolishness were the whole of it. I unthinkingly tried to satisfy the insatiable, fulfilling the unfulfillable. I have lived long enough. It is time for my life to end. I surrender; do with me as you will."

"So gallant, always the Paladin. Well, Mr. McLeod, before pain forces you into unconsciousness and death provides the escape from the forthcoming, I would like to salt your emotional wound."

As stated earlier, my father is the Russian you seek; his only value was the location of his bearer shares. A few days after my mother's death, the segregated GRU agent stationed helplessly by my dear mother was with me on his boat. I tortured him like a cat playing with an injured bird. Until I finally secured the location of his bearer certificates. Then, mercifully, per my tradeoff pledge for the whereabouts of the bearer shares. I dosed him with a toxic brew of fentanyl and heroin, my father, the rapist, the once intimidatingly fearsome, before my eyes faded into a lifeless shell. With difficulty, I slid him off the gurney onto a positioned-on-wheels dolly, an oversized metal garbage can. I moved him onto the fantail, dosed the body with a flammable, lit a match, and set the garbage can contents on fire. After an hour, I dumped the charred remnants and all into the ocean.

 Mr. McLeod, my mother, was a person of great erudition and love. Mother was genuine, kind, and considerate. Isn't it ironic, Mr. McLeod, that you killed the person who bore the daughter who finalized your quest for revenge?"

"I assume you have plans for me. Let's get on with it," McLeod suggested.

"Sounds like the beginning of your begging, Mr. McLeod; today is the last day of your life. The forthcoming will be excruciatingly painful, so tense up and render me my due."

While Charlie talked, the butchers started sharpening their knives preemptively.

"My mother never mentioned my father; when I asked, she said it did not matter. So, after my mother's death, I did my investigation, and you fit perfectly as a possibility. On one night of sex with you, I saved your sperm in a plastic tube. Upon analysis, there is no doubt you are not my father. Since I am Eurasian, there was another possibility. Having the opportunity, I assessed Maximillian's DNA and found that the rapist monster is my father."

"Then what purpose did the shadowing and seduction of me serve?" McLeod asked.

"What purpose! You eliminated my and Old Dutch's enemies. Because of the management of your revenge, attending the shareholders' meeting and finalizing the acquisition was safe. You inadvertently removed Confield and Calvo, two board members who were embezzling from Old Dutch. Because of you, Marin is dead. I believe my sensual allure and your delusional pretentiousness as Sir Galahad forced you to attend your execution.

Of course, I had many motives other than simply to exchange sexual nothings. Besides, I genuinely enjoy shagging, and you did provide a vibrant body. However, I could not duplicate what I had fantasized about as a girl. The anxiety of war consumed my mother's longing. You were young, innocent, and free of complications. That was then; today, revenge and guilt have fatally infected your being. You are forever tainted as the murderer of my dear mother."

"I have no rebuttal. I am, as you describe. I have sorrows, and admittedly, killing your mother was cold-blooded murder. The others I killed deserved to die."

"Mr. McLeod, if you are satisfied with that response, so be it. What matters is that you're here. You would not be here if I had not lustfully sexed you. You are another simple-minded SUPERALFA, seduced, managed, and boldly betrayed by a woman."

"Yes, so very true," McLeod conceded.

With her seductive success and boastful, coldly assertive demeanor, Charlie had McLeod in a painful acknowledgment of her truthfulness. Like a savagely beaten prizefighter, McLeod's body language begged the ringside physician to throw in the white towel, whereas the words I quit could not be formed.

Insistent on talking, Charlie drags out the preliminaries of the execution, asking, "In pursuance of your revenge, do you remember who you initially connected with?"

"Yes, I asked Jasper, who operated the Central and South American junket business, if he knew anyone connected to Cuban military intelligence; I told him it was personal. I thought if I were confined to Jasper, he might run into such a connection. It was a wild guess."

"Well, Jasper's got to the Panamanian via a Mexican family connection. That connection alerted the Cuban consulate in Nicaragua, which passed the information to his boss. Eventually, after it was too late, the Ochoa family was alerted to the possibility of your presence. At the time, it was not known that Rojo's report was incomplete. This transfer of information took months. But shortly after your initial meeting with Cornfield in Vegas, my mother knew that Sepúlveda, hired by you, was seeking and searching for information on Cubans serving in Vietnam. Nonetheless, she did not make your pursuance a danger to her because she did not consider the traditional Ochoa family Christmas vacation that she usually attended on your revengeful docket.

"Well, my intention with General Ochoa was known only to me," McLeod asserts.

"The point is that because of Rojo's disclosure to you but not to Cuban authorities, particularly to my mother, my mother is dead. After the killing, Sepúlveda suspected, just based on your timeline unavailability and an innocent disclosure of Delores, that you were in Spain, the gateway to the islands."

"I was unaware of his knowing; at any rate, he is dead, and soon so will I. Let's get on with the execution," McLeod demanded.

"Your naivety is astounding. Did you think that Sepúlveda's knowledge of my mother was inconsequential?"

"At the time, I believed that Raymond was a man who confided in no one about another man's business," McLeod emphasized to Charlie. "I did not tell Raymond of my past relationship with your mother; his regret of her death was palpable in his words and expressions."

"Well, you bet your life on that assumption of confidentiality," Charlie replied.

"Raymond passed on to me an investigative report...."

"My mother failed to warn you of Team 33's pending danger; I know she knew something was wrong. She could have done something, but she didn't. She regretted not having warned you. She did love your sweet innocence. And unlike her, I warned you that you were playing a dangerous game," Charlie revealed, emphasizing the emotional impact of her mother's regret.

"Yes, Raymond did betray me?" McLeod noted.

"In the strictest of terms, yes," Charlie confirmed. "Of course, from the beginning, he was conflicted and had forsaken his lifelong neutrality pledge. He said he would never work for one client in conflict with another. But his mistake was aligning with Marin and attempting a coup within Old Dutch. Nonetheless, Raymond was more benign than lethal."

"Then why?" McLeod asked. "Force him into suicide?"

"I did no such thing," Charlie adamantly denies.

'Then it was Marin," McLeod offers.

Charlie guesses, "I assume Marin decided that Raymond knew too much and was no longer needed with the Spanish insurance company sufficiently aligned. So, a greedy, no need for a partner, Marin found Sepúlveda's Achilles heel and flung an arrow into it."

"You knew of his out-of-wedlock son," McLeod asserted.

"Yes, my mother's research verified that fact long ago. This information was not common knowledge, but was also not a secret."

"I assume you had Lucy do your dirty work?"

"Lucy was my informant, not my assassin. Marin initially hired him. I hired Luke as a professional, and he worked for me. For Marin to scare Raymond was a simple task. Although Raymond's family was never in danger, the fear of their endangerment, exemplified by the note on the kindergarten teacher's desk, was enough. And you should know I was not aware of the action. I had no part in it; now, Marin's death was another matter. He had to die, and I used you to aid and assist in that endeavor."

"You knew I was intent on killing General Ochoa? Why didn't your mother know that and warn Ochoa?" McLeod inquires.

"You look perplexed; as I said earlier, it was because Rojo left that part out of his debriefing report. He was the only member of that team left alive; no one to dispute his testimony. Besides, Rojo rightly thought that information would end his career, if not his life."

"Yes," Charlie concedes. "I'll give that to you; I never envisioned that information so commonly known in Cuba would be critical information for you. The fault was my mother's."

"You found out the truth about Rojo's report?" McLeod stated.

"Yes, but this knowledge came to us after you murdered my mother."

"And you still have Rojo as an employee?" McLeod questioned.

Charlie looked at her watch and said, "He has another two hours of employment before termination."

"I thought keeping Rojo as your liaison was a signature touch. Someone indirectly at fault for your mother's death adds flavor to your revenge," McLeod comments.

"Hmm, you approve; that warms my heart."

"My dear Charlie, so cold, calculating, and deadly; I never imagined your culpability in my death," McLeod added.

"I had a mother," Charlie insisted, "never a father. We are all characters in this retelling of a Greek tragedy, actors reading our lines and performing our parts in a Sophoclean melodrama. The lover kills the mother. The daughter sleeps with her mother's killer and then tortures him until death is considered merciful."

"How very praying mantis of you. Okay, when do we get to the killing part?" McLeod asked.

"When I'm ready, Mr. McLeod," Charlie declared.

"All that incredible sex we enjoyed. I always thought," McLeod expressed, 'There was a sense of loving regard."

"You are a fool, Mr. McLeod. Women have sex with multiple partners, wherein the only motivation is self-serving desire. Sex has little to nothing to do with love, and the only true love is the love of mother and family; the exception in your case, sadly, is your love of the Corps."

"Mr. McLeod, Chidiock Tichborne wrote an elegy to his wife: On the Eve of His Execution, have you heard of it?

"Can't say that I have," McLeod replied.

"Well, it's a very moving poem. Tichborne wrote it in the Tower of London the night before his execution for plotting the assassination of Queen Elizabeth I."

Hmm, interesting, I had no idea you were an English history buff, but then I knew little about you. I assume that this poem has to do with my death." McLeod offered the conclusion as more than a mere possibility.

"You are right on; Chidiock, a Catholic, plotted to assassinate the Protestant Queen of England. The penalty for such a crime was to be drawn and quartered. I assume you're unfamiliar with this execution process; I'll explain. First, eviscerated, an interesting word that means your stomach's innards are cut open from top to bottom and your innards exposed. Then, to keep the tempo, you will be hanged just to the edge of death, only to be drawn and quartered by a large butcher knife. My executors will do their best to keep you alive, but you'll more than likely die of shock; regardless, the process is painful. A death well deserved for murdering my mother. I am filming this pending ordeal to replay your anguish at my pleasure."

"You are imaginative," McLeod countered. "It's been said all is fair in love and war."

"You're sounding like a victim. But of course, I know you as a convincingly feigned person who has rationalized the killing of my mother. Only a sociopath could kill with such cold-blooded disdain and continue a life of normality. Mr. McLeod, you may feel remorse, but this sense of guilt is no more than fodder to feed your behavioral dysfunction. I have supplanted your position as a vengeful judge and jury. I am judging a wrong by charging W.R. McLeod with the strangulation of my dear mother."

The guard to Charlie's left pulls out a revolver and points it at McLeod.

"Pass me the canvas bag covering your hand, and I'll unzip it, Charlie ordered." McLeod interrupted with a comment, "You mean this canvas bag?" Charlie answered. "Yes, that very one. You are gripping a 45-caliber pistol. It's your favorite. I will insert one bullet into the chamber with the safety off. The pistol will be aligned and positioned to fit about an inch inside your mouth. The index finger of your right hand will have enough rope to reach the trigger. The rest of your fingers will be taped and useless. Because I am kindhearted, once eviscerated and before hanged, your right hand is strung free, so you may then have the choice to kill yourself."

"Extend your right hand!" Charlie shouts as the two men in black, pistols drawn, take a step forward.

"Please, no need to raise your voice." McLeod moved as if to comply.

"You're right; in minutes, you'll be doing the screaming," Charlie foretells.

 At that moment, obeying Charlie's demand, McLeod raised his canvased bagged right hand and fired two rounds without pulling the pistol from the bag. The first shot hit the bodyguard with the pointed pistol in the chest, and the second guard in the midsection. The 45-caliber bullet's velocity knocked both men on their backs.

"McLeod grabs a startled Charlie by her hair, turns her about, and drags her heels on the floor toward the gangplank. Charlie reaches up with both hands onto McLeod's arm. McLeod releases his grip, pushing Charlie before him while continuing to disembark.

"Well, surprise, surprise," Charlie said, turning to face McLeod. As she realizes the turn of events, she says, "I have miscalculated. Where did I go wrong, Mr. McLeod?"

"You have thought of everything except the loyalty of one of your operatives."

"Nonsense, all our employees are trustworthy," Charlie declared.

"Well, one skipped the morning elixir. Rojo and I chatted about his debriefing in Cuba after being released from confinement. As I suspected, he left out the details of the Ochoa family vacation. I thought his reinstatement as a loyal soldier of the cause could only have occurred if there had been a memory lapse. Of course, I did wonder why you picked Rojo. Why insert Rojo into this drama solely to pass on information? Well, then it occurred to me. You thought of the justice of it all, Rojo delivering me to you, and you would kill both of us, a clean settling of the old and lingering. I explained his pending destiny, and we contrived a mutually beneficial solution. First, I wired his bank account, and then he would hand me the unzipped canvas bank bag. So, I could slip my hand in and grip the loaded pistol."

One of the wounded guards raises his pistol. McLeod fires off two rounds to end that attempt. He then fired once more into the other guard for good measure.

Aiming the pistol directly at Charlie's mid-body, McLeod ordered, "I think now is the time for me to demonstrate my loving regard. Walk five yards in front and head for the gangplank. I am disembarking. If other bad guys ride to the sound of gunfire, I cannot be held responsible for your safety."

Charlie, Anh Li's daughter, walked out onto the gangplank. "Mr. McLeod, I just have to know why you agreed to meet me if you knew I intended to kill you."

"Because it suited me and, naively, a faulty characteristic of mine as you so poignantly described. I held out for the possibility that you were being forced into this situation. If that was the case, I came to rescue the damsel kidnapped by the Black Knight."

"A knightly gesture; well, as you can see, I am the Black Knight," Charlie stated.

Within minutes, a truck arrived; Billy, dressed in jeans and a T-shirt, stepped out and opened the passenger door. McLeod fitted the pistol into his waistband.

Charlie stopped and turned. "I have no regrets. You killed my mother, and I will kill you."

"I will die soon enough," McLeod conceded. "You will have your revenge by living your life to its fullest. Take it from the revenger; I found satisfaction in all but one of the killings. You are a remarkable, tenacious person. Though unrequited, I have experienced the illusion of loving and the delusion of being loved. You are extraordinary. However, your bloodlust pursuit has added more hostility to this hostile world. Goodbye, Charlie..."

McLeod walked past Charlie onto the ground toward the truck. Realizing the opportunity, Charlie reached down inside her left pant leg and stood up, revealing a snub-nosed thirty-eight taken from her ankle holster. Reaching down, she aimed the pistol in both hands and called out his name, "Mr. McLeod! Soon enough is now."

McLeod stopped and turned, exposing his shoulder. Charlie squeezed the trigger and hit McLeod high on the upper part of the left upper arm. The impact was significant; it smacked the unsuspecting McLeod to the ground. In anguish, he cried out. Focused on her victim while walking closer for the headshot, Charlie loudly rants, "McLeod, you killed the only person that meant anything to me."

Three feet away, Charlie aims the pistol barrel directly at the target. "Mr. McLeod, the last of Team 33."

McLeod stared into her eyes. A lifetime of images traversed in panorama, people, situations, and animated, indistinguishable bouncing lights grew bright and dim. Charlie began to squeeze the trigger of the coup de grâce that would end the last living member of Team 33, but before the hammer could strike, Billy, the unseen driver, rushed from the blindside and smashed his body into hers. The pistol dislodged from her hand and fell to the ground.

"Billy! Do not hurt her," McLeod pleaded.

McLeod stood up and leaned against the truck; he asked Billy to help him stand and ensure he was not hurt. With her arms pinned to her back, Billy placed one hand firmly against the nape of her neck. Charlie was now physically restrained.

"Well," Charlie asked, "now what, Mr. McLeod?"

"Now," McLeod announced as he reached down and threw the thirty-eight into the water, "I'll stop the bleeding, and Billy releases you."

"You'd better kill me now," Charlie warned. "I will come after you."

"Yes, my love, but all you can do is kill me.

I am suffering from a loss I never possessed. From what I know of love, I can honestly say I loved you. The testament of my love is my foolishness.

At the top of my regrets is killing your mother; in truth, I am a sorry fellow." With Charlie firmly held, he closed the distance to Charlie and gently touched her face. She vehemently spat upon his face. McLeod gave Billy the high sign, facing Charlie while wiping his face, and said, "Finally, dear Charlie, after all the deceptiveness, finally, an expression of genuineness." Billy released Charlie and guided McLeod back to the van's passenger side. Charlie turned to walk away. At the top of the gangplank, Charlie paused for a moment. She faced in the direction of McLeod and begrudgingly shouted, "This is not over, you murderer. I will kill you."

"Do what you must, and I will wrestle with the thought of living with your hate and my many regrets. If it is too much for me to manage, I'll rid you of the trouble of killing me."

Again, Charlie faced McLeod and cried, "You're a fortunate man. But luck is a commodity that ebbs and flows; eventually, for the murder of my mother by my hand, I swear you will endure a painful death."

With that threat, Charlie walked on the gangplank and onto the yacht. McLeod, helped by Billy, struggled onto the vehicle. Team 33's revenge has ended.

TABLE OF CONTENTS